Personnel Administration in Higher Education

Handbook of Faculty and Staff Personnel Practices

Ray T. Fortunato

D. Geneva Waddell

Personnel Administration in Higher Education

Jossey-Bass Publishers

San Francisco • Washington • London • 1981

PERSONNEL ADMINISTRATION IN HIGHER EDUCATION
Handbook of Faculty and Staff Personnel Practices
by Ray T. Fortunato and D. Geneva Waddell

Copyright © 1981 by: Jossey-Bass Inc., Publishers
433 California Street
San Francisco, California 94104
&
Jossey-Bass Limited
28 Banner Street
London EC1Y 8QE

Library of Congress Cataloging in Publication Data

Fortunato, Ray T.
  Personnel administration in higher education.

  Includes bibliographies and index.
  1. College personnel management. I. Waddell,
D. Geneva.   II. Title.
LB2342.7.F67   378'.0068'3   81-47769
ISBN 0-87589-506-9   AACR2

Manufactured in the United States of America

JACKET DESIGN BY WILLI BAUM

FIRST EDITION

Code 8120

*The Jossey-Bass
Series in Higher Education*

❧ Preface ❧

Higher education administrators who take a "seat of the pants" approach to administering personnel policies are not likely to survive the challenges and demands of the 1980s. Methods for accomplishing much more with fewer human resources are needed in order to meet rapid changes in technology, as well as the needs of the changing workforce and environment.

In *Personnel Administration in Higher Education,* we explain the elements of viable faculty and staff personnel programs and focus on improved methods and techniques used in the field; our goal is to enable administrators and practitioners to (1) develop and implement prudent personnel policies and procedures, (2) increase productivity and minimize human resources costs, and (3) deal effectively with problems stemming from the current economic strain as well as with future challenges and demands. Drawing on our hands-on experience in personnel administration over the past three decades, we provide a compendium of practical information for those whose responsibilities include influencing or recommending personnel policies, promoting effective interaction among various groups in the institution, and making cost-effective decisions. The handbook is intended primarily as a resource and guide for both academic and nonacademic administrators and for personnel specialists. It is also designed for administrators new to higher education, for faculty involved in managing human resources, and for faculty and graduate students in higher education administration programs.

The existing literature does not cover, or show the interrelationships of, faculty and staff personnel administration within higher education institutions. By providing an understanding of the similarities and differences in faculty and staff administration, this handbook should help readers develop efficient and effective policies and practices. In addition, most works on personnel administration are theoretically based and tend to focus on industrial models, public service governmental practices, or personnel practices in small colleges and universities. We have attempted to fill the gap between theory and practice and to meet the needs of large as well as small, four-year as well as two-year, institutions of higher education.

The handbook presents information and samples relative to positions, people, and processes and is, therefore, divided into three distinct parts. Part One illustrates the importance and urgency of improved personnel administration, outlines position control needs, offers techniques for documenting position responsibilities, suggests position categories and position analysis methods, highlights evaluation plans, and summarizes equal employment opportunity and affirmative action requirements. Part Two focuses on the employment process (recruitment and appointment), mandated and optional benefits, academic freedom and tenure, human resources development, performance standards and evaluation, faculty and staff relations, grievance procedures, and retirement, resignation, retrenchment, and disability. Part Three follows the various processes associated with personnel policies and procedures, records, collective bargaining, and the personnel function and organization in general.

The list of exhibits directs readers to dozens of examples of forms, policies, and practices that are currently being used effectively in a variety of colleges and universities; the exhibits serve as useful guides to developing personnel administration materials appropriate to one's own institution. We acknowledge with special thanks the following organizations for giving permission to reproduce their materials: the College and University Personnel Association, Cornell University, University of Georgia, University of Michigan, University of Oklahoma, Pennsylvania State University, Purdue University, and Virginia Polytechnical Institute and State University.

Over the past few decades, we have visited many educational institutions and attended numerous conferences, workshops, and short courses. During those years ideas have been exchanged freely, and many of them have found their way into this handbook. Unfortunately, the sources of some of these ideas are no longer known, but it has not been our intent to use the materials of others without proper credit; we gratefully acknowledge all the people who have contributed not only to our understanding of personnel administration but especially to the development of sound policies and practices in the field.

It is our hope that the information provided in the following chapters will assist administrators in making more effective decisions, allow for improved interaction among the various groups within institutions, encourage further study of the various personnel functions and methods with a view toward continued improvement, and contribute to the professionalism of personnel administration.

September 1981   Ray T. Fortunato
University Park, Pennsylvania

D. Geneva Waddell
Rockville, Maryland

❦ Contents ❦

Focuses on changes that necessitate improved faculty and staff personnel administration; asks how this need can be met; stresses the importance of "doing more with less" (increased productivity and minimized cost); suggests personnel research needed to help improve decision making; and highlights the role of the faculty in higher education personnel administration.

Part One: Positions

Illustrates the need for and process of position control; suggests alternatives to the meat-ax approach to cutting budgets; defines and describes elements and uses of position descriptions for faculty and staff as tools for a variety of decision-making functions; outlines responsibility associated with supplying information for position control and descriptions; and suggests shortcuts to position description writing.

effective probationary periods for faculty and staff; provides sample forms useful in the performance review for tenure promotion of faculty; describes the job ownership phenomenon; describes approaches to effective performance evaluation; and provides sample standards for faculty and staff, and forms for use in evaluating performance.

Reveals the reverse side of the appointment process— retirement, including mandatory age, early retirement programs, and preretirement counseling programs; resignation and dismissal; retrenchment, including layoff and recall policies; and disability, including policies on sick leave with pay and leave without pay; provides sample policies and forms for emeritus rank, reduction in force, and exit interview.

Stresses that administrators' recognition of faculty and staff relations facilitates an effective climate for reducing conflicts; highlights the sometimes conflicting needs of faculty, staff, administrators, institutions, unions, and government; discusses motivation and the importance of effective communication; describes discipline and dismissal policies, due process, grievances, and early warnings of problems. Explores policies for handling grievances including arbitration.

Part Three: Processes

Focuses on who should originate policies and procedures, the review and approval process, and the basic difference between policy and procedure; suggests methods for developing policies and procedures; explores effective dissemination of policies; and provides samples of policies peculiar to higher education such as definitions of academic ranks, affiliate appointments, and private consulting practices.

❧ Exhibits ❧

❧ The Authors ❧

RAY T. FORTUNATO is assistant vice president for personnel administration at The Pennsylvania State University. He received his B.A. degree in business administration and his M.A. degree in music/economics from Pennsylvania State. With over thirty years experience in higher education personnel administration, he has served as past national president of the College and University Personnel Association (CUPA), and has received both the Donald Dickason and Diedrich K. Willers awards from the association for professional service in the field. He has also been chairman of the Eastern Universities Personnel Group and president of the Centre County Personnel Association, an affiliate of the American Society for Personnel Administration. He is the author of many articles on personnel administration in higher education, coauthor with J. M. Elliott and J. V. Pezzoni of *College and University Personnel Policy Models* (1974; revised 1980), and coordinator of *Guidelines to Better College and University Personnel Administration* (2 vols., 1969 and 1972). He is on the faculty of the annual College Business Management Institute at the University of Kentucky and has served as a consultant to several institutions on university personnel matters.

D. GENEVA WADDELL is a personnel specialist at Montgomery Community College, a multicampus college in Maryland. Prior to joining Montgomery College in 1970, her work experience included personnel functions at the National Institutes of Health, Clinical Center in Bethesda, Maryland. She received her B.A. degree in business and management and her M.A. degree in education administration/journalism, both from the University of Maryland, and is currently in the Higher Education Administration Doctoral Program at George Washington University. She is past president of the Greater Washington Chapter of the College and University Personnel Association and serves on that association's Research and Publications National Advisory Board.

Personnel Administration in Higher Education

Handbook of Faculty and Staff Personnel Practices

1

Urgency of Improved Personnel Administration

The need for improved and enlightened personnel administration in colleges and universities is urgent because of the forces for change now evident. For example, major shifts in curricular emphasis have taken place in the last decade, as illustrated, by one institution's undergraduate enrollments between 1970 and 1980 (see Table 1). At this institution, the most popular undergraduate majors are now accounting, with 770 students; electrical engineering, with 737; mechanical engineering, with 619; individual and family studies, with 581; biology, with 566; nursing, with 550; computer science, with 526; chemical engineering, with 472; and administration of justice, with 470. What happens—and what should happen—to tenured faculty members when the mix of undergraduate majors changes this drastically in just ten years and in the direction of such specialized programs? What obligation does an institution have to retrain tenured faculty members for new assignments? And is such retraining realistic?

1

**Table 1. An Institution's Changes in Undergraduate Enrollments
Between 1970 and 1980**

Majors	Undergraduate Student Majors 1970	Undergraduate Student Majors 1980	Percentage of Change
Public service	4	50	+ 1150%
Mining engineering	24	251	+ 940
Forest products	7	64	+ 814
Horticulture	38	284	+ 647
Petroleum and natural gas engineering	39	285	+ 631
Agricultural business	27	169	+ 526
Microbiology	57	357	+ 526
Communication studies	16	93	+ 481
Sociology	159	63	− 60
Elementary education	1101	438	− 60
Art education	190	64	− 66
History	258	86	− 67
Community development	244	70	− 71
Health and physical education	603	165	− 73
Secondary education	1202	199	− 83

A second factor facing higher education personnel administration in the 1980s is the demographic evidence that in most sections of the country fewer persons will be in the traditional college age range. How will this affect the required number and mix of faculty and staff during the decade? For instance, how will it affect the granting of tenure? Should alternatives to tenure be instituted? Should tenure be granted for only a set number of years? How can institutions with many older and tenured faculty ensure the flow of new and energetic faculty into their programs? Will the future see more and more courses in the hands of temporary faculty? If so, what problems will this cause? Will retrenchment policies provide for maintaining a qualified faculty in the face of serious cutbacks? And can recent gains in affirmative action and equal employment opportunities be sustained in such an environment?

Besides changes in curricular emphasis and projected lower enrollments, increased costs are causing competition for the personnel-related budgetary resources of colleges and universities. Among them are charges for benefits programs such as hospital, surgical, and major medical insurance; increases in both the tax base and percentage of contributions for social security; rising unemployment compensation costs caused by retrenchments and more rigorous tenure denials; requests for additions of benefits such as dental and vision care insurance; litigation connected with equal pay, age discrimination, sexual harassment, and other alleged breaches of equal employment opportunity regulations; the proliferation of union activities and the resulting high cost of collective bargaining; and high salaries needed to deal with inflation.

A fourth factor affecting higher education personnel policies has been the proliferation of state and federal legislation affecting faculty and staff members since the late 1960s and early 1970s. The list of laws and regulations to which higher education has adjusted during this period includes the Age Discrimination in Employment Act, the Comprehensive Employment and Training Act, the Fair Credit Reporting Act, the Occupational Safety and Health Act, the Employees Retirement Income Security Act, the Vietnam Era Veterans Readjustment Act, new pregnancy benefits regulations, the introduction of unemployment compensation, wage and price freezes, the assertion of the National Labor Relations Board over private institutions, public employee relations acts passed by many states and the resultant proliferation of academic unionization, regulations concerning the handicapped, changes in social security legislation, coverage of higher education under the Fair Labor Standards Act, equal pay legislation, affirmative action regulations, and fast escalation of the minimum wage. These and other government requirements forced development of a "legalistic" approach to personnel administration and absorbed the attention of personnel professionals during the recent past. Now, however, colleges and universities must progress beyond these legal issues and provide leadership in personnel administration in order to do more or at least hold steady with fewer resources.

Will institutions of higher education be able to continue their mission of exploration and discovery with the budget constraints they face? Obviously, not unless they can manage better their main budgetary expenditure—people. Changes in attitudes at all administrative levels will be required. Concepts like "productivity" and "minimized costs" will have to be implemented rather than remaining only words, and they will have to be used carefully so as not to destroy the sense of professionalism in higher education that is so essential to academic quality.

What Is Effective Personnel Administration?

C. Wayne Vanderwill of the University of Michigan defines effective personnel administration as having the right numbers and the right kinds of people, at the right places, at the right times, acting in a way that provides both the organization and the individual with maximum long-range benefits. Under this definition, personnel administration involves asking such questions as:

1. How few faculty or staff members are needed to accomplish a specific task?
2. What safeguards can be used to avoid the adding of unnecessary faculty or staff members?
3. Have standards of performance been established for positions at all levels to ensure productivity? For example:
   - How many undergraduates and course sections should half-time graduate assistants teach, by discipline?
   - How many advisees should a typical faculty member be expected to counsel?
   - What are desirable teaching loads and dissertation advisor loads for faculty members, by discipline?
   - How many salads should a salad maker make in an average day?
   - How many students should a health service physician be expected to see in an average day?
4. Are faculty and staff members paid properly?
5. Are faculty and staff members properly trained?
6. Are the most cost-effective methods being used to perform all tasks?

7. Have the proper people been selected to do the tasks required? Are staff being paid excessive rates because overly qualified personnel were selected?
8. Are positions properly defined?
9. To undertake a new program or project, will adequate staff be available?
10. Can competition for staff to fill difficult-to-recruit positions caused by scarcity of applicants be met successfully?

Administrators in higher education—including everyone who has responsibility for people and budget, whether department heads, director of food services, or president—would like to have simple answers to such staffing questions. For example, administrators frequently ask us, "How many clerical employees should an institution of higher education have in its academic areas?" There is no simple answer to such a question, since the complexity of academic areas varies by such factors as the amount of research that is conducted, the number of graduate students enrolled, and the physical layout of the department. Furthermore, the answer to such a question depends on an institution's answer to a prior question, "What can we afford to have our clerical staff do?" This question suggests the need for a set of institutional standards for clerical employees in academic units, to answer such questions as these: Should clerical employees be permitted to type graduate assistants' theses, faculty members' manuscripts, or material for informal, unfunded research done by faculty members? Should clerical employees be assigned to one senior professor or to the department head only? If so, under what conditions? Should all clerical employees in academic departments be hired on a twelve-month basis or should some be hired on a school-year basis? Should the luxury of personal dictation be permitted despite the fact that it is less cost-effective than machine dictation? What other equipment could be used to increase productivity? Effective personnel administration requires that these kinds of questions be dealt with in order adequately to determine staffing needs.

Proper data collection to answer such questions can result in accumulating information useful for other personnel decisions.

Personnel data, however, serve only limited utility unless put to work in research projects and studies. Here are examples of studies generated by such data that can help improve personnel planning, policy, and practice:

- Multiyear studies by academic discipline of the various awards of probationary tenure granted to new faculty members upon appointment. Are a variety of standards being used within the institution?
- Multiyear studies by academic discipline on the numbers of faculty members denied tenure versus those eligible. Are there trends by disciplines?
- Studies by discipline of the ratio of tenured to nontenured faculty members. Do certain disciplines have a dangerously high percentage of tenured faculty?
- Studies by discipline of the ages of faculty members. Which areas lack young faculty members?
- Studies by discipline of the mix of faculty ranks. Are certain disciplines advancing more quickly than others in promotions to higher ranks?
- Studies by academic discipline of the ratio of part-time to full-time faculty. Are certain disciplines using too many part-time faculty? Should others use more?
- Studies comparing the size of the administrative structure of each major academic unit of the institution. What is a reasonable structure? Are there areas of excess?
- Studies of the male, female, and minority salaries in similar position levels to uncover any unequal relationships.
- Studies by discipline of the number of requests for sabbatical leaves of absence in relation to those eligible. Are some administrators denying these opportunities?
- Studies by classification category showing the ages at which individuals have retired over each of the past five years. How many waited until the mandatory retirement age? How many retired in each age bracket below the mandatory age? What kinds of planning do the patterns suggest? Are incentives needed to encourage earlier retirement?

- Studies by unit of the results of performance evaluations. What percentage of faculty and staff received the highest rating? Are there any drifts toward leniency in evaluation?
- Studies by discipline of the appointments of faculty members on tenure-eligible versus non-tenure-eligible appointments. Is there any relation between a faculty member's sex and race and eligibility for tenure?
- Studies by unit of the numbers of leaves of absence without pay, the reasons and durations of the leaves, and individuals' employment status following a leave. Is the policy on leaves effective? Are leaves given for improper reasons?
- Studies by department and classification group of the uses of sick leave. Does the amount of sick leave in a unit suggest a serious morale problem?
- Studies by unit and classification category of turnover. Why is turnover higher in some units?
- Annual studies of the grades of positions by classification groups to monitor the activities of position analysts. Is there an upward drift in the grades?
- Studies by unit of participation in the various training and development offerings within the institution. Are some units neglecting staff development?
- Studies by unit of the number of requests for upgrading positions. Are some units overactive in the number of requests they make?
- Studies by unit and classification category of the usage and patterns of overtime. Is overtime used judiciously? Is it affecting employees' morale?
- Studies of the cost effectiveness of classified advertisements placed in order to determine future advertisement procedures. Can recruitment be made more effective or less costly?
- Studies of the longevity of employees recruited from different sources and locations. Is heavy and costly turnover of employees related to certain sources?
- Studies of the position evaluation factors and degrees assigned to positions within categories of jobs. Are there any inconsistencies?

- Studies by unit of the numbers and types of grievances submitted and the final decisions reached in those grievances. What is the employee relations climate in individual units?
- Studies on the effectiveness of outside arbitrators. Were decisions fair and just?
- Studies by unit and by classification category on the length of service of employees. Do longevity patterns suggest the need for policy revisions?
- Studies by unit of the relationship between employees' length of service and their place on the salary schedule. Are all areas of the institution consistent in the salary treatment for employees with longer service?
- Studies by unit and classification category outlining the benefits plan chosen by those employees who were offered options. Should certain plans be discontinued?

This is only a sample of possible studies and not all of these would be applicable to all institutions, but decisions about desirable ones need to be made as part of the personnel administration process so that appropriate personnel data are not only collected but also maintained. For more details on conducting field research see Fiedler, (1978); for survey research methods see Babbie, (1973); for statistical methods see Hue and others (1975).

Who Is Responsible for Personnel Administration?

An effective program of sound personnel administration requires the cooperative participation of administrators at all levels in the institution. A personnel officer can accomplish very little if he or she is isolated from the principal decision makers. In order to be effective, the personnel officer must be included in institutional operational planning. Additionally, if the actions of the chief officers of the institution make it obvious that sound personnel administration is not important to them, the effectiveness of the personnel administration will be seriously hampered. The president should be responsible for establishing among the members of his or her staff in both the academic and business affairs areas and among deans and all other administrative officers an understanding of the importance of sound personnel administration and the personnel function. Meeting the challenges before higher education by improving personnel administration requires commitment on the part of all segments of the institution.

Faculty members also have a role in personnel administration. The relationship between the faculty and the administration is different than that between employee and employer in most employment settings. An enlightened faculty, as a group and as individuals, assumes a managerial and decision-making role in many personnel matters. They assist in recruiting new faculty members and approve the backgrounds of candidates for appointment. They set standards of performance for their peers and participate within their disciplines in peer review for the granting of tenure, promotion, dismissal, and so forth. They serve on search committees that make effective recommendations for the selection of academic administrators at all levels. They sit on committees to hear faculty grievances. As a group they form faculty organizations (senates) that legislate in areas such as curriculum, research, faculty status, entrance requirements, student life, and so forth. In some cases, such organizations make effective recommendations regarding benefits granted to faculty members. (For more details on faculty organizations, see Mortimer and McConnell, 1978.)

The governance and managerial role of faculty was made particularly evident in the U.S. Supreme Court ruling on the Yeshiva University case in 1980. The Court ruled that faculty members at Yeshiva University are managerial employees and, as such, do *not* have the right to bargain collectively under general labor law. In its decision, it upheld the U.S. Court of Appeals statement that full-time faculty members at Yeshiva University, a private institution, have so much authority over academic matters and institutional policies that they, in effect, operate the university. Of course, not all faculty organizations have the degree of authority given to Yeshiva University's faculty. Their level of authority differs from institution to institution. For more details on the Yeshiva University case (National Labor Relations Board v. Yeshiva University 100 S. CT. 856–1980), see Daponte (1980), Douglas (1979), Roots and Shepard (1980), and *College and University Personnelite* (1980d).

Managerial authority is not granted to employees other than faculty, although some institutions establish employee councils that discuss general matters affecting employees. Some councils exist to clarify the institution's personnel policies and benefits and others explore or suggest new approaches. In institutions whose employees are unionized, salaries, benefits, and working conditions are negotiated prior to being implemented. Employees, particularly younger employees, expect to play a greater role in decision making than heretofore. Therefore, some institutions are developing participatory management programs that promote discussion of preliminary plans for change to provide employees opportunities to understand and make recommendations about the proposed plans. In none of these cases, however, do these employees exercise the right to evaluate their peers and make recommendations for their promotion, dismissal, discipline, and so forth. That is a unique role for faculty.

The remainder of this book is devoted to information about the tools administrators and faculty need to meet the personnel challenges confronting higher education. The chapters in Part One discuss how to control, describe, categorize, evaluate and determine salaries for all the positions at an institution. Then the chapters in Part Two offer advice about hiring, motivating and evaluating the people placed in these positions. Finally, the chapters in Part Three explain desirable personnel processes and the staffing of the personnel administration in order to apply these tools effectively.

❧ 2 ❧

Defining Duties and Controlling Numbers of Positions

The central administrators of a major American university were recently embarrassed when a technician improperly discarded chemicals into a drain and caused the massive death of fish in the streams and river below the campus. In order to prevent future incidents, they created a position for a high-salaried expert in the disposal of chemicals. Three months after employing the expert, the university put revised waste disposal procedures into effect, and the basic problem was solved. However, the institution now had the expensive employee on its payroll. If the university's leaders had analyzed the need adequately and had had a proper position description drafted, it would have been apparent to them that the university needed expensive expertise only for a short time and that after existing problems were solved, an employee with less technical background and experience could maintain the new program. Employing an outside consultant temporarily for the needed expertise would have been more appropriate than creating the new position.

11

Mistakes such as this one are caused by less-than-adequate attention to the basic principles of proper position control, description, classification, analysis, evaluation, and salary administration. Are such incidents infrequent and far-fetched? Unfortunately they are not. They happen quite often, and they point up the need for institutional leaders to pay attention to the matter of institutional positions themselves as well as to the characteristics of individuals filling these positions. Controlling the numbers of positions, reallocating positions, describing and analyzing the positions, and setting appropriate salary levels for these positions must of necessity normally precede decisions about the occupants of the positions.

How Can The Number of Positions Be Controlled?

Whether or not a specific position is needed should be a matter of concern at any time. During the 1960s and early 1970s, however, some institutions were able to maintain some positions of questionable need. It has been said that if a higher education institution had an Edsel department, it would still be there. To respond to inflation, changing curricular desires of students, and shrinking financial resources, administrators need to consider the most cost-effective manpower planning feasible.

What systems can be used to eliminate unnecessary positions? While several different approaches can be used, practically all of them are variations of two basic types of fiscal management systems, either (1) giving deans and other equivalent administrative officers both the total responsibility for and the control of how to spend the funds assigned to them, or (2) centrally controlling major expenditure of funds.

Consider each of these two systems in turn. The first, or decentralized, system requires that deans and other division directors assume the budget responsibility and be judged on their ability to handle that responsibility. It precludes "bailing out" a dean who mismanages funds and comes up short. With this system in place, a central institutional budget committee can determine total institutional needs and then assess the areas of least need and reallocate funds to those areas of greatest need. For example, enrollment in instructional areas such as computer science, accounting, and engineering may be growing while other areas, such as education, history, and sociology, may be in decline. The central budget committee may then tell the dean of the college of education to relinquish $125,000 in salary money, which will be reallocated to the areas of need. In this model, the dean of the college of education would then decide by one means or another how to reduce the college's budget. Such a system permits great flexibility but requires that deans be capable fiscal managers.

Under the second system, central administration "owns" all positions centrally. Therefore, if a vacancy occurs in any area, the unit must seek permission from the top administration to fill the vacancy. Obviously, centralization provides tight control. However, in a large institution it is difficult for top administrators to understand the specific needs of every area for every position. Therefore, a centralized approach works better in small institutions or in subsections of larger institutions. For example, the dean of the college of education mentioned above might impose this system on the department heads within the college of education as a means to meet the college's assessment.

How Should Requests for New Positions Be Handled?

The most important strategy under either of these systems is to prevent the establishment of a new position unless it is absolutely needed. Even in periods of declining enrollments, however, some new positions will be required in some areas while positions are being eliminated in others. In order to create any new position, the dean or administrative officer should submit the request to central administration together with details of activity changes that have taken place to make the new position essential, a standard position description (illustrated later in this chapter), and information about how the position will be funded. Such justification reports should be sufficiently detailed for decision making regarding the need to establish the position.

Two different committees are desirable for reviewing such requests—one for academic positions and another for other positions. In large institutions it may be cost effective to employ industrial engineers to assist the committee concerned with non-academic positions. Such engineers should be able to save considerably more than their salaries by finding the most efficient ways to solve manpower problems. For example, a request for an additional secretary may be eliminated by establishing more cost-effective means to provide the services, such as machine dictation instead of oral dictation, relocation of existing staff for more effective work flow, reassignment of duties among existing clerical staff, or elimination of nonessential duties in existing positions.

Just the fact that administrators know that when they request additional positions, their request will be examined in such detail is a deterrent to less-than-justifiable requests.

Should a "Meat-Ax" Approach Be Used to Cut Positions?

The "meat-ax" approach to position reduction dictates that all budgets be cut by the same fixed percentage; for example, an executive decision that each administrative officer cut his or her clercial staff by ten percent. This approach is based on "treating everyone alike," and it may sound logical to a budget planner or a president. However, it kills managerial morale and future effectiveness.

The unfairness of this across-the-board approach is demonstrated by the fact that it penalizes equally those administrators who have been practicing efficient methods and sloppy administrators. Good managers already have trimmed fat from the budget, while inefficient managers can easily agree to a percentage of cutback because they still have the fat to cut.

Observe what is likely to happen to the efficient administrator who has tried to manage well. First because he or she is efficient, the cuts will be made, perhaps at the cost of effective programs and certainly at the cost of morale. Second, in the future, the manager will develop self-protective strategies to avoid ever again being penalized by across-the-board cuts. The manager will store pockets of funds against future cutbacks, and in all probability, will make few new recommendations for efficiency. This manager will have received clearly the message that efficiency and effective management do not pay off and that inefficiency is tolerated. Thus, a good manager will be destroyed.

Why is the meat-ax approach to reductions in force used? Perhaps because top administrators lack the courage and imagination needed to devise better approaches. It is an easy approach. It avoids making difficult decisions. Everyone appears to be treated the same. But perhaps administrators simply lack the management tools and data to determine where to cut most effectively.

What alternatives exist to the "meat-ax" approach? Here are five: (1) Cut an entire program instead of upsetting large numbers of faculty and staff members in a variety of programs; strengthen the better programs by dropping those that are marginal; (2) identify and cut dead-wood personnel; (3) establish performance standards for all positions; identify ineffective employees and identify tasks that can be eliminated or greatly reduced in scope; (4) identify effective administrators and apply their methods in other areas of the institution; and (5) examine the proliferation of gadgetry; for example, does everyone need a computer?

What Is a "Position Description"?

Position description usually refers to a formally drafted list of duties that define a position. However, position descriptions also include any statement of the responsibilities of an employee: a letter to a new faculty member that outlines his or her duties; an annual understanding between a department chairperson and a faculty member about the emphasis of assignment for the next academic year; a list prepared for a management by objectives program; a work schedule that states that Gene makes coffee at 7:30 A.M. and Tom cleans the serving areas at 1:30 P.M.; or guidelines about the number of square feet of floor to be waxed during a shift or the number of salads to be made in an hour.

The combination of all such statements—the formal position description and any supplementary lists of duties or responsibilities—define the position.

What Are the Uses of Position Descriptions?

Position descriptions can help avoid the creation of unnecessary positions. Sometimes an administrator wishes to create a position to solve a nagging problem. By writing down the specific duties that the incumbent will perform, the administrator may see clearly that to solve the problem will require someone with specialized training, but that a specialist will not be needed once the problem is solved.

In such cases the administrator could hire a consultant to solve the problem and a lower-paid employee to carry out the routines recommended by the consultant. Individuals with specialized backgrounds, who must be paid accordingly, should be hired as permanent employees only if the administrator can foresee a long-term need for their specialized skills.

Position descriptions can serve as a check against hiring unqualified or overly qualified faculty or staff members. As a final step after choice has been narrowed to a final pool of candidates, administrators with hiring authority need to consult again the various lists of duties and responsibilities of the position to assure that those final candidates meet the specified requirements. In the absence of such a check, the administrator may compromise the standards originally established for the position.

They can be the basis for planning work. By listing the expectations of an incumbent of a position, one may uncover the strengths and weaknesses of the way in which tasks are expected to be performed. The exercise of listing the tasks enables an administrator to improve the structure of the job. By comparing the description with descriptions of other positions in the department, one will discover gaps and overlaps with other positions.

They can provide a basis for determining which positions are exempt and nonexempt under the Fair Labor Standards Act. The relevant provisions of the Fair Labor Standards Act are discussed in Chapter Three.

They can be the basis for setting pay rates. Position descriptions are used in the evaluation and comparison of positions in order to establish equitable rates of pay. (See Chapter Four on position evaluation.) Position content rather than position titles should be used when comparing the relative value of positions within the organization. A well-structured position evaluation system based on well-written position descriptions should assure that differences in pay are related to differences in the duties and not on external bases such as sex or race. The position descriptions must be accurate for the position evaluation plan to be effective in meeting this goal.

They can provide standards for evaluating the performance of employees. Performance evaluations should be based on the employee's fulfillment of the duties and responsibilities of the position rather than on temperament or behavior unless the manifestation of the temperament or behavior is directly related to the performance of duties and responsibilities of the position. Thus, the position description can and should be used as the basis of the evaluation.

They provide a means for settling grievances regarding scope of the position and remuneration for the position. A dispute about duties, responsibilities, or level of pay requires factual data for resolution. The position description should serve as the basis for the settlement of such formal or informal grievances. Additionally, it can be used to determine when a change in the level of duties of a position is significant enough to require a change in pay level. Too often an employee is given an unwarranted pay increase when duties are changed or added yet are of the same level as those already being performed.

They are the basic tool for making salary surveys. Factual comparisons of positions for salary surveys must include comparisons of duty and responsibility levels. (See Chapter Five on salary surveys.)

They can be used to identify training needs. Human resources planning requires administrators to anticipate future needs. When skilled employees retire or terminate their employment, will other employees have the necessary experience, skills, and knowledge to fill the needs? Studies of individuals by age will identify a probable schedule of departure of skilled employees. A study of their position descriptions will determine the skills that will be lost. A study of the remainder of the work force will uncover the deficiencies and identify training needs.

What Information Should a Position Description Provide?

There are at least two basic philosophies about writing the information for position descriptions. One is to tailor each description to each position. The other is to have a series of standard descriptions and match the duties performed with duties listed in the standard description that most closely resemble the particular position.

Using standard descriptions can require less work than writing tailor-made descriptions. The use of such descriptions may invite certain inaccuracies. Standard descriptions are not fully dependable in assuring that the descriptions match the actual duties, that incumbents are paid properly in relation to other employees, and that positions are properly classified as exempt or nonexempt under the Fair Labor Standards Act.

Whichever procedure is used, the description should provide a picture of the responsibilities and tasks of the position. While higher-level positions should be described with broad statements of responsibility, lower-level positions should be characterized by rather specific statements of tasks. Positions between the extremes may be described by a combination of responsibility statements and statements explaining the methods for implementation of those responsibilities.

Exhibits 1, 2, and 3 (see pages 25–28) present sample descriptions for three positions. These descriptions illustrate the following elements:

1. *Position title.* Position descriptions and titles must be free of any references that imply sexual preference. For example, titles such as maid, janitor, houseman, should be replaced by maintenance or janitorial worker. In order for titles to properly reflect responsibility, a centralized system of classification is needed. In the absence of a central system, titles such as director, assistant or associate dean, manager, and so forth might be assigned to positions of different levels in the total organization.

2. *Department.* Description should identify the home base for the position.

3. *Date of review.* The date helps administrators and personnel staff to identify position descriptions that have not been reviewed for a while.

4. *Code number.* Some form of code is normally used to identify the position, its grade level, the numbers of similar descriptions used, or other data that will help in identifying, studying, comparing, and otherwise using the descriptions.

5. *Supervisor.* The title of the next higher-level authority responsible for the position should be listed. A record of the name of the administrator who verified the information contained in the position description is also helpful.

6. *Functional statement.* The position description should begin with a statement of the basic purpose of the position. For example, Exhibit 1, the sample position description for an Assistant Supervisor, Motion Picture Services, states: "Responsible to the Supervisor, Motion Picture Services, for the scheduling and supervision of personnel and professional motion picture production equipment on location and in the studio."

7. *Most significant duties and responsibilities.* The position description should summarize the most significant tasks and responsibilities. Not every detail of every task that might ever be performed need be included. The tasks should be described in enough detail to provide a basis for position evaluation. However, if the detail is too specific, the descriptions will need constant updating to keep them accurate. Examples of statements that may be too specific are: "is responsible for a budget of $353,000," or "supervises seven clerical employees." Better statements might be: "is responsible for a budget between $300,000 and $399,000," or "supervises six to ten clerical employees." Notice that the classification category (for example, clercial employees) of those supervised is used to provide information about the scope of the position. If specific technical equipment is important to the execution of the position, that equipment should be mentioned. Since equipment is modified from time to time, the general type of equipment should be mentioned; trade or brand names should be avoided unless absolutely essential to the description.

8. *A catch-all duties statement.* Because it is not feasible to publish all the duties that might be performed, a catch-all statement should be included. Such a statement might be "performs additional duties as assigned." Although supervisors have the right to assign appropriate work and duties to an employee, employees may dispute the right of a supervisor to assign duties not listed in the description. A catch-all statement provides the supervisor with some latitude. However, duties that require skills or knowledge beyond the level of the position should not be assigned under the catch-all provision.

Nor should supervisors use the provision to justify the assignment of tasks substantially below the level of the position, lest employees feel demeaned by such request.

9. *Position requirements.* Position requirements include the education, knowledge, and experience needed to fulfill the position's duties. The educational requirements are subject to review under federal guidelines intended to preclude any discrimination that may result from unnecessarily stringent prerequisites to employment. Therefore, administrators must be prepared to prove that the educational requirements listed are necessary for the position; the educational and knowledge requirements must relate directly to the duties listed in the position description. In this area, it is troublesome to defend the requirement for a master's degree.

   Since not all knowledge is gained through formal degree granting institutions, one can state equivalencies to degrees; for example, "A bachelor's degree or equivalent experience in accounting." Too, a combination of a lesser degree than that required for a position plus very pertinent experience might produce such an equivalency; each case must be measured on its own merit. Since some experience may be needed to perform the duties, a statement about the work experience should be included in the position specifications. Typical statements are: "up to one year of related experience required," "up to two years of effective experience required," and "demonstrated ability to _____." Because working experiences are of many different types, the statement should specify the effective or relevant prior experience, needed to fulfill the basic needs of the position. Again, experience requirements are subject to review under federal guidelines.

10. *A statement on scope of supervision received.* The position description should include the scope of independent judgment that the individual filling the position may exercise. Such statements are derived from a list of previously determined levels. Here is a sample list:

    a. Under immediate supervision with assignments of work at frequent intervals and a regular check of performance.

b. Under general supervision with standard practices enabling the employee to proceed on regular duties, referring questionable cases to supervisor or others.

c. Under direction with definite established objectives that require the use of a wide range of procedures; the employee plans and arranges his or her own work, referring only unusual cases to supervisor or others.

d. Under general direction, the employee works from policies and general objectives with little functional guidance and rarely refers specific cases to superior unless clarification or interpretation of policy is involved.

e. Under administrative direction, the employee establishes his or her own standard of performance within overall policy or budgetary limits and with direct accountability for final results; employee is virtually self-supervising, using an independent approach to highly creative work or basic research and evaluating the phenomena encountered without direction except as to general areas of original exploration.

For more details on writing job descriptions, see American Management Association (1977); and College and University Personnel Association (in press).

Who Is Responsible for Supplying Data
for the Position Description?

Positions are created because of an organizational need. Thus, the management of an institution needs to determine the duties and responsibilities of a position. The responsibility for job content rests with the administrator. If a new position is to be created, the administrator has the responsibility for prescribing the duties and responsibilities of the new position. However, if a review is undertaken of an existing position, the incumbent should be asked to review the description to make sure that the position description accurately describes the duties performed.

After the incumbent reviews the position description, the supervisor should reviewed it again. Such a review may uncover differences of opinion between the supervisor and the incumbent about the duties to be performed, revealing both duties performed by the incumbent that should have been discontinued and necessary duties performed by the incumbent about which the supervisor was unaware. In any case, the result of the combined review should be a position description that satisfies management's needs rather than the employee's habits or preferences.

Normally, the formal position description is prepared by a member of the personnel department from data supplied by the administration. Centralized description writing should assure a consistency of style and format. However, small colleges and universities simply may not have the resources, time, or staff to assign the description writing to the personnel department. Such institutions should consider the following procedures. Have the personnel department prepare a format for a position description and delegate to the employee and supervisor the responsibility for writing the position description. The supervisor should prepare the specifications of education and experience requirements for the position. Or, implement an employee representative system in which one person in each department or college is responsible for position descriptions and specifications within that area. Institutions could also employ a consultant or other outside help on a temporary basis. Too, graduate students could conduct analyses and temporary workers could type and edit the documents. Of course, all these practices carry certain risks and disadvantages. These risks and disadvantages must be weighed according to need, purpose, and consequences depending upon the organizational circumstances and philosophies.

Sample forms useful for recording data for writing position descriptions are presented in Exhibits 4 and 5 (see pages 29–36). The following discussion about the completion of the form shown in Exhibit 4 explains the purposes of the various sections of the form. The form should be prepared by the supervisor if the position is a new one and jointly by the supervisor and the incumbent if an existing position is under review. It should be approved by the next level of supervision before being submitted to the personnel specialist.

First, The supervisor designates the institutional unit of the position. Determination of the classification category rests with the personnel office. Then, Section I asks, "Why is this position being created?" and "Is any portion of this position supported by general funds?" Neither of these questions is related to the position description. Rather, they are directed to the process to obtain ultimate approval to create the position.

Section II asks for a list of duties and responsibilties, and the approximate percentage of time that will be spent on each of these duties. These data are needed when the position is evaluated to determine whether the position is exempted or not from the overtime provisions of the Fair Labor Standards Act (see Chapter Three). The primary duties and responsibilities should be listed first, with secondary duties following, and occasional duties listed last.

Section III asks specific questions to determine the education and experience needs for the position. Determining these requirements often requires discussion between the personnel specialist and the supervisor so that like requests can be assigned to relatively similar positions throughout the institution. These facts are used when evaluating the position and, also, when filling the position.

Section IV lists specific statements that designate levels of supervisory control. This information will be used by the personnel specialist. Section V raises questions about the types and nature of contacts the incumbent would experience, the scope of confidential data handled, and the probable errors the individual might be subject to. Section VI includes questions on physical demand, equipment operated, and working conditions.

Section VII requests an organization chart that places the position in the context of other positions in the area. It provides a basis for review of the descriptions of the other positions to assure that there are no gaps or overlaps in the duties and responsibilities. It helps to measure the levels of responsibility by placing the position in its working relationship with those positions above and below.

This form thus provides not only information about the duties and responsibilities needed to write the position description but also information about the position's place in the organization, the educational and experience requirements, and other information needed to evaluate the position. All this information assists the personnel staff in writing an accurate formal position description.

After a formal position description is developed, it should be verified by the supervisor and the employee.

How Often Should Position Descriptions Be Reviewed?

Every position title should be routinely reviewed at least annually. Since a small cadre of personnel specialists usually monitors such a review program, it is probably desirable to divide the institution into twelfths and work on one twelfth each month. One procedure is to provide the administrators with a copy of the current description and ask that the supervisor and the incumbent review it. They both sign and return it if there are no changes in content. If changes are indicated, they sign and indicate agreement with the changes. The suggested revisions are then sent to the personnel specialist for review and correction. The review process should be kept simple and the benefits of the review should be made known so that supervisors and employees are encouraged to accurately report changes in position content.

Certain events will force descriptions to be reviewed early. For instance, a decision not to replace an employee who resigns probably will have an effect on the duties of the other employees in that work group. Similarly, if programs and positions are retrenched, the duties of the remaining individuals will be affected. If two units merge or any basic reorganization occurs, the duties and responsibilities of those employees involved are likely to be affected. Such actions suggest an active program of updating for accuracy. If regular updating is not practiced, an employee grievance may develop that is caused by an employee's resentment at being required to do higher-level duties, or more work, without additional compensation. Outdated descriptions could also result in a determination by a regulatory agency that pay inequities have developed between male and female employees in similar positions and that a substantial cash award is due employees who suffered this inequity.

In summary, adequate methods to control positions and properly written descriptions of duties and responsibilities provide administrators with the primary and beginning tools for effective management of positions.

Exhibit 1. Position Description: Assistant Supervisor

Title of Position: Assistant Supervisor, Motion Picture Services
Classification: Staff exempt
Department: U.D.I.S.

Function of Position:

Responsible to Supervisor, Motion Picture Services, for the scheduling and supervision of personnel and professional motion picture production equipment on location and in the studio.

Principal Duties and Responsibilities:

1. Supervise assigned personnel and the operation of professional motion picture production equipment on location and on studio assignment.
2. Under the general direction of the supervisor, plan, schedule, and make work assignments for the crew.
3. Check invoices against services performed or materials received; prepare or check laboratory work orders; handle problems that arise with the laboratory; check billings before they are sent to clients.
4. Maintain control of inventory and order film stock, magnetic materials, or other operating supplies when needed.
5. In the absence of supervisor, assume full responsibility for the operation of the section. This responsibility includes conferring with clients, preparing quotations and estimates, and solving operational problems.
6. Advise faculty and staff on motion picture techniques.
7. Prepare reports for the supervisor and inform the supervisor about the status of all jobs in progress.
8. Operate professional motion picture equipment such as cameras, lighting instruments, recorders, and editing equipment.
9. Maintain delicate optical and electronic equipment.
10. Perform additional duties as assigned by supervisor.

Supervision:

Determines own work assignments based on an understanding of the limits of established practice within the position. Supervises the activities of two to ten professional, clerical, and technical-service employees. Assists with occasional special assignments.

Minimum Qualifications:

Bachelor's degree or equivalent in motion picture production with three to four years of effective experience working in an active production unit.

Exhibit 2. Position Description: Academic Department Head

Title of Position: Academic Department Head

Function:

The academic department head is the chief administrative officer and educational leader for disciplines within the described department and is responsible through his or her leadership for the direction of programs in resident instruction, continuing education, research, public service, and creative endeavor.

Principal Responsibilities:

1. To organize the department, taking the initiative in developing departmental policies and programs in resident education, research, and continuing education.
2. To recommend to the dean the section heads for major areas within a department.
3. To recruit capable faculty members, with the concurrence of appropriate administrative officers, to encourage excellence in teaching, and to develop means for its evaluation and improvement.
4. To encourage faculty in research, writing, and other creative endeavors.
5. To organize and supervise appropriate faculty seminars and convocations.
6. To recommend individuals for membership in the graduate faculty.
7. To make effective recommendations to the dean relative to hiring, promotions, salary adjustments, tenure, leaves of absence, transfer, suspension, termination, and discipline.
8. To serve as a channel of communication between the faculty and the administrative or executive committee, dean, and general university offices.
9. To administer the departmental budget, supervise the department's secretarial and service staff, and supervise physical facilities under jurisdiction of the department.
10. To prepare schedules of course offerings.
11. To plan appropriate arrangements for advising undergraduate students majoring in the department.
12. To plan appropriate arrangements for the supervision and approval of graduate theses and dissertations, and for the advising and guidance of graduate students within the department.
13. To encourage the organization and operation of appropriate student seminars, convocations, student groups, and clubs within the department.

14.   To participate in teaching and research, as feasible, and to maintain relationships with the technical, scientific, and scholarly organizations in his or her field.

15.   To cooperate with and assist the associate or assistant deans for resident education, research, and continuing education in his or her college in promoting and developing undergraduate and graduate programs in instruction, opportunities for research, and participation in continuing education programs.

16.   To develop and maintain appropriate contacts with research organizations, foundations, business, labor, professional, and public groups.

17.   To serve as liaison between the department and other academic departments of the college, the university, and the graduate school.

Appointment:

The academic department head is appointed by the president of the university upon recommendation of the dean of the college and with the advice of faculty. He or she holds office at the pleasure of the president and dean and is administratively responsible to the dean.

Exhibit 3. Position Description: Carpenter

Code No.: 40-001-01-04
College or Department: Maintenance and Operations
Grade: 4
Job Title: Carpenter A

Under normal supervision, the following duties are to be performed:

1. Perform a variety of carpentry work to construct, alter or repair woodwork within campus buildings and offices, such as office partitions, wood trim and general repairs and alterations, repairs to roofs, stairs, and floors, and construction of small buildings.
2. Fit and hang doors, install hardware on millwork, doors, windows, screens, and cabinets.
3. Install laboratory equipment such as wood or metal cabinets, tops, hoods, and the like.
4. Interpret orders and drawings; plan work in proper sequence.
5. Set up and operate woodworking machines such as power saws, planers, joiners, routers, portable power morticers, power planes, power caulkers, hinge jigs, nailers, and a variety of carpenter's hand tools.
6. Erect various types of partitions, such as prefabricated wood and metal.
7. Lay out and mark openings in masonry walls for masonry crew.
8. Occasionally may be required to perform special jobs using styrofoam or cork or installation of floating floors and the like.
9. Install acoustic ceilings such as suspended, adhesed, splined, and stapled.
10. Install various types of lathe, corner bench, and the like.
11. Install glass and hardware on windows, doors, and partitions.
12. Construct concrete forms; cut and place steel reinforcement.
13. Build and erect wood or metal scaffolding.
14. Work with plastic laminates such as formica.
15. Apply wood preservatives as required.
16. Direct the work of helpers or laborers as assigned by supervisor.

Date _____

Exhibit 4. Request for Evaluation of New Position

College or Department: Office of Physical Plant

Please indicate the type of new position you wish to have evaluated:

☒   staff   ☐   clerical   ☐   technical-service

This form and any related information should be forwarded through the designated Personnel Representative to the Manager, Salary Administration, and Classification Division.

   I.   Why is this position being created?   Increased work load requires better organization of the management of this function.

      Is any portion of this position supported by general funds?

      ☒   yes   ☐   no

  II.   Duties and Responsibilities: Please list the duties and responsibilities of the position. Indicate the approximate percentage of time which will be spent performing each duty. (If desired, some duties may be grouped and a composite percentage given.)

Approximate Percentage of Time	Duties and Responsibilities
5%	1. Supervises and administers the Service Garage clerical function. This includes scheduling of vehicle maintenance, billing for services and associated clerical activities.
5%	2. Supervises and administers the Maintenance Building Reference Room which includes the microfilm area, manuals, periodicals, and office and audiovisual equipment check-out.
10%	3. Responsible for the operation of data-processing accounting system within the office of Physical Plant. Supervises and coordinates the collecting, verifying, preparation and processing of data relevant to the system.
10%	4. Supervises the Physical Plant data-processing time card payroll system for technical-service employees. Responsible for the resolution of discrepancies and ensuring that corrective action has been initiated.

Exhibit 4 (continued)

Approximate Percentage of Time	Duties and Responsibilities
10%	5. Responsible for planning and scheduling assigned personnel to effectively meet priorities and established workloads.
10%	6. Responsible for interviewing, hiring, supervising, training, orienting, and coordinating the work of assigned employees to include clerical, technical-service, and wage payroll personnel. Represent management in administering the university-union agreement.
10%	7. Acts as paymaster for the division and ensures that paychecks are dispersed according to policy and procedure.
10%	8. Calculates and administers the payroll for those employees eligible to receive Worker's Compensation Benefits.
5%	9. Supervises the operation of the Physical Plant taxi system.
8%	10. Responsible for the administration of the two-way radio and page-master systems and for ordering and recommending modifications to equipment and systems.
7%	11. Counsels and disciplines employees within established guidelines. Recommends appropriate action.
5%	12. Responsible for evaluating and performance of assigned personnel. Completes performance reviews and conducts appraisal sessions.
5%	13. Responsible for verifying key requests for university community and overseeing associated records.
2%	14. Schedules vacations and other absences according to priorities and workload demands and oversees associated records.
2%	15. Performs other duties as assigned.

III.   Education and Experience Requirements

What is the minimum level of formal education and specialized knowledge required?   Associate Degree or equivalent and knowledge of data processing.

What amount of experience and on-the-job training are required to meet the minimum requirements? (Do not include education or training after competency has been reached.)   Two to four years in data-processing routines and supervision of employees.

IV.   Supervisory Control: Check any of the following statements that describes how the employee's duties and responsibilities will be carried out day to day.

_____   Performs under almost daily oral or written instruction from supervisor.

_____   Performs under immediate supervision; work assignments given at frequent intervals and checked regularly.

_____   Performs under general supervision, regular work assignments within standard practice.

___✓___   Determines own work assignment where a definite objective has been set up, requiring a wide range of procedures.

_____   Initiates broad programs under general direction, working from policies and general objectives.

_____   Other: _____

V.   Complete this section for *staff* or *clerical* positions only.

Contacts: List the titles of individuals with whom the person in this position has contacts (face-to-face, telephone, correspondence) and the nature of these contacts (furnishing information, discussion, persuasion).

Titles of contacts	Nature of Contacts
Directors and Managers	Meetings, Payroll, Procedures
Bursar/Payroll	Checks, Worker's Compensation
(Various) Sales Representatives	Radio and pagecom equipment

Exhibit 4 (continued)

Titles of contacts	Nature of Contacts
Mgr. of Systems Engineering Management Services	Computer problems
Secretary, Risk Management	Worker's Compensation

Confidential data: List all confidential university data to which the person in this position has full and complete access. (Examples: university salaries, knowledge of classified research, department budgets, personal records).
University salaries, department budgets, personnel records, computer information, worker's compensation.

Errors: Describe the probable results of an inadvertent error in judgment, interpretation, accountability, or exercise of authority in the performance of the position. Give examples.
Payroll check incorrect requires possibly going to the Bursar with an explanation of what happened and have check rewritten. Computer information used for billing if incorrect must be called in to Management Service for correction. Error in calculating Worker's Compensation results in giving employees false information on which to make their financial decisions. Failure to expedite paperwork could result in an employee owing money to the university.

VI.   Complete this section for *technical-service* positions only.

Physical demand: List the types and weights of materials lifted or moved.

Materials   Weights

Equipment operated: List the types of equipment operated.

Working conditions: List any disagreeable working conditions, such as dust, heat, noise, vibration, water, and the like.

VII. Organization Chart: Complete as follows:

Block #1	Title of this position and name, if filled.
Block #2	The name and title of the immediate supervisor of this position.
Block #3	The name and title of the supervisor's supervisor.
Blocks #4A and 4B	The names and title of two positions on the same level as this position.
Blocks #5A, 5B, 5C, and 5D	If applicable, the number of full-time and part-time employees under the direct supervision of this position.

```
┌─────────────────────────────────────────────┐
│ 3.          William Henry                     │
│ Director, Physical Plant Administration       │
└─────────────────────────────────────────────┘
                      │
          ┌───────────────────────────┐
          │ 2.        Carl James        │
          │ Mgr., Business Operations   │
          └───────────────────────────┘
                      │
┌──────────────────┬─────────────────────┬──────────────────┐
│ 4A. Supervisor,  │ 1.Maintenance Bldg.  │ 4B. Supervisor,  │
│ Office and       │ Supervisor, General  │ Office and       │
│ Accounting       │ Helen Holmes         │ Accounting       │
│ Elsie Smith      │                      │ Carol Nystrom    │
└──────────────────┴─────────────────────┴──────────────────┘
┌──────────────┬──────────────────┬──────────────┬──────────────┐
│ 5A.          │ 5B.              │ 5C.          │ 5D.          │
│ Staff Exempt │ Staff Nonexempt  │ Clerical     │ Tech-Service │
│ No. of 0     │ No. of 0         │ No. of 9     │ No. of 4     │
└──────────────┴──────────────────┴──────────────┴──────────────┘
```

VIII. Remarks

Form prepared by _____   _____
                              Signature   Date

Approved by _____   _____
                          Signature   Date

Personnel
Representative _____   _____
                            Signature   Date

Exhibit 5. Request for Classification Action

Please have this form typed and retain a copy for your files.

Action Requested   Date: _____

☐   New position
☐   Reclassification of an occupied position
☐   Reclassification of a vacant position
☐   Other. Specify: _____

Name of Incumbent: _____
                          (Present or most recent if classified)
Position Title: _____
                                  (If presently classified)
Position Code: _____
                                  (If presently classified)

Department Name: _____
Department No.: _____ Department Phone No.: _____
Account No.: _____ Budget Position No.: _____

For more information on this position, please contact:

_____
(Name)

_____
(Department)

_____
(Building)

Please answer each of the questions listed. If you need additional space, attach separate sheets and identify the question by number.

1. Specific duties. First, list your duties in order of importance. Second, estimate the percentage of time for each task based on the time spent in a day, week, month, or any other unit of time. Total percentage should equal 100%. *Percentages must be assigned.*

Specific Duties (list in order of importance)	Percentage
	100%

2. Most difficult duties: What are the most difficult or complex duties of your position? Which duties require the most training or assistance from others?

3. Responsibility and decision making: What kinds of decisions are you required to make?

4. Assignment, review, and approval of work: How do you receive your assignments? How is your work reviewed? Who would help you with a problem? What type of problem do you refer to someone else?

5. Position requirements: Are there any special courses or formal training programs required for your position? Are you required to have a special license? Please explain.

6. Working Environment: Explain any presence of radiation or environmental hazards in your work. Describe any other hazards on your job.

7. Machinery and equipment operated: Describe any machinery or equipment used in your position.

8. Reporting relationships: List the titles of persons reporting to you and summarize their basic duties.

9. Nature of supervision: Describe the type of supervision *you* provide, including how often you review work and the types of problems that are brought to your attention. Do you have the authority to make hiring and dismissal decisions?

Exhibit 5 (continued)

Review of form by immediate supervisor

What do you consider to be the most important duties of this position?

Reviewed by: _____
                    (Signature)   (Title)   (Date)

Review by department head

Please confirm or deny the content of this position description.

Reviewed by: _____
                    (Signature)   (Title)   (Date)

Fiscal approval for classification action
(Sign appropriate statement)

Fiscal approval for new position

This request for the establishment of a *new position* is submitted with the understanding that funds will be available from within my budgetary area to enter this position in my budget at the appropriate rate of pay immediately upon classification.

_____
(Signature of dean or director)

Fiscal approval for reclassification

This request for reclassification is submitted with the understanding that, if the position is reclassified to a level having a higher pay range, funds will be available from within my budgetary area, *exclusive of salary increase funds,* to fund the position at the appropriate rate at the beginning of the next fiscal year.

_____
(Signature of dean or director)

❧ 3 ❧

Categorizing and Analyzing Positions

Once methods have been estab-
lished for position control and for gathering written data about
position content, effective personnel administration requires the
categorization and analysis of the positions. One step in categorization is to distinguish positions as "exempt" or "nonexempt" under the Fair Labor Standards Act for those institutions covered by
the act.

The Fair Labor Standards Act is federal legislation that contains provisions covering minimum wages, equal pay, age discrimination, and payment of overtime for work in excess of forty hours a
week. On June 24, 1976, the United States Supreme Court, in the
case of the *National League of Cities* v. *Usery,* exempted public institutions from the overtime and minimum wage provisions but not
from the equal pay and age discrimination conditions of the act.

Under the act, positions are classified as nonexempt or
exempt from the overtime provisions. Administrative, executive,
and professional positions that meet the conditions specified in the
act are exempt. (See Exhibits 6, 7, and 8, pages 46–47, for the act's
definitions of such positions.)

37

A sample form for classifying exempt and nonexempt duties is presented in Exhibit 9, page 48. Each duty listed in the description of the position is declared to be exempt or nonexempt. The percentage of time that duty is performed is entered on the form. If 80 percent or more of the time is spent performing exempt duties, the position is declared to be exempt. Thus, in the position description, the time element for each duty is very significant. Similarly, it is important to audit positions frequently to determine whether the time elements originally assigned remain the same. If a position that has been exempt loses its exemption by a change in the amount of time spent on exempt duties, and if that employee has been working more than forty hours a week, the employee is due retroactive overtime pay.

Academic positions should be exempt positions and usually meet the requirements quite readily. However, the lowest paid academic staff member's position should be examined to avoid a claim for overtime by a disgruntled faculty member. Such positions might lose their overtime exemption in two ways: by not meeting the minimum salary for the professional exemption or by including routine tasks that do not meet the exempt criteria. The pay requirement is sometimes not met if a doctoral candidate is given an appointment under a research contract that provides limited funds.

It is possible that of two positions with identical duties, one is exempt and the other nonexempt. For example, two graduate architectural engineers work in the physical plant department as architectural drafters, and both perform design drafting (exempt work) and detail drafting (usually nonexempt work). The employee who performs design work at least 80 percent of the time is exempt from overtime payments. The other employee, who performs nonexempt work more than 20 percent of the time, is categorized as nonexempt and is entitled to overtime payments for work in excess of forty hours a week.

Since public institutions were required to follow all the provisions of the act from 1967 through 1976, many still operate under its provisions. These provisions offer a sound basis for classifying positions and assist an institution in offering competitive conditions of employment. Thus, employers should study the act to become familiar with its recordkeeping obligations and its definitions of hours worked, on-call time, hours worked by employees living on the employer's premises, bona fide meal breaks, travel time, work week, and so forth.

How Many Broad Categories of Personnel Are Needed?

The Fair Labor Standards Act uses the two broad categories exempt and nonexempt, with the exempt category divided into the three subcategories of professional, administrative, and executive. Most institutions use more categories than these to classify their personnel. Four principle considerations affect such decisions. First, faculty members are usually placed in a category separate from other staff professionals because of differences in application of such policies as tenure, academic freedom, sabbatical leaves, compensatory time for consulting, and the like. Second, some institutions combine supervisors, administrators, and professionals into a single group to avoid problems of status that cause hurt feelings. For example, the position of a dietitian in the food services unit is both supervisory and administrative, and the practitioners consider themselves to be professionals.

Third, for similar reasons, most secretarial and clerical staff members do not want to be grouped with service personnel. Thus many institutions have a secretarial-clerical category and a separate service, or service-technical category. Fourth, institutions consider the relationship between position categories and potential unionization. Employees with a community of interest and similar policies and benefits often are placed in a single unit for collective bargaining purposes. When unions present petitions to labor boards for unit determination, the institution will have a better chance of influencing that determination if the position categories appear reasonable. Thus, in devising a categorization scheme, administrators should ask themselves: "If we were approached by a union, what kinds of bargaining units would we prefer? What combinations of employees in a single unit would cause administrative anguish?" Definitions of employee categories and benefits should be established to reflect those wishes.

Two samples of personnel categories used in higher education follow. The first system is that used by the federal government in requesting information regarding affirmative action efforts. (For details on institutional reporting for affirmative action, the EEO-6 report, see Chapter Seven and Commerce Clearing House, 1979.) Several institutions have adopted these categories simply because they must provide the government with data based on them. This system defines seven categories of employees:

Executive, administrative, and managerial. All persons whose assignments require primary (and major) responsibility for management or general business operation of the institution, or a customarily recognized department or subdivision thereof. These persons exercise discretion and independent judgment and direct the work of others. This category includes all officers holding positions such as president, vice president, dean, director, associate dean, assistant dean, executive officers of academic departments such as chairpersons and heads if their principle activity is administrative, and officers subordinate to any of these administrators. However, supervisory personnel of technical, clerical, craft, and service or maintenance force should be reported within those specific categories.

Faculty. All persons whose specific assignments are made for the purpose of conducting instruction, research, or public service as a principle activity and who hold academic-rank titles of professor, associate professor, assistant professor, instructor, lecturer. Deans, directors, associate deans, assistant deans, executive officers of academic departments should be reported in this category if their principle activity is instructional.

Professional and nonfaculty. All persons whose assignments require either a bachelor's degree or experience of such kind and amount as to provide a comparable background. Included are all staff members with assignments requiring specialized professional training.

Clerical and secretarial. All persons whose assignments typically are associated with clerical activities or are specifically of a secretarial nature. This category includes persons who are responsible for internal and external communications, recording and retrieval of data (other than computer programmers) or information, and other paper work required in an office: bookkeepers, stenographers, clerk-typists, office-machine operators, statistical clerks, payroll clerks, sales clerks, library clerks (but not librarians), and the like.

Technical and paraprofessionals. All persons whose assignments require specialized knowledge or skills that require experience or academic work such as is offered in two-year technical institutions, junior colleges or equivalent on-the-job training. This category includes computer operators, computer programmers, drafters, engineering aides, junior engineers, mathematical aides, nurses (licensed, practical, and vocational), dietitians, photographers, radio operators, scientific assistants, technical illustrators, and all technicians (medical, dental, electronic, physical sciences, and the like).

Skilled crafts. All persons whose assignments typically require special manual skills acquired through on-the-job training or through apprenticeship or other formal training programs: mechanics, repairers, electricians, stationary engineers, skilled machinists, carpenters, compositors, and typesetters.

Service and maintenance. All persons whose assignments require limited degrees of previously acquired skills the performance of which results in or contributes to the comfort, convenience, and hygiene of personnel and the student body or which contributes to the maintenance of buildings, facilities, or grounds of the institutional property. This category includes chauffeurs, laundry and dry cleaning operatives, cafeteria and restaurant workers, truck drivers, bus drivers, garage laborers, custodial personnel, gardeners and groundskeepers, refuse collectors, construction laborers, and security personnel.

Although this scheme is, as we noted, the one that must be used for affirmative action reports to the federal government, some institutions use other categories for classification. One sample system uses eight categories:

Executive. An executive is the president, a senior officer, a staff officer of the university, a dean of an academic college or an administrative head of a four-year or upper-division campus.

Administrator. An administrator is a person responsible directly to the president, a senior officer, or a staff officer of the university *and* who has been delegated by that executive officer the responsibility for a nonacademic department or nonacademic function of major scope. Examples are the director of physical plant operations, or the director of housing and food services.

Academic administrator. An academic administrator is one who holds academic rank *and* who holds an administrative position in a major academic function. A person holding any of the following or similar titles in an academic area is included: assistant vice president, assistant to the vice president, associate dean, assistant dean, assistant to the dean, department head, director of a school, director of a major research unit, chairman of an academic division, assistant or associate director, assistant department head, or coordinator.

Academic. An academic employee is one who is qualified to hold academic rank and whose major responsibility is in the academic pursuit. Academic ranks are as follows: professor, associate professor, assistant professor, instructor, assistant, librarian, associate librarian, senior assistant librarian, assistant librarian, senior research associate, research associate, research assistant, and lecturer.

Staff exempt. A staff-exempt employee is one whose primary duty is the performance of office or nonmanual work directly related to management policies or general business operations and who customarily and regularly exercises discretion and independent judgment. Also in this category is an employee whose primary duty requires knowledge of an advanced type in a field of science or learning, or original and creative work in an artistic field. The work requires the consistent exercise of discretion and judgment, and the work must be predominantly intellectual and varied in character as opposed to routine mental, manual, mechanical or physical work; and of such character that the product or the result accomplished cannot be standardized in relation to a given period of time. (Assignment to this category is based on rules and regulations under the Fair Labor Standards Act.)

Staff nonexempt. A staff-nonexempt employee is one whose work is semiprofessional, administrative, or technical in nature and subject to provisions for overtime payment under the Fair Labor Standards Act.

Clerical. A clerical employee is one who performs duties usually referred to as office duties that entail one or more of the following: typing, stenography, filing, public contact, operation of office machines, and recordkeeping. Duties may involve directing the work of employees performing the same or similar work.

Technical-service. A technical-service employee is one who performs unskilled, semiskilled, or skilled work usually referred to as manual. Duties require the use of tools, machinery, or equipment, and involve one or more of the following: the fabrication of apparatus, equipment, machinery, buildings, or tools; the supply of materials, apparatus, machinery, equipment, or tools; the operation of apparatus, machinery, equipment, or vehicles; the maintenance of apparatus, machinery, equipment, vehicles, livestock, buildings, grounds, or fields. In addition to performing such duties, a technical-service employee may be required to lead and give direction to employees performing the same or similar work.

What Is Position Analysis?

Position analysis is the process of reviewing the duties, responsibilities, and qualification requirements of a position and relating the results of the review to other facets of the personnel function—recruitment, selection, development, appraisal of performance, and position evaluation. Position analysis takes the information provided from the review of the formal position description and places it in an institutional context; thus position analysis is preliminary to position evaluation. The process of position analysis addresses the relatedness of duties and responsibilities to experience, skills, knowledge, and abilities required for the tasks to be performed. Such analysis facilitates nondiscriminatory employment, the setting of standards for performance evaluation, and the implementation of policies on training and development, promotion, demotion, and the like.

The multiple and varied uses of information about positions suggest a need for systematic development of techniques for position analysis. Caution should be taken, however, not to load the analysis with multiple purposes to the extent that the method becomes cumbersome and the results ineffective. Among the many uses of position analysis are: (1) to verify that position descriptions are written to insure proper recruitment, selection, and placement; (2) to assure that required data are available for proper job evaluation; (3) to monitor job design for adequacy of the mix of duties and responsibilities and provisions for upward mobility; (4) to verify equal employment opportunity for protected groups such as handicapped individuals; (5) to set standards for appraising and measuring performance; (6) to identify possible occupational health and safety hazards; (7) to identify training needs; (8) to collect data for human resources planning; (9) to resolve union grievances; (10) to specify division of labor expected to yield maximum productivity; and (11) to develop career ladders that provide upward mobility for employees.

Sound position analysis procedures contribute to successful and effective results. The most basic position analysis procedures require the analyst to first choose a representative sample of positions and become thoroughly familiar with each position before the actual analysis. The analyst should then identify the duties of each position in rank order of importance or frequency; identify the skills, knowledges, and abilities needed to perform the work; and identify the physical and mental demands, environmental conditions, and the like. The analyst should also identify both the degree of supervision received and supervision given. Having gathered this information, the analyst should invite comments from the administrator (and the position holder, if there is an incumbent) on the accuracy of position analysis record.

More specifically, the four steps of the position analysis process, along with their substeps, are:

1. Preparation. The analyst should (a) learn the technologies of the position; (b) set objectives, organize the approach, and select and plan the position analysis method to be used; and (c) discuss the position with experts in the field either at the institution or at similar institutions. Examples of ways to learn the position technologies include consulting the dictionary of occupational titles; reading books, trade, or professional journals; searching catalogues, position descriptions, training manuals; studying organization and flow charts; and talking with experts in the field.
2. Information gathering. The analyst should (a) observe the unit, department, or office; (b) interview individuals or groups;

(c) use a questionnaire to solicit information; (d) keep a diary about the position; (e) keep a critical incident record; (f) use equipment design information (blueprints or company specifications); (g) record job activities; (h) map jobs using flow charts or other visual aids. A combination of observation, interview, and questionnaire is most effective for most jobs. However, in determining the most effective data collection technique, the analyst should consider the personnel available to conduct the position analysis, cost, time, and the complexity of occupation to be analyzed. Usually a combination of techniques yields the most useful and reliable information. A greater risk of error or omission exists when only one method is used.

3. Analysis. The analyst should organize the data and select a position analysis method. Five position analysis methods are presented in Exhibit 10 (see pp. 49–51). The choice of position analysis methods depends on the purpose and use of the analysis (performance appraisal, training, employee selection) and the constraints of the proposed project. The analyst must understand the exact kind of information needed to satisfy project requirements and the focus of available position analysis methods. For example, some methods focus on the tasks, while others look more closely at worker characteristics; some emphasize the tools, products, and environment of the job, while others ignore these factors. Additionally, if the analysis is to be used to obtain information upon which work comparisons, ratings, or standards will be based, the analyst must carefully read and interpret any program requirements and federal regulations or guidelines that must be followed or satisfied.

4. Summary and documentation. The analyst should prepare an interview and observation summary (job analysis schedule), a job description, and job specifications.

The end products of position analysis—the position description and the specifications—may be provided in a variety of formats. Most computerized position analysis procedures (CODAP, for example) provide numerical summaries, whereas more traditional methods (classification, for example) provide descriptive summaries. While the specific features of position descriptions and position specifications are quite varied, the basic patterns have much in common. For more details on position analysis methods and techniques, see McCormick (1979), Smith (1979), U.S. Department of Labor (1972), and Fine (1974).

Once the position analysis information is summarized and documented, the information may be put to a variety of uses. One such use is position evaluation, the subject of the next chapter.

**Exhibit 6. Administrative Employee:
Fair Labor Standards Act Definition**

Test: A, B, D, and E must all be met along with one of the three tests in C.

A. Primary duty is the performance of office or nonmanual work directly related to management policies or general business operations of the employer or the employer's customers; and
B. Customarily and regularly exercises discretion and independent judgment; and
C. (1) Regularly and directly assists a proprietor, or an employee employed in a bona fide executive or administrative capacity, or (2) performs under only general supervision work along specialized or technical lines requiring special training, experience, or knowledge, or (3) executes under only general supervision special assignments and tasks; and
D. Does not devote more than 20 percent of hours worked in the workweek to activities which are not directly and closely related to the performance of the work described in subsections (A) through (C) above.
E. Receives payment on a salary or fee basis at a rate of not less than $155 a week ($8060 a year).

Source: Commerce Clearing House, *Guidebook to Federal Wage-Hour Laws* (1970, pp. 83–85) for Exhibits 6, 7, and 8.

Exhibit 7. Executive: Fair Labor Standards Act Definition

Test: All six of the following conditions must be met.

A. Primary duty is the management of (1) the enterprise in which employed, or (2) a customarily recognized department or subdivision thereof.
B. Customarily and regularly directs the work of *two or more* other employees.
C. Has authority to hire or fire other employees or to make recommendations as to hiring, firing, and the advancement, promotion, or change of status of employees.
D. Customarily and regularly exercises discretionary powers.
E. Receives payment on a salary basis at a rate of not less than $155 a week ($8060 a year).
F. Does not devote more than 20 percent of the hours worked in the workweek to activities which are not *directly and closely related* to the performance of exempt work.

Exhibit 8. Professional Employee: Fair Labor Standards Act Definition

Test: One of the alternate requirements under A and all of the requirements B, C, D, E, must be met.

A. Employee must have as the primary duty either (1) work requiring knowledge of advanced type in a field of science or learning, *or* (2) original and creative work in an artistic field.
B. Work requires the consistent exercise of discretion and judgment.
C. Work must be (1) predominantly intellectual and varied in character as opposed to routine mental, manual, mechanical, or physical work; and (2) of such a character that the output produced or the result accomplished cannot be standardized in relation to a given period of time.
D. Time spent in activities not "an essential part of and necessarily incident" to professional duties may not exceed 20 percent of employee's own weekly hours worked.
E. Received payment of a salary or fee basis at a rate of not less than $170 a week ($8840 a year).

Exhibit 9. Exempt/Nonexempt Classification Form

Job Title: _____

College or Department: _____

Estimated Percentage of Time	Executive	Exempt		Nonexempt
		Administrative	Professional	
1. _____				
2. _____				
3. _____				
4. _____				
5. _____				
6. _____				
7. _____				
8. _____				
9. _____				
10. _____				
11. _____				
12. _____				
13. _____				
14. _____				
15. _____				
Subtotal _____				
Total _____				

Remarks: Classification

Executive   _____
Administrative   _____
Professional   _____
Nonexempt   _____
                          Initials _____
                          Date _____

Exhibit 10. Summary of Five Common Position Analysis Methods

Background	Major Characteristics	Initial Uses
1. The *Position Analysis Questionnaire* (PAQ) a. Developed in the 1950s at Purdue University, Occupational Research Center by Ernest J. McCormick. b. Approaches work from the perspective of the characteristics required to perform the task. c. Defines worker-oriented job elements (physical and mental behaviors that remain constant across jobs and throughout changes in technology). Job elements are based on a stimulus-organism-response model (stimulus=sensory activity; organism=reasoning, decision making, and other mental processes; response=psychomotor aspects of work including tools used).	A. Defines approximately 200 elements and groups them in six categories: (1) information input, (2) mental processes, (3) work output, (4) relationship with other persons, (5) job context, (6) other job characteristics. B. Provides scales for employees, supervisors, or job analysts to record degree to which each element applies to the job being analyzed. C. Provides checks for data consistency among raters before data are analyzed by computer program. D. Yields results showing relative involvement of a job with the predefined job elements in comparison with a varied sample of jobs from the U.S. economy. Involvement is presented in score format and from the scores, estimates are made of expected ability characteristics of incumbents as a group.	A. Used to aid in development of worker selection procedures and to clarify abilities relevant to a position.

Exhibit 10 (continued)

Background	Major Characteristics	Initial Uses
2. *Job Element Method*		
a. Developed at Personnel Research and Development Center, U.S. Civil Service Commission (Now Office of Personnel Management), Washington, D.C.	A. Provides scales for supervisors or workers to identify job elements crucial to success and to rate them in terms of: (1) degree to which barely acceptable workers possess the element, (2) degree to which it helps identify superior workers, (3) problems caused in the job if the element is ignored in selecting applicants, and (4) the practicality of demanding this element of applicants.	A. Used extensively by federal government as a basis for developing fair selection procedures;
b. Approaches work from the perspective of human characteristics required to perform the tasks.	B. Computer analysis of the data provides a list of important elements of the job and a basis for analysis.	B. Used to define important elements in federal wage-grade jobs;
c. Emphasizes skills and knowledge a worker needs to perform the job well.		C. To a limited extent, used with other factors to select people for jobs and for entrance into upward mobility programs.
3. *U.S. Department of Labor Method*		
a. Developed in 1930s by the U.S. Employment Service, which sought to classify individuals in the working population according to their occupational characteristics.	A. Provides standard form for trained analysts to obtain information on tasks and traits required of the worker to perform the task. Uses both interview and observation techniques.	A. Used to categorize and classify broad families of work into discrete job groups.
	B. Describes tasks in terms of (1) worker function relative to people, data, and things, (2) major actions performed, (3) machines, tools, and	B. More recently used to analyze both work tasks and worker characteristics.

b. Originally focused mostly on tasks themselves; however, has been refined to capture information both about the tasks of the job as well as the skills, aptitudes, and knowledge needed to perform the job.

4. *Functional Job Analysis* (FJA)
a. A variation of the Department of Labor method, FJA was developed by Dr. Sidney A. Fine, of the Department of Labor and later the W. E. Upjohn Institute for Employment Research.
b. Focus is mostly on tasks themselves, but the method retains the worker function concept, description of machines/tools, definition of products/services and some of the worker traits contained in the Department of Labor method.

equipment used, and (4) results of the task (materials, products, services).
C. Describes worker traits required for the job as a whole in terms of aptitudes, temperament, interests, physical demands, and environmental demands.
D. Provides codes and scaled ratings to rate the job in terms of required worker traits.

A. Provides protocol for experienced workers or people outside the profession trained in FJA to interview and observe workers. Secondary sources compile initial task traits and refine the list through interview and observation processes. Tasks are edited by a few people to assure clarity of language and these lists are verified by larger groups of experienced workers.
B. Uses a systems approach to define the basic purpose of the work in its broadest terms. Each task is then described in terms of (1) the goal to which it contributes, (2) the objective to which it contributes, (3) a standard set of content elements, (4) measures of the level of involvement with and orientation to data, people, and things, (5) the level of complexity and general educational development required, (6) performance standards, and (7) training content.

C. Used to collect data on jobs in the U.S. that are listed in the Dictionary of Occupational Titles.

A. Frequently used to gather information about two or more jobs to ascertain their comparability.

Exhibit 10 (continued)

Background	Major Characteristics	Initial Uses
5. *Comprehensive Occupational Data Computer Program (CODAP)* a. Developed in the 1950s at the Occupational Research Division, Lackland Air Force Base (Texas), Human Resources Lab. b. Focus is mostly on tasks themselves, and develops extensive task inventories (500 tasks per occupational area) to identify tasks most appropriate for training and the kind of training most appropriate. Data must be collected from at least 2,000 workers in each occupational area in order to be valid and reliable.	A. Provides a task inventory to be constructed by individuals specifically trained in gathering and writing task information. The completed inventory is reviewed by five to ten supervisors in the occupational area. The inventory contains general worker background information and tasks stated in terms of results. For each task respondents indicate factors such as performance or nonperformance, time spent, criticality to the job, learning difficulty, frequency of performance, time intervals between training and initial performance, and amount of guidance provided before or during performance. B. Provides relative scales (with a defined numerical range) for worker to rate each task relative to other tasks. C. Offers some forty computer programs for analysis of data. Standard analyses include (1) list of tasks performed, (2) percentage of group performing the tasks, and (3) percentage of time spent performing the task. Analysis identifies the tasks to be included in training, the type of training to be provided, the level of proficiency needed.	A. Used initially to extract important aspects of a job for which training may be needed. (Used mostly in U.S. Air Force since 1960 and in other branches of military with some adaptations). Some state and local governments have recently adapted some of the concepts of CODAP for training and job evaluation purposes.

Note: This information was compiled from information provided by Smith (1979).

❧ 4 ❧

Evaluating
Positions

Equal pay is an essential ingredient of good personnel management for several reasons. Unfair pay policies may subject an institution to lawsuits by employees claiming discrimination, to employees' demands for unionization, and to low morale and productivity. To assure that pay rates are equal and fair, institutions need a detailed system for evaluating position content. Such evaluation identifies the fair wage for old and new positions, thereby preventing "promotions" at higher pay to positions with less responsibility, improper employee selection, and unfair pay.

Position evaluation is a systematic process of rating a position in relation to other positions in the organization in order to determine the relative worth of a position to the organization. Position descriptions and position analyses, the first steps in position evaluation are discussed in Chapters Two and Three. Job pricing, the last step in position evaluation and salary surveys are discussed in Chapter Five.

Basic to the design and formulation of a position evaluation plan are sound position analysis procedures, complete and accurate position descriptions and position specifications, and a clear definition of the institutional goals to be realized as a result of the position evaluation efforts. The goals of a position evaluation plan must relate to fair compensation among all positions within the institution. Once position descriptions and position specifications are developed and the goals of the position evaluation plan are determined and clearly stated, the evaluator must determine objectives that will facilitate attainment of the goals, choose an evaluation plan to meet these objectives, communicate and install the plan, and maintain the plan. These procedures are the subject of this chapter.

Although the position evaluation itself may be made by the personnel department or selected administrators, administrators at all levels within an institution of higher education have certain responsiblities for position evaluation. These responsibilities, which should be understood throughout the institution, include providing accurate, factual, and complete descriptive information about positions to be evaluated; keeping position descriptions up to date as changes occur in duties, responsibilities, methods, and technology; assigning employees tasks that are within the limits of their descriptions; understanding the position evaluation system utilized at the institution and supporting it in discussions with subordinates. ordinates.

What Are the Uses of Position Evaluation Plans?

Position evaluation systems are not normally used for faculty positions. However, faculty positions represent one of the earliest forms of hierarchical ranking in that the standard ranks of instructor, assistant professor, associate professor, and professor represent levels of positions. Faculty ranks, however, are usually not related to duties and responsibilities but rather to the scholarship of the incumbent. This is one basic difference between academic positions and support staff positions.

In general, then, position evaluation plans are used to objectively analyze nonacademic positions in order to establish an equitable pay plan that provides for equal pay for work of comparable value. They are also used to develop salary surveys, to correct salaries that are "out of line," and to aid in setting the wages for positions. More specifically, position evaluation provides sound foundation for fair salary relationships among positions based on position content rather than other factors. This evaluation assists administrators in thinking objectively about each position under their control and helps administrators explain the differences to employees. Evaluation facilitates making salary surveys because of the reliability of the data base, and it provides a system for determining when changes in positions merit changes in evaluation and pay. For more details about uses of position evaluation plans and methods see Chesler, 1948; Harris, 1976; McCarthy and Buck,1977; Robinson and others, 1975; Smith, 1978.

What Are Appropriate Position Evaluation Methods?

Four position evaluation methods are commonly used. A description of each follows together with the principal uses, advantages, and disadvantages.

Ranking method. Under the ranking method, a rater (or a group of raters) simply makes a judgment about each position in its entirety as it relates to each other position within the entire organization. Typically, the position's title and the rank of the incumbent are placed on an index card and the cards are arranged in order from top to bottom. If several raters participate, their differences are settled through debate. This system works best for a small and simply organized institution.

A sample ranking for secretarial and clerical support staff in a small institution is (a) secretary to the president, (b) secretary to the provost and secretary to the chief business officer, (c) secretary to an academic dean, (d) secretary to an academic department head, and (e) clerk-typist in an academic department.

The advantages of this method derive from its simplicity. The method is fast and inexpensive, and the results usually reflect the general climate of the institution. However, in the absence of criteria for measurement, each rater may look at only one criterion such as "importance to the institution" and overlook other important criteria. Also, ratings of the value of the position may relate to the incumbent rather than to the duties and responsibilities of the position

Classification method. Under the classification method, a variety of class definitions are established which delineate various levels of responsibility, experience, education and training needed, and complexity of trades. These specifications are organized to yield levels or zones, each of which contains positions of equal value. These selected specifications or levels are then used as the bench marks with which all other positions are compared. Positions are compared in their entirety, not by their component parts. Federal, state, and local governments, and colleges and universities under governmental civil service systems are most likely to use this method of position evaluation. Exhibit 11, pp. 61–62, presents a sample class specification.

The advantages of this method are that it is relatively easy to use for large numbers of positions and that redesigned positions can be easily placed in new appropriate categories. However, this method may invite administrators to "beat the system" because they know in advance the position levels, and levels are open to argument by the position holder. Further, position descriptions may be inaccurate if they are drawn up to meet a specification rather than to reflect the actual duties and responsibilities.

Factor comparison method. Under the factor comparison method, each position is divided into elements or factors, such as skills required, position responsibility, and effort expended. These factors are then measured against a set of bench marks. The sellected factors are weighed according to their relative worth, and grades or levels are thus assigned for each position so compared. Exhibit 12, p. 63, presents a sample of factor comparison data.

The advantages of factor comparison are its simplicity, adaptability, and accuracy. Because there are usually few factors, the method is less cumbersome than some others, and the factors can be modified to meet the institution's needs. The relative accuracy of factor comparison results from the position being divided into several parts, each of which is measured. However, factor comparison may be difficult to defend to employees, particularly if the factors cover a wide variety of positions. Too, some bias may be inherent in the selection of the few bench marks. Finally, this method may invite administrators to "beat the system" because they know in advance the bench marks.

Point method. Under the point method, a position analyst measures each position against a number of yardstick factors. Sample factors are education, experience, initiative and ingenuity, supervision received, hazards, working conditions, and the like. Each factor has a number of gradations that define different levels of the quality or quantity of that factor. For example, the factor for education may be divided into five different degrees (levels), each with an assigned point value. The point values for all the factor degrees are totaled, and the total determines the grade and salary level of the position.

Ready-made point plans are readily available and can be used as they are or with slight modification. The point method is the most widely used system in the United States, and many colleges and universities use it. Exhibit 13, p. 64, shows a sample list of factors and degrees. Exhibit 14, p. 64, provides details for one factor, showing five degrees of difficulty. Exhibit 15, p. 65, presents a sample position evaluation worksheet. The position evaluated is Carpenter A, the position description of which is given in Exhibit 3, p. 28.

The advantages of the point method are substantial. Of the four methods described here, it offers the most complete means to assure equal pay. Each position is evaluated independently from all other positions, and a wide variety of positions can be measured using the same basic measurement criteria. Employees and administrators can be supplied factual information on why their positions fall in a certain salary grade level, and administrators cannot easily interfere with the objectivity of the method by second-guessing the grade a position will receive. The obvious disadvantage of the point method is that it requires more work and time to plan and implement than the other methods.

In addition to the four position evaluation methods listed, there are other unconventional methods that are rarely used in higher education. For example, a time span of discretion method was introduced by Elliott Jaques. Positions are evaluated in terms of the maximum period of time during which the employee is expected to use discretion without review by a supervisor. This factor is similar to the responsibility factor in most point or factor methods. However, most higher education positions are too complex to be measured adequately by a one-factor method.

How Does an Institution Install a Position Evaluation Plan?

In deciding to initiate a position evaluation plan, the administration must make determinations about the scope, goals, and procedures of the evaluation. Among the questions to be answered are: What groups of positions are to be evaluated? What are the institutional objectives for evaluating the positions? What position evaluation method should be used? Should a prepackaged plan be used or is a tailor-made plan necessary? Which employees or groups will need to be consulted? Is a union involved? Is there an employee council or a university senate involved?

Unless a very simplified approach such as ranking can be used, the installation of a plan takes a considerable amount of time and expertise. While simple approaches like ranking may be adequate for small institutions, they are not recommended for larger or more complex institutions. The institution's administration must decide whether a plan can be developed and implemented by personnel available within the institution or whether it is necessary to turn to an outside consultant to accomplish the task. Outside consultants are available who specialize in position evaluation programs and who have experience in installing plans in institutions of higher education.

The authors recommend that the installation be done by internal personnel if the institution has personnel with both the experience and expertise to handle the task, and those personnel can be released from other duties and responsibilities to accomplish the task in a timely manner. This process, however, is effective only if the institutional climate is such that faculty and staff members will trust an installation by internal experts.

If installation by internal personnel is unfeasible or inappropriate, an institution can hire outside consultants. These consultants could be hired to perform the entire task, or they could be employed to advise institutional personnel in performing the task. Consultants can also be asked to assign to institutional personnel certain time-consuming parts of the task and hold themselves in reserve to handle other parts. For example, a cadre of institutional personnel could be temporarily assigned to the personnel department and trained by outside consultants to collect data and write position descriptions. The consultants could then evaluate the positions from the data collected. Thus, a time-consuming part of the task could be accomplished more quickly at a minimum cost for outside consultants, and the cadre of individuals selected would develop an interest and understanding of the evaluation process. If a consultant is to be used, the authors recommend inviting several to make bids on the variety of services needed.

How Does an Institution Maintain a Position Evaluation Plan?

Communicating the position evaluation plan to top management, line supervisors, and faculty and staff members is an important first step in gaining acceptance of the plan and crucial to success of installing and maintaining the plan. Oral and written presentations may be used to explain the administrative, financial, and procedural aspects of the plan. Presentations should be kept as simple as possible and should encourage participants to ask questions, offer suggestions, dispel rumors, and verify facts. In order to gain the participants' commitment to the plan, the administration should explain how the plan relates to the institution's philosophy, policy, past practices, present needs, and future plans.

Resistance to a new plan (as well as grievances after installation) may be minimized if some precautionary steps are taken to gain employees' acceptance before installation. To facilitate employees' acceptance, the management and supervisors should communicate the purpose and procedures of the plan to their employees and employee groups (unions, councils and caucuses). Supervisors should tell employees about the plan before rumors start and assure them that the plan will not result in loss of pay or jobs. Supervisors should emphasize the benefits of the plan to employees and the institution, but without promising any results that cannot be delivered. Employee position evaluation committees could be established to provide direct involvement and commitment, or meetings with top management, governance bodies, or the union could be arranged so that these groups could express their support for the plan.

Once the plan is installed, routine maintenance of the plan is crucial to sound wage and salary administration. To assure proper maintenance, the personnel staff must set up the necessary records and controls, and establish and follow a schedule for reviewing jobs. (As noted earlier, all positions should be reviewed at least once a year.) Effective maintenance also requires that position analysts, supervisors, and employees be instructed as to their roles and importance in the evaluation plan. For such instruction, a job evaluation manual should be prepared. For example, a position evaluation manual for a point evaluation method might include the following:

> Introduction
> Objectives and scope of the job evaluation program
> Directions for using the position evaluation manual
> Definitions of certain position evaluation terms
> Procedures for collecting information about positions
> Table of factors, degrees, and points
> Definition of each factor and degree
> Sample job descriptions
> Sample rating forms
> Brief explanation of how position evaluation results are used
>   in job pricing
> Table of point ranges and pay grades

"Substantially Equal" Versus "Comparable Worth"

An issue is currently unfolding in the courts that could have a great bearing on the future of position evaluation. Traditionally, positions are compared and evaluated against positions within the same general occupational category. For example, clerical positions are compared with clerical positions, and technical-service positions with technical-service positions. Indeed, often the factors used to evaluate clerical positions differ from those used for technical-service positions. The comparison of positions within an occupational category—but not across categories—is based on the substantially equal concept.

However, the Equal Employment Opportunity Commission (EEOC) alleges that discrimination may be inherent in such techniques because women and other protected groups are often employed in occupational categories that are low paying. Therefore, EEOC officials feel that positions in all categories should be compared to determine their relative worth. For example, the value of nurses, truck drivers, secretaries, and counselors should be compared in order to determine each position's fair rates of pay.

To date, revelant court rulings have not yielded a set of precedents for this issue. Some courts indicate that to advance the comparable worth principle exceeds the intent of federal law, while others confirm the concept. Ultimately, this issue will be settled through a variety of court cases and probably a decision from the Supreme Court. If the equal value concept of comparable worth prevails, many position evaluation systems will need to be replaced or modified.

Exhibit 11. Classification Method: Sample Class Specification

Assistant Librarian:

An assistant librarian performs professional work in cataloguing library materials, discharging reference activities, and providing other library services.

Work involves original cataloguing of library materials or direction of circulation, periodicals, acquisitions, reserve or reference activities in accordance with standard library operations practices. The employee uses judgment in interpreting and adapting guidelines and recommends new acquisitions and work methods or procedures to enhance services. Work is reviewed for effectiveness in meeting users' needs, for appropriateness, and for conformity to policy requirements.

Examples of Duties:

Catalogue and prepare library materials for processing; code and catalogue cards in format compatible with computer printout; participate in development and implementation of new cataloguing procedures; oversee preparation of new materials.

Analyze book collection by comparing standard bibliographies to those on file; select newspaper and magazine articles and pamphlets for inclusion in information files; proofread bibliographical records; make recommendations for acquisition of new materials.

Provide advice to library users for locating and using library materials.

Direct the work of circulation, periodical, and reserve areas of library.

As required, instruct and guide lower-level employees in work to be done, and review their work for accuracy and completeness.

Perform related work as required.

Exhibit 11 (continued)

Recommended Preparation for Employment:

Possession of a bachelor's degree in library science, and considerable experience in cataloguing library material and in performance of the duties of the various functional areas of a library; or an equivalent combination of training and experience that would provide the following:

- Considerable knowledge of library practices and procedures, including cataloguing, processing, acquisitions, reference and research techniques, and related terminology.
- Considerable knowledge of computerized library systems.
- Knowledge sufficient to catalogue foreign language materials, as required.
- Skill in the use of standard office equipment.
- Ability to instruct and guide lower-level employees.
- Ability to accurately analyze and process a variety of detailed data.
- Ability to communicate effectively, orally and in writing.

Physical Demands: Primarily sedentary

Work Environment: Involves normal, everyday risks and discomforts

Special Requirements: An employee in this class may be required to work evenings and weekends

Exhibit 12. Factor Comparison Method: Judgment Factor Rating Scale

Impact of decisions and recommendations made and their importance to the university.	Scope of Judgment Required			
	A	B	C	D
	Application of prescribed, standard practices. Use of several procedures and making of minor decisions that require some judgment.	Diversified use of judgment to analyze facts in individual problems or transactions within limits of standard practice.	Considerable use of judgment required to apply policies and procedures to cases not previously covered. Independent work and decision making based on precedent and policy.	High degree of judgment used to make decisions based on little precedent, to evaluate complex factors, to solve new or constantly changing problems.
1. Limited	10 18 27	18 27 37	27 37 48	37 48 59
2. Moderate	27 37 48	37 48 59	48 59 71	59 71 83
3. Significant	48 59 61	59 71 83	71 83 95	83 95 108
4. Major	61 73 85	83 95 108	95 108 121	108 121 135

Instructions: Select scope A, B, C, or D as applicable. Then select range 1, 2, 3, or 4 as applicable. To refine the factor value compare the two selections with bench marks and select the appropriate score.

Exhibit 13. Sample List of Factors and Degrees

Points Assigned to Factors and Degrees

Factors	1st Degree	2nd Degree	3rd Degree	4th Degree	5th Degree
Education	15	30	45	60	75
Experience	20	40	60	80	100
Judgment	20	40	60	80	—
Supervision received	15	30	45	60	75
Responsibility	10	20	30	40	50
Access to confidential data	10	15	20	25	30

Score Range for Salary Grades

Score Range	Salary Grade	Score Range	Salary Grade
75–100	1	255–280	7
105–130	2	285–310	8
135–160	3	315–340	9
165–190	4	345–370	10
195–220	5	375–400	11
225–250	6	405–430	12

Exhibit 14. Five Degrees for the Factor of Supervision Received

The factor of supervision received considers the amount and the character of that supervision. It appraises the degree to which the immediate supervisor outlines the methods to be followed or the results to be attained, checks the progress of the work, or handles exceptional cases. Consideration is given to the place this position occupies on an organization chart and the accountability of the position measured in terms of responsibility for costs, methods, or personnel.

Degree 1   15 points

Work is performed under immediate supervision and is checked regularly. Work is generally a short assignment or project, and as questions arise they are referred to supervisor.

Degree 2   30 points

Work is performed under general supervision, and the employee is expected to proceed alone following standard practice and any of several procedures. Decision making is part of the job, but questionable cases may be referred when they arise outside of standard practice.

Degree 3   45 points

Duties are performed under general direction, and the employee plans and arranges his or her own work, which is directed toward an established objective. Employee determines action to be taken handling all but unusual cases. Knowledge of established policy, procedure, and practice is required.

Degree 4   60 points

Duties and responsibilities are performed under general direction and from interpreting university policy with regard to general objectives. Thorough knowledge of university policies and procedures is required in their application to cases not previously covered. Work is performed independently toward general results and requires devising new methods or modifying or developing standard procedure to meet new conditions. Problems are rarely referred.

Degree 5   75 points

Responsibilities are executed under administrative direction. Incumbent establishes standard of performance and is self-supervising. Complex work on involved projects requires solutions to new or constantly changing problems. Ability is required to deal with complex factors not easily evaluated. Decision making process is directed toward developing policy for which there is little precedent.

Exhibit 15. Sample Position Evaluation Worksheet

Code No.:   40-001-01-04
College or Department: Physical Plant Maintenance and Operations
Grade: 4
Job Title: Carpenter A
Total Points: 299

Factors	Substantiating Data	Degree	Points
Education	Requires the use of advanced shop mathematics, complicated drawings, specifications, charts, tables, handbook formulas, all varieties of precision measuring instruments and the use of broad training in a recognized trade or craft, equivalent to a complete, accredited, indentured apprenticeship.	4	56

Exhibit 15 (continued)

Factors	Substantiating Data	Degree	Points
Experience	Over one and up to two years of effective experience.	3	66
Initiative and ingenuity	Requires the use of judgment to plan, perform, and make decisions as to the set-up and operation of a particular job or process. Works within limitations of recognized or standard methods and procedures.	3	42
Physical demand	Moderate physical effort consisting of frequent lifting or moving average weight materials or occasional lifting or moving heavy materials.	3	30
Mental or visual demand	Continuous mental and visual attention on diversified operations requiring constant alertness or activity.	3	15
Responsibility for equipment or process	Probable damage to tools, equipment, and vehicle would exceed $25 but seldom exceed $250.	3	15
Responsibility for material or product	Probable damage to wood and other raw materials would exceed $10 but seldom exceed $100.	2	10
Responsibility for safety of others	Inattention, thoughtlessness, or careless operation of tools and other equipment may cause lost-time injury to others such as crushed hands or feet, loss of fingers or toes, eye injuries.	3	15
Responsibility for work of others	Responsible for own work, or occasionally for one person.	1	5
Working conditions	Somewhat disagreeable working conditions. Exposed to some sawdust and outside weather conditions.	3	30
Hazards	Injuries, should they occur, may result in loss of time due to crushed hands or feet, loss of fingers or toes, eye injuries.	3	15

Remarks

❦ 5 ❦

Determining
Salary Ranges

Salary administration is the for-
mulation of policy regarding rates of pay for duties performed and
the implementation of this policy. Some administrators use the
term compensation to include the total pay picture (of benefits and
salary), but the importance and extent of benefits in higher education institutions warrant separate discussion of these benefits in
Chapter Eight.

Since approximately 80 percent of most college and university operating budgets is related directly to salaries, the development of sound salary policies as well as prudent administration of
the policies is crucial to accomplishing the mission of educational
institutions. Basic to effective salary administration are: a clear institutional philosophy of objectives, well-defined pay policies and
pay plans to complement those policies, consideration of pay controls imposed upon the institution, and competent wage and salary
administrators. In this chapter, we specify the procedures for implementing an effective policy.

The basic activities of salary administration include:

1. Defining the institutional pay objectives
2. Assigning responsibilty and authority for administering the
   pay policies and objectives

3.   Selecting an effective position analysis method
4.   Selecting or constructing a position evaluation plan to measure the relative worth of jobs, and for compliance with legislation such as the Equal Pay Act, Fair Labor Standards Act, and the like
5.   Selecting a pay plan or plan
6.   Conducting salary surveys
7.   Relating the pay plan to the position evaluation plan
8.   Determining the levels of pay within the pay plan(s)
9.   Administering the pay plan
10. Establishing internal controls and maintaining records

For more details about developing and administering effective wage and salary programs see Davidson (1979) and Rock (1980).

Do Institutional Philosophies Differ Regarding Competitiveness in the Marketplace?

Some higher education institutions adopt the philosophy that they can best meet their objectives by striving to remain at the top of their various labor markets. More frequently, however, institutions adopt a low to middle-of-the-market philosophy. Depending upon competition and funding, other institutions strive for the upper quartile of their labor markets. Philosophies about market competitiveness thus vary among institutions.

However, effective salary administration requires that each institution clarify its attitude toward competitiveness. In the absence of an institutional philosophy, various administrators may adopt different philosophies for their areas. Some administrators may feel that the institution must top marketplace salaries, while others may react more conservatively; often such attitudes depend on the administrator's source of funding. Lack of uniform policy may result in the improper use of institutional funds and could lead to lawsuits charging unequal pay.

The institution's philosophy will determine which pay objectives are appropriate. Certainly all institutions must comply with relevant laws, regulations, and executive orders, and all will seek to provide pay equity and fairness among faculty and staff members, while spending payroll monies effectively. Other valuable objectives are to attract and retain qualified faculty and staff members, to maintain a proper relationship to the institution's various labor markets, and to motivate faculty and staff members. The policy should thus be a systematic method understood by administrators, faculty, and staff members.

Six main factors influence pay levels: availability of funds, ability to hire, institutional policies, marketplace conditions, productivity, and merit ratings.

Who Has the Responsibility to Establish, Administer, and Change Pay Policies?

In almost all higher education institutions, the governing board (the board of regents or trustees) has the authority to establish policies, review effectiveness, change policies, and approve budgets. An administrative office, usually the personnel office, is responsibile for setting objectives, implementing the competitive pay policy, and determining procedures. The personnel office typically provides recommendations on policy matters to the president and technical assistance to line managers (administrators, academic department chairpersons, and supervisory staff). Line management's responsibility usually includes: providing accurate, factual information about positions; keeping position descriptions current; assigning work that is within the limits of the position descriptions; understanding the procedures used to implement pay policies; supporting the pay plan and position evaluation method; and recommending changes needed to respond to changes in methods or technology.

How Do Legislation and Pressures for Accountability Affect Faculty Salary Administration?

Formalized salary administration for faculty members historically has been quite limited because of the individual entrepreneurship of faculty members and the highly diversified environment in the academic arena. However, pressures for greater institutional accountability have developed because of legislation regarding equal pay. To preclude charges of violations of this legislation, institutions must devote careful attention to the development of defensible rationale for salary differences among faculty members. (For more details about equal pay legislation, see Smith, 1978).

Should charges of discrimination be made, an investigator may ask the institution to name the criteria used in determining the salary level of the faculty. The investigator may then use these criteria to evaluate whether the institution has acted in a discriminatory manner. Thus institutions of higher education must carefully assess the bases for faculty salary determinations in each individual academic unit. Clearly defined criteria should be distributed to each of the academic units in which salary determinations are recommended, and these criteria should serve as a uniform guide for the salary determinations. Criteria for faculty salary determinations may include the following:

> Educational preparation, including degrees attained
> Teaching and research experience
> Publications, quality and number
> Participation in professional conferences and symposiums
> Community contributions
> Teaching effectiveness
> Advising and counseling expertise
> Academic rank attained
> Marketplace difficulties
> Student evaluations

How Is a Pay Plan Built?

The institution's position evaluation plan is the foundation for the establishment of pay rates because it provides a systematic method for assigning pay grades. The position evaluation plan yields a framework that relates positions to one another so that the more complex, responsible, and skilled positions are placed at the higher grade levels and less skilled jobs are placed at the lower grade levels. When the pay plan is based on the position evaluation plan, both intra- and interinstitutional comparisons are feasible.

Properly described and evaulated positions provide the basis for conducting salary surveys, which are essential to the establishment of competitive pay plans. An institution's philosophy about its relative position in the marketplace can be maintained only by collecting accurate information about what others are paying for the same kinds of occupations.

How Are Salary Surveys Conducted?

First one must decide which positions are to be surveyed. The geographical areas and the types of employers to be surveyed depend upon the normal recruitment area for the positions under consideration. An examination of hiring records of the positions to be surveyed should assist in disclosing the geographical areas in which applicants are found and the former employers of those applicants. This information should assist in the determination of the areas to be surveyed and the types of employers to survey. For example, faculty members, senior academic administrators, and professional employees may be sought nationwide or within a major portion of the nation (such as the northeast or the midwest). Usually, they are recruited from other educational institutions. Accountants, dieticians, and engineers may be recruited from business, education, and industry within an entire state. Clerical, service, or maintenance personnel may be found from business, education, and industry in the local marketplace. Salary surveys should be made accordingly.

Next, one must determine the comparability of positions to be surveyed. Surveys produce valid comparisons only if the positions are common to all the employers surveyed and are truly comparable positions. Determining comparability among positions is the most time-consuming and most important step. Similarity of job titles does not imply comparability of positions. Positions must be compared by duties, responsibilities, educational and experience requirements. To facilitate comparisons, detailed position descriptions should be used. Ideally, the exchange of information should be by personal contact; however, telephone or mail (or a combination) may be necessary. The final survey instrument should not be so complicated as to discourage potential respondents. A survey that covers twelve to fifteen positions is reasonable.

The survey instrument should elicit certain basic information beyond rates of pay. The list should be kept simple, but will probably include questions about total compensation (paid time off, employee and employer contributions to benefits programs), hours per week worked, type of incremental increases provided, and so forth. In addition, the survey should ask how many employees are in each surveyed position, when the next increase will be granted and its projected amount, and if the rates are negotiated through a union. It is helpful to know the ranges specified for each position (at least the hiring rate, midpoint, and maximum rates) as well as the weighted average salary paid to all incumbents in each position.

To preserve equity of survey results within an institution, one office should oversee the collection of all survey data. If decentralized, some administrators might choose to survey only high-paying employers, and their survey will not produce a true market picture.

Following a survey, the results are usually shared with the respondents. Such reports typically list the employers surveyed, but display the rates by code to preserve confidentiality.

The College and University Personnel Assocation regularly conducts a salary survey of a number of higher education academic administrative and other administrative positions. See Exhibit 16, p. 80, for an excerpt of that survey. Two additional sources of survey information are surveys made by other employers and data that can be gathered from information contained on applications for employment. For more details about administrative compensation, see College and University Personnel Association (1975–1976, 1980a).

What Kinds of Pay Plans Are Used?

After positions are evaluated and a salary survey is conducted, the positions need to be placed into a pay plan. There are three basic kinds of pay plans: (1) a single-rate plan with a single rate for each grade; (2) a scale with fixed steps for each grade level; and (3) a rate range indicating at least a minimum and maximum for each grade level.

A single-rate plan is composed of a single wage or salary for a given position or grade. Such a plan may include trainee rates that precede the single job rate. Exhibit 17, p. 83, shows a sample single-rate plan. Single-rate plans are sometimes used by colleges and universities that employ a large number of janitorial, maintenance, craft, or trades personnel. A disadvantage of the single-rate plan is that it does not provide opportunity for recognition of merit. An advantage is that the pay administrator does not have to justify specific merit raises for employees. For some jobs, there are no significantly different levels of merit; for example, a janitorial employee either meets the basic standards or does not meet them. There are fewer shades of differences understood by employees on such jobs.

A pay scale with fixed steps is sometimes used by higher education institutions that are partially funded by state or local governments. Exhibit 18, p. 83, illustrates a sample plan with fixed steps. A disadvantage of scale plans is that they often inhibit the recognition of real merit. Both employees and supervisors may assume that promotion to the next step is automatic, and frequently only totally incompetent employee's do not receive the increase.

A third type of pay structure sets rate ranges by grade or class. Exhibit 19, p. 84, presents a sample of a range plan. Under this structure, a range of pay is indicated for each job class or grade. A new employee normally starts at the minimum of the class or grade in which the position falls and advances within the range through the scale on a merit or longevity basis.

Some institutions operate effectively with one pay plan for all staff employees, other institutions use separate pay plans for different categories of staff personnel. Since many higher education institutions that have formal position evaluation plans use a point method for evaluating at least some positions, our discussion of pay plans is based on a point plan for position evaluation. We must determine the best relationship between the total points assigned to the position and both the present rate of pay for the position and the salary rate for similar positions surveyed in the marketplace.

Each position to be evaluated can be located on a graph whose horizontal axis is the series of point values and whose vertical axis is the range of present salaries. Figure 1 shows a sample scatterplot for twenty positions. The present actual salary is identified by the diagonal line through the scatterplot that represents the line of best fit. This graphing allows an examination of the internal

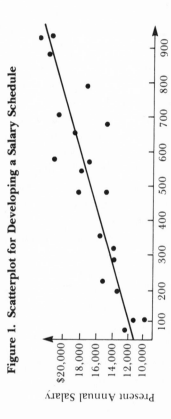

Figure 1. Scatterplot for Developing a Salary Schedule

equity of the compensation program. To examine the compensation program in relation to the marketplace, one would construct a scatterplot on a graph whose vertical axis is the average salary rate for similar positions as determined from salary surveys.

If one is seeking to compare large numbers of positions and employees, a more statistically accurate projection technique is the least squares method, a common statistical approach for data analysis of this type. For more details on the least squares technique in salary administration, see Davidson (1979).

The final step in completing a pay plan is to establish the number of grades and the salary range for each grade. The number of grades and the spread in salary ranges depend on the institution's pay philosophy about competitiveness. Typically, however, a salary chart is made up of several grades whose relations to one another are based on three general principles. First, the difference between the minimum of a grade and the minimum of the grade immediately above it should be 8 to 10 percent at the lower-level grades. The percentage of difference between the minimums may increase as the grades progress to include more responsible positions. Second, each lower-level grade should have a smaller span between the minimum and the maximum of that grade than the span for the higher-level grades. That is, the spans within a grade should be progressively larger at the higher grades. In each of the lower grades, a span of 20 to 30 percent from the minimum to the maximum of that grade is typical. In the higher-level grades, the span may be 40 to 50 percent. Third, the upper and lower limits for the salary ranges may be determined by using the ranges obtained from the marketplace survey or by using fixed percentages above and below the salary established for each grade by the line of best fit.

Should Outside Consultants Be Hired?

While it is possible, and in some instances preferable, for the pay administrator of an institution to establish a pay plan, there may be advantages to hiring an outside wage and salary consultant. Circumstances that prevent the pay administrator from establishing and administering an effective pay plan include lack of time, poor organizational communications, politics within the institution, or the lack of qualifications.

The advantages of employing a wage and salary consultant are several.

- The consultant can assist management in clarifying and specifying the objectives of the pay plan.
- The consultant can be effective in conditioning the organization of the study.
- The institution's investment in a consultant indicates the institution's priorities and interest in equitable systems.
- The consultant can bring a proven degree of competence, objectivity, and problem-solving skills.
- The consultant may be able to complete the task in a shorter period of time than an in-house analyst.
- A consultant may have relevant salary comparison information.
- Independent and objective analysis may enhance the reliability of position ranking and grading.

How Is the Pay Plan Administered?

Once the pay plan is established, decisions must be made about how to apply it to individual positions. The most important decisions to be made are:

Exceptions. Will special rates be permitted beyond the normal ranges to meet special market conditions? In all probability, in unusual cases special rates will be required. However, someone in the central personnel administration should monitor all such requests to ensure that the request is based on a proper evaluation of the marketplace. Some adminstrators may preselect only high-paying employers in their survey samples.

Merit. If increases are to be given based on merit, what is the institution's definition of merit? Does it mean "satisfactory performance" or "outstanding performance"? A statement defining merit is essential, and the definition must be understood by all administrators within the institution. If performance is used as the basis to give or deny pay increases, what assurances are there that similar standards are used throughout the institution? For example, in any institution, a variety of supervisors with a variety of standards evaluate clerical employees, whereas on the other hand, some positions are supervised by a single administrator (dietitians, personnel professionals, for example). Merit increases are more apt to be more evenly applied in the latter than in the former case.

Some very basic positions may not lend themselves to variances that provide for defensible differentiation with merit pay adjustments. For example, the work of a janitor with an assigned area to clean is either satisfactory or not. If not, the employee needs training. If the employee does not respond to the training, dismissal may be called for. Attempts to provide varying levels of merit adjustments to persons in such basic positions often lead to distrust and unionization. Usually, one of the demands of unions whose members have basic positions is a single-rate plan.

Cost-of-Living Increases. What actions should be taken in an inflationary economy? In order to stay competitive, an institution must appropriately increase pay ranges. However, if all projected resources are committed to cost-of-living increases and none to merit, salaries will not advance within the range in the salary progressions. For example, if an employee's rate is at the minimum of a range and all available funds are used to increase the range by 8 percent to meet an increase in the cost of living, that employee will receive the 8 percent but will still be at bottom of the new range. Consideration should be given to providing a portion of the available funds to boost the ranges while reserving another portion for merit increases. Most institutions of higher education do not tie increases to a cost-of-living index. Since most institutions are not in control of their sources of funds, it is usually not feasible to schedule automatic increases tied to an index of inflation. Such a practice (usually known as COLA, cost-of-living adjustments) is more common in business and industry.

Seniority. What part should seniority play in pay adjustments? Ideally, all pay adjustment systems should be driven by considerations of merit in performance. However, providing increases based on longevity (with satisfactory service) through at least part of the pay scale is a common practice. In addition, some institutions offer special increments above the normal scale for individuals who achieve exceptionally long service.

Promotion. What pay policy should apply in the case of a promotion to a higher-level position? The institution should have a percentage increase (or range of percentage increases) established for promotion. A sample policy might be: "A promotion will be accompanied by a pay increase of between 7 and 10 percent."

Trainees. What rate should be paid to an individual who does not meet the minimum qualifications established for the position? Provisions should be made for paying below the minimum rates for specified periods of time to enable such individuals to meet the established qualifications.

Inherent in the detailed practices and processes such as position analysis, position descriptions, position evaluation, and pay plans should be systems for internal controls. However, since changes occur over which institutions have no control (inflation, changes in management, improved technology, and the like), additional internal controls are needed to stabilize the pay system.

The responsibility for setting pay controls should be designated to the personnel office, which shares responsibility for implementing and administering the controls with department heads. The responsibilities of the personnel office should include:

> Conducting salary surveys
> Developing pay plans
> Preparing position descriptions and analysis
> Establishing implementation procedures and informing supervisors of the procedures
> Evaluating positions and resolving disputes concerning position evaluations
> Monitoring each recommended pay increase
> Approving bona fide exceptions to the pay plans
> Recommending revisions to policies and procedures
> Maintaining records
> Establishing a position control numbering system

The responsibilities of administrators are to:

Know the content of positions

Control the content of positions by assuring that employees' duties are within the limits of the position descriptions

Provide accurate, factual, and complete descriptive information on positions to be evaluated

Review and keep current position descriptions as changes occur

Recommend pay increases or adjustments

Conduct and support performance reviews based on the duties of the positions

Know and understand the position evaluation and pay plan procedures

All pay plans must conform to federal legislation. Exhibit 20, p. 85, provides an overview of the provisions and major characteristics of federal legislation that affects pay plans. Also, in Chapter Six, we discuss equal employment opportunity and affirmative action legislation, regulations, and guidelines that apply to pay plans.

Exhibit 16. Sample Administrative Compensation Survey

Distribution of Salaries
All Institutions

Salary	51	52	53	54	55	56	57	58	59	60
$81,000–$81,999										1
$74,000–$74,999										1
$71,000–$71,999										
$69,000–$69,999						1				
$68,000–$68,999	2							1		
$67,000–$67,999	1	1								1
$66,000–$66,999		1								
$65,000–$65,999	1	2	1			1				2
$64,000–$64,999										1
$63,000–$63,999				1				1		4
$62,000–$62,999	1							2		1
$61,000–$61,999	1						1	1	1	
$60,000–$60,999		1						2		3
$59,000–$59,999		2						1		
$58,000–$58,999	2	1			1		1	3		3
$57,000–$57,999	1	3					1	2		6
$56,000–$56,999							1	6	2	4
$55,000–$55,999	1	3					1	3		2
$54,000–$54,999	4						1	1		4
$53,000–$53,999	1		2							2
$52,000–$52,999	3	2					3	3		10
$51,000–$51,999	2	2			1		4	3	3	11
$50,000–$50,999	2	3	3			1	2	4		13
$49,000–$49,999						1	3		2	6
$48,000–$48,999							3	3		5

Salary Range										
$47,000–$47,999	4	2					2		3	9
$46,000–$46,999	1	2					3	3	2	7
$45,000–$45,999		7		2			3	6	3	13
$44,000–$44,999	2	6			1		8	1	1	11
$43,000–$43,999		5	1			1	1	3	3	15
$42,000–$42,999	2	4	1	1	1		2	1	5	15
$41,000–$41,999		1	1	1	2	2	1	2	1	16
$40,000–$40,999	5	10	1	2	1	3	4	3	5	19
$39,000–$39,999	2	6	1	1	3		2	2	2	14
$38,000–$38,999	3	4	5	3	1				7	24
$37,000–$37,999	1	4	5	3	3	2		5	7	9
$36,000–$36,999	7	4	1	3	1		1	2	5	16
$35,000–$35,999	2	7	5	1		3	1	4	5	17
$34,000–$34,999	2	5	5	3	4	1	1	2	2	14
$33,000–$33,999	4	3	6	3	3	3	3	1	3	13
$32,000–$32,999	4	10	7	5	4	4		1	2	10
$31,000–$31,999	1	5	4	4	3	5		5	2	14
$30,000–$30,999	2	13	7	8	2	7		1	3	19
$29,000–$29,999	7	8	11	6	2	5		9	2	10
$28,000–$28,999	2	10	5	5	5	7	3		4	12
$27,000–$27,999	2	8	12	3	3	5		4	7	8
$26,000–$26,999	1	2	12	8	8			1		10
$25,000–$25,999	1	3	11	6	6	5		3		6
$24,000–$24,999	2	7	11	6	6	3		1		1
$23,000–$23,999	2	2	6	9	9	7		1	2	2
$22,000–$22,999	4	8	9	1	1	4		1	3	3
$21,000–$21,999	4	5	10	4		8			2	5
$20,000–$20,999	1	5	15	6		5		1	2	1
$19,000–$19,999		2	17	6	3	4			2	1
$18,000–$18,999		3	10	4		3			1	1

Exhibit 16 (continued)

Salary	51	52	53	54	55	56	57	58	59	60
$17,000–$17,999	1	1	13	1		2		1	1	
$16,000–$16,999		2	9	6		1			1	
$15,000–$15,999	1	1	11	3	1	1				
$14,000–$14,999	1	1	10	3		1				1
$13,000–$13,999	1	1	8					1		
$12,000–$12,999			3	1					1	
$11,000–$11,999			1							
$10,000–$10,999			2	2					1	1
less than $10,000			2							
N	90	188	245	125	50	99	61	101	101	398
Mean Salary	$38,755	$34,784	$24,634	$27,335	$32,570	$28,529	$44,107	$41,701	$34,977	$39,770

Note: Code for Positions Surveyed

  Number—Title

  51—Chief Planning and Budget Officer
  52—Chief Development and Public Relations Officer
  53—Director, Personnel and Affirmative Action
  54—Director, Admissions and Financial Aid
  55—Director, Housing and Food Services
  56—Director, Development and Alumni Affairs
  57—Dean, Architecture
  58—Dean, Agriculture
  59—Dean, Arts and Letters
  60—Dean, Arts and Sciences

Source: College and University Personnel Association, 1980a, p. 92.

Exhibit 17. Sample Single-Rate Pay Plan

	Hourly Wage	
Grade	Hiring Range	Grade Rate
10	$7.54–$7.95	$8.37
9	6.98– 7.36	7.75
8	6.47– 6.82	7.18
7	5.98– 6.31	6.65
6	5.55– 5.86	6.16
5	5.13– 5.41	5.70
4	4.76– 5.02	5.28
3	4.41– 4.65	4.90
2	4.09– 4.31	4.54
1	3.78– 3.99	4.20

Note: An individual is hired in the appropriate grade at a rate in the hiring rate range according to the time required to learn the job. The more experience and training the new employee has, the higher the hiring rate.

The job grade rate is achieved when the individual can perform all of the duties under minimal supervision. In no case, shall the job grade rate be offered before at least three months following appointment.

Exhibit 18. Sample Scale Pay Plan

Grade	Step 1	Step 2	Step 3	Step 4	Step 5	Step 6
10	$27,852	$30,504	$32,156	$34,808	$37,460	$40,112
9	23,796	25,932	28,068	30,204	32,340	34,476
8	20,508	22,248	23,988	25,728	27,468	29,232
7	17,832	19,260	20,688	22,116	23,544	24,972
6	15,636	16,812	17,988	19,164	20,340	21,516
5	13,836	14,808	15,780	16,752	17,724	18,696
4	12,348	13,152	13,956	14,770	15,574	16,378
3	11,124	11,796	12,468	13,140	13,812	14,484
2	10,104	10,656	11,208	11,760	12,312	12,864
1	9,264	9,732	10,200	10,668	11,136	11,604

Annual Salary

Exhibit 19. Sample Range Pay Plan

| Grade | *Annual Salary* | | |
	Minimum	*Midpoint*	*Maximum*
10	$27,852	$33,984	$40,112
9	23,796	29,136	34,476
8	20,508	24,876	29,232
7	17,832	21,408	24,972
6	15,636	18,576	21,516
5	13,836	16,272	18,696
4	12,348	14,364	16,378
3	11,124	12,804	14,484
2	10,104	11,484	12,864
1	9,264	10,440	11,604

Exhibit 20. Major Legislation Affecting Pay

The Fair Labor Standards Act of 1938 (as amended)

Provides for minimum wage, equal pay, age discrimination, and overtime regulations. A Supreme Court decision of 1976 exempts public institutions from the overtime and minimum-wage obligations but not the equal pay and age discrimination conditions of the act.

Civil Rights Act of 1964 (as amended)

Provides for nondiscrimination in conditions of employment including compensation.

Age Discrimination in Employment Act of 1967 (as amended)

Provides for nondiscrimination in conditions of employment including compensation for employees between the ages of forty and seventy.

Rehabilitation Act of 1973 (Section 503 and 504)

Provides for nondiscrimination in conditions of employment including compensation for qualified handicapped individuals.

Davis-Bacon Act of 1931 (as amended)

Provides for payment of local "prevailing wages and fringe benefits" for laborers and mechanics employees on federal construction projects.

Walsh-Healey Public Contracts Act of 1936

Provides for payment of local "prevailing wages and fringe benefits" for employers having contracts to supply goods to a governmental agency.

Service Contract Act of 1965 (as amended)

Provides for payment of local "prevailing wages and fringe benefits" for employers, both contractors and subcontractors, holding a service contract with a governmental agency.

❧ 6 ❧

Assuring Equal Employment Opportunities and Affirmative Action

Equal employment opportunity is the right of all persons to work and advance on the basis of merit, ability, and potential. By law, this policy must not only be stated, it must be the ongoing practice. To practice equal employment opportunity is to forbid discrimination on the bases of sex, race, color, age, religion, handicap, or national origin in all employment practices including hiring, firing, promotion, compensation and other terms, privileges, and conditions of employment. The most pervasive discrimination arises from thoughtless and deeply entrenched stereotypical thinking. For example, recently a chairman of the board of trustees of a major university made the following statement regarding that institution's search for a president: "We are looking for a bright young man for the position." Although the statement may not have been intended to be discriminatory, it contains sexual and age biases.

Affirmative action, as the name suggests, is a series of active policies and practices aimed at the elimination of current and past discriminatory practices. Educational institutions with one or more federal contracts of at least $50,000 and fifty or more employees must execute a written affirmative action program. It must contain hiring goals and timetables for the employment of minorities and women in a proper mix representative of the various marketplaces used for the recruitment of faculty and staff members.

What Is the Legal Basis for Equal Employment Opportunity?

Five major pieces of legislation and two executive orders provide the legal basis for equal employment opportunity and affirmative action. We briefly summarize these; the reader is referred to the documents themselves for details.

Title VII of the Civil Rights Act of 1964 prohibits discrimination on the basis of race, color, religion, national origin, and sex in all employment transactions. As amended in 1972, it provides the Equal Employment Opportunity Commission (EEOC) access to the courts and covers educational institutions.

Executive Orders 11246 and 11375 require employers, including higher education, who have fifty or more employees and who have federal nonconstruction contracts totaling $50,000 or more, to conduct a self-analysis of the work force and employment practices, and to implement an affirmative action plan to correct inequities.

The Equal Pay Act of 1963, an amendment to the Fair Labor Standards Act, requires equal pay for males and females who perform equal work in jobs that require equal knowledge, skill, effort, and responsibility and that are performed under similar working conditions. A 1972 amendment extends this act to include professional employees.

The Age Discrimination in Employment Act of 1967 protects individuals between the ages of forty and sixty-five from age discrimination. The recent amendments extend the maximum age to age seventy for all except high-policymaking executives, who are protected only until age sixty-five; tenured individuals are protected only up to age sixty-five until July 1, 1982.

The Rehabilitation Act, Sections 503 and 504, protects individuals with handicaps. A handicapped worker is defined as one who has a physical or mental impairment that substantially limits one or more of such a person's major life activities and who has a record of such impairment or is regarded as having such an impairment. (Obviously, that definition is open to a wide range of interpretation.) Sections 503 and 504 require employers who have federal grants and contracts totaling $2,500 or more to make recommendations and take affirmative action on behalf of handicapped individuals. Section 503 requires affirmative action regarding employment. Employers must develop and use lists of internal and external recruiting sources such as training centers for the handicapped, social service agencies, state employment agencies, and so forth. The setting of goals and timetables is not required. Employers must make reasonable accommodations in the physical and mental job requirements for handicapped but otherwise qualified individuals. Section 504 requires nondiscrimination regarding handicapped students.

The Vietnam-Era Veterans Readjustment Acts of 1974 requires affirmative action by employers with federal contracts totaling $10,000 or more and applies to qualified disabled veterans and veterans of the Vietnam War era (August 24, 1964 to May 7, 1975). Goals and timetables are not required. However, institutions are required to list with state employment agencies all vacancies which pay up to $18,000 a year.

For more details about the legal basis for equal employment opportunity, see Commerce Clearing House (1979).

How Does an Institution Develop an Affirmative Action Plan?

Each institution with the qualifying federal contracts is required to develop a written affirmative action plan. The Office of Federal Contract Compliance Programs (OFCCP) is the federal agency responsible for review of the affirmative action plans of higher education institutions.

The most important steps in developing an affirmative action plan are:

- Adopt a strong, written policy statement of commitment. (See Exhibits 21 and 22, pp. 97–99, for sample policy statements.)
- Assign the responsibility and authority for the program to a top institutional official.
- Analyze the present work force to identify jobs, departments, and units where minorities and females are underutilized.
- Set specific, measurable, and attainable hiring and promotion goals with target dates in each area of underutilization.
- Make every dean, department head, and supervisor responsible for meeting these goals.
- Examine job descriptions and hiring criteria to assure that they reflect actual job needs.
- Review all employment procedures to assure that they help attain the goals and that they are nondiscriminatory.
- Focus attention on involving minorities and females in upward mobility and relevant training programs.
- Develop systems to monitor and measure progress regularly.
- Allocate sufficient resources to do the job.

Exhibit 23, pp. 99–100, presents a sample table of contents for a written affirmative action plan. In reviewing these plans and their results, the OFCCP analyzes both the results and the strength of the institution's good faith effort. Success is not required; a good faith effort is.

How Is Sexual Harassment Defined?

Sexual harassment is an act of discrimination on the basis of sex within the meaning of Title VII of the Civil Rights Act. Employers may be held legally liable for such misconduct by supervisory personnel. Sexual harassment is defined as: Unwelcome sexual advances, requests for sexual favors, and other verbal or physical conduct of a sexual nature when:

- submission to such conduct is made either explicitly or implicitly a term or condition of an individual's employment,
- submission to or rejection of such conduct by an individual is used as the basis for employment decisions affecting such individual, or
- such conduct has the purpose or effect of substantially interfering with an individual's work performance or creating an intimidating, hostile, or offensive working environment.

All institutions should make a strong statement that sexual harassment will not be tolerated; faculty should be informed that this policy also holds for their relationships with students.

What Recordkeeping Is Needed?

Recordkeeping is an important aspect of the affirmative action program. Records on all personnel transactions related to recruiting, hiring, promotion, training, tenure, demotion, transfer, layoff or termination, pay and other terms of compensation should be retained. Should an employee file a complaint regarding any such transaction, the institution will be asked to supply records outlining all the elements in the personnel transaction under question. Federal and state regulations vary on how long records must be kept. It is recommended that they be retained for at least three years. Exhibit 24, pp. 101–102, shows a sample report used to record the recruitment efforts for a faculty or staff member. Exhibit 25, p. 103, shows a sample report used to record the reasons for not hiring certain candidates for a position.

Biennial EEO-6 reports are required by educational institutions, both public and private, with fifteen or more employees. The EEO-6 report is a joint report of the OFCCP and the EEOC. Institutions are to report their number of employees by sex, race, and salary within the following basic categories: executive, administrative, and managerial; faculty; nonfaculty professionals; clerical and secretarial; technical and paraprofessionals; skilled crafts; and service and maintenance.

How Does One Determine the Race or Ethnic Identification of Candidates for Employment?

Institutions are permitted to seek racial or ethnic identification of applicants for employment. A form similar to the applicant data card shown in Exhibit 26, p. 104, may be sent to job applicants for self-identification. Of course, self-identification on the part of an applicant prior to employment is optional. If such a program is used, it is recommended that the cards be retained separately from the applications for employment in order to avoid charges of discrimination. The standard racial and ethnic identifications are as follows:

- White (not of Hispanic origin): All persons having origins in any of the original peoples of Europe, North Africa, or the Middle East.
- Black (not of Hispanic origin): All persons having origins in any of the black racial groups.
- Hispanic: All persons of Mexican, Puerto Rican, Cuban, Central or South American, or other Spanish culture or origin, regardless of race.
- Asian or Pacific Islander: All persons having origins in any of the original peoples of the Far East, Southeast Asia, the Indian subcontinent, or the Pacific Islands.
- American Indian or Alaskan Native: All persons having origins in any of the original peoples of North America and maintaining their cultural identification through tribal affiliation or community recognition.

What Hiring Procedures Conform to Equal Employment Opportunity Policies?

Under the federal Uniform Guidelines on Employee Selection Procedures, which became effective on September 25, 1978, the "four fifths rule" was adopted to help determine whether the total selection process for a position has an adverse impact on a protected class. If the total selection process results in an adverse impact on a protected class, the individual selection procedures used in making the hiring decision (application forms, tests, interviews, and so forth) must each be examined for adverse impact. If one or more of the procedures results in adverse impact an employer must either (1) modify the procedure so that the adverse impact is eliminated; (2) stop using the procedure; or (3) validate the procedure in accordance with the guidelines' rules for validation.

It is important to note that, in most cases, adverse impact determinations do not have to be made for individual selection procedures unless it is first determined that the total selection process results in adverse impact on protected groups. In order to make such a determination, the institution must keep and evaluate records for each job opening. These records must indicate the sex, race, and ethnic identity of applicants, using the same classification as that required for the EEO-6 report.

An adverse impact determination must be made for each group that constitutes at least 2 percent of the labor force in the relevant labor area or 2 percent of the applicable work force. To make an adverse impact determination for a specific position: (1) calculate the rate of selection for each group by dividing the number of persons selected from a group by the number of applicants from that group; (2) determine which group has the highest selection rate; (3) calculate the impact ratios by comparing the selection rate for each group with that of the highest group; and (4) apply the "four fifths rule" by checking to see if any of the impact ratios is less than 80 percent. If the impact ratio is less than 80 percent for a group, that group may have experienced adverse impact. The "four fifths rule" is only a rule of thumb. The guidelines provide for instances in which a finding of less than 80 percent is not determined to indicate adverse impact and, conversely, a finding of greater than 80 percent does not indicate lack of adverse impact.

Here is an example of the use of the adverse impact formula. Two hundred persons apply for a job. Of these applicants, 140 are male, 60 are female; and 100 are white, 60 are black, and 40 are Hispanic. Institutions must make two determinations, one for sex and another for racial and ethnic groups; determinations need not be made for white males, white females, black males, black females, and the like. Of the applicants, 60 whites, 20 blacks, and 20 Hispanics are chosen; and 75 are male and 25 are female.

Following the adverse impact formulas, one obtains the following:

1. Rates of selection
    Whites: 60 chosen/100 applied = .60
    Blacks: 20 chosen/60 applied = .33
    Hispanic: 20 chosen/40 applied = .50
2. Whites have highest selection rate (.60)
3. Impact ratios
    Blacks: .33 ÷ .60 = .55
    Hispanic: .50 ÷ .60 = .83
4. Impact ratio for blacks is less than .80, which may indicate adverse impact.

Similarly, for determination by sex, the selection rate for men is .54, for women .42. The impact ratio for women is .42 ÷ .54, or .78, which indicates possible adverse impact.

Figure 2 summarizes the basic procedure to determine whether or not employee selection procedures have had adverse impact on protected groups.

Litigation

Litigation abounds in the field of equal opportunity. The regulatory agencies frequently try for settlements in such cases. Of course, if the institution has acted improperly, settlement and proper action must be initiated as soon as possible. Some of the regulatory agencies, however, in their zealousness appear to extend the laws beyond their intent and seek settlements in cases where there is no proof of discrimination. When this happens, some institutions make "settlements without prejudice" as a way to be rid of the problem at a lower cost than litigation. This practice can lead to the expectation of more and more of such settlements on the part

Figure 2. Procedures for Determining Adverse Impact

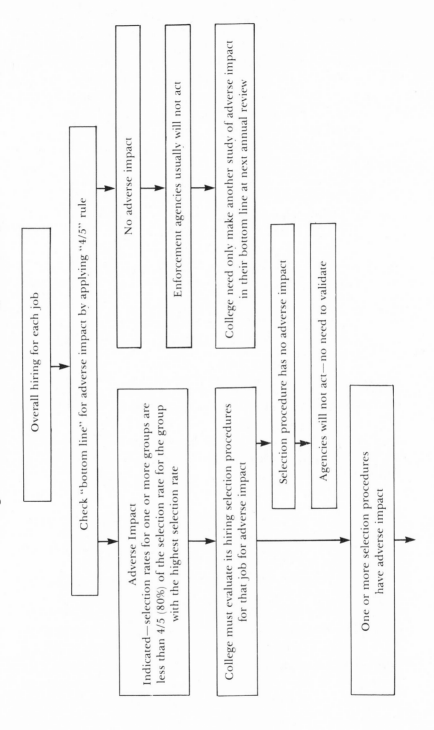

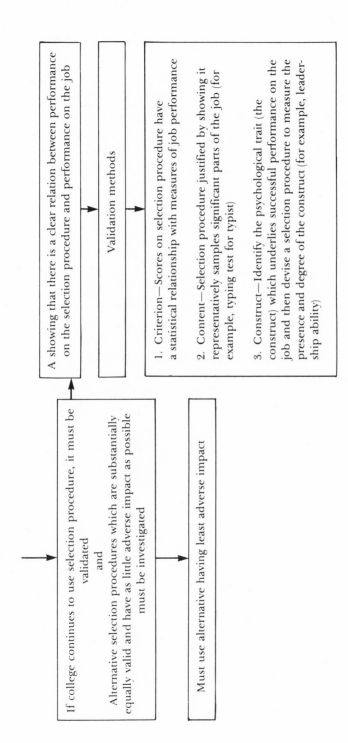

If college continues to use selection procedure, it must be validated

and

Alternative selection procedures which are substantially equally valid and have as little adverse impact as possible must be investigated

Must use alternative having least adverse impact

A showing that there is a clear relation between performance on the selection procedure and performance on the job

Validation methods

1. Criterion—Scores on selection procedure have a statistical relationship with measures of job performance

2. Content—Selection procedure justified by showing it representatively samples significant parts of the job (for example, typing test for typist)

3. Construct—Identify the psychological trait (the construct) which underlies successful performance on the job and then devise a selection procedure to measure the presence and degree of the construct (for example, leadership ability)

Source: College and University Personnel Association (1979, pp. 2–3).

of the regulatory agencies. Institutions should feel the responsibility to obtain legal advice and to seek remedial actions in the courts if the regulatory agency's request for settlement is questionable. Four issues of discrimination that probably will cause considerable court activity before there is clarity of purpose and definition are sexual harassment, hiring of the handicapped, age discrimination, and the question of comparable worth of jobs.

This chapter presents only an overview of equal employment opportunity and affirmative action. Ongoing court decisions and legislative actions make this subject an actively changing area of concern. Thus educational institutions need to designate an affirmative action officer who will keep up-to-date in the field, create an affirmative action awareness, and assure that programs meet the requirements of the various laws and regulations. Further implications of affirmative action and equal employment opportunity are discussed in the chapter covering position descriptions, salary administration, employment (recruitment and appointment), retirement, employee development programs, and performance evaluation.

Exhibit 21. Sample Fair Employment Practices Policy

The university as an equal opportunity employer:

The university is an equal opportunity employer and, as such, takes affirmative action to ensure that both applicants for employment and employees are treated in compliance with applicable laws and regulations governing equal employment opportunity and nondiscrimination in employment on the basis of race, color, religion, national origin, handicap, age, sex, or status as a disabled or Vietnam-era veteran.

Affirmative action and nondiscrimination concept:

The university is committed to the concept of affirmative action to accelerate the achievement of equal opportunity for minority groups, women, the handicapped, and disabled and Vietnam-era veterans at all levels and to ensure equal opportunity in all aspects of employment, and all other personnel actions, including, but not limited to, compensation, benefits, transfers, layoffs, return from layoff, termination, educational privileges, and selection for training, including apprenticeship training. Any person responsible for employment or promotion decisions should ensure that these decisions are based solely on an individual's qualifications for the requirements of the position for which he or she is being considered.

Employee recruiting through agencies or societies:

In all solicitations to placement agencies or societies, a statement must be made indicating that all qualified applicants will receive fair and equitable consideration for employment. Since it is the responsibility of the Employment Division to coordinate all help-wanted advertising, that office will see that suitable statements are included in the appropriate advertisements. Unless clearly necessary (that is, in the case of approved bona fide occupational qualifications for employment) advertisements will make no reference to sex or age.

Reports on fair employment practices:

The Employment Division is responsible for answering requests for reports concerning employment practices. Therefore, any contacts from agencies or groups requesting such information or reports should be directed to that office.

Exhibit 22. Sample Policy for Affirmative Action in Employment

Policy:

It is the policy of the university to provide equal opportunity in all terms and conditions of employment, as described in the university's Affirmative Action Compliance Plan for all persons. The intent of this policy is to prohibit discrimination and to promote the full realization of equal employment opportunity through a continuing affirmative program in each administrative unit outlined in the plan. This policy of equal opportunity applies to and must be an integral part of every aspect of personnel policy and practice in the employment, development, advancement, and treatment of employees and applicants for employment at the university.

Responsibility:

The head of each administrative unit identified in the Affirmative Action Compliance Plan, and subunits as identified by the Affirmative Action Office, shall be responsible for working with the staff of the Affirmative Action Office in implementing the requirements of the plan. It is the responsibility of each unit head to provide sufficient resources to administer such a program in a positive and effective manner; assure that recruitment activities reach appropriate sources of job candidates; provide reasonable opportunities to employees to enhance their skills so they may perform at their highest potential and advance in accordance with their abilities; provide training and advice to managers and supervisors to assure their understanding and implementation of the university's policy of equal opportunity and the affirmative action plan; and provide for a system within the unit for periodical evaluation of the effectiveness with which the plan is being carried out. Compliance with the intent of university policy and the Affirmative Action Compliance Plan shall be part of the acceptable standards of performance for all employees.

Leadership and guidance:

The Affirmative Action Office, under the auspices of the president and reporting to the provost of the university, shall provide leadership and guidance to administrative units in the conduct of their programs affecting employees and applicants for employment. The Affirmative Action Office shall periodically review and evaluate administrative unit program operations, obtain such reports as deemed necessary, and report to the provost of the university as appropriate on overall progress. The Affirmative Action Office will consult from time to time with such individuals, groups, or organizations as may be of assistance in improving the university's program and realizing the objectives of the plan.

Resolution of complaints:

The university shall provide for the prompt, fair, and impartial consideration of all complaints of discrimination in employment. Each administrative unit shall provide access to counseling for employees who feel aggrieved and shall encourage the resolution of employee problems on an informal basis. Procedures for the consideration of complaints shall include at least one partial review within the administrative unit and shall provide for appeals.

Administrative guidelines:

The Affirmative Action Office shall be responsible for preparing guidelines and instructions necessary and appropriate to carry out the intent of the university policy and the Affirmative Action Compliance Plan.

Exhibit 23. Table of Contents for an Affirmative Action Plan

Introduction

Section I	Policy Statement
Section II	Dissemination of Policy
	Internal Dissemination of Policy
	External Dissemination of Policy
Section III	Responsibility
	Affirmative Action Officer
	Affirmative Action Specialist
Section IV	Utilization of Resource Analysis
	Collection Method for Protected Category
	Identification
	Faculty Utilization
	Staff Utilization
	Staff Exempt and Staff Nonexempt
	Secretarial and Clerical
	Technical-Service
	Location and Utilization Analysis
	Utilization Analysis by Unit
	Labor Force Analysis by Labor Market Location
	Analysis by Major Employee Category
	Academic Personnel
	Part-Time Faculty
	Staff Personnel
	Clerical and Technical-Service

Exhibit 23 (continued)

Section V   Identification of Problem Areas
                 Underutilization
                 Promotion
                 Internal Promotion Policy and Guidelines
                 Tenure
                 Salary Equity
                 Action Programs for Correction of Deficiencies and
                     Utilization
                     Faculty Employment Procedure
                     Staff-Exempt and Staff-Nonexempt Position
                         Vacancies
                 Job Classification

Section VI   Establishment of Goals and Timetables

Section VII   Development and Execution of Programs
                 Job Classification
                 Grievance Procedures

Section VIII Internal Audit and Report System

Section IX   University Support Programs Related to Affirmative
                 Action
                 Affirmative Recruiting Practices
                     Academic Recruiting
                     Staff Recruiting
                     Clerical and Technical-Service Recruiting
                 Evaluation of Personnel

Section X   Compliance with Sex Discrimination Guidelines

Section XI   Compliance with Handicap Discrimination Guidelines

Section XII   Compliance with Veterans' Affirmative Action Regulations

Section XIII Graduate Student Exclusion

Section XIV   Part-Time Employment

Exhibit 24. Affirmative Action Recruitment Report for Faculty or Staff

1. Title of Position:	Salary Level:
College or Administrative Unit:	Department/Division:
Contract Type:	EEO-6 Classification:

2. Was a written position announcement and description prepared?
    Yes ☐   No ☐
    If yes, please attach a copy of each.
    If no, indicate why not:

3. Was the announcement published?
    Yes ☐   No ☐
    If yes, please list the names of the publication(s) and referral organizations, and the number of responses from each. (Use continuation sheet if necessary.)

4. Were efforts made to determine the availability of qualified minorities, women, veterans, and handicapped persons for the position?

    Yes ☐   If yes, please describe efforts below: No ☐   If no, indicate why not:

5. How many applications (vitae) were received? _____
    A. Minority (male and female) _____   D. Handicapped _____
    B. Women (except minority) _____   E. Veterans _____
    C. Nonminority male _____

6. How many applicants were considered candidates (beyond preliminary screening)? _____
    A. Minority (male and female) _____   D. Handicapped _____
    B. Women (except minority) _____   E. Veterans _____
    C. Nonminority male _____

7. Give name, sex, and race/ethnic group of each candidate interviewed but not selected. Indicate the specific criteria by which the selected candidate was determined to be *better qualified* for the particular position than those persons interviewed but not selected.

    Name, Sex, Race/Ethnic Group: (Use continuation sheet if necessary.)

    _____   _____
    _____   _____
    _____   _____
    _____   _____

Exhibit 24 (continued)

8. Give name, sex, and race/ethnic group of the candidate selected:

		Race/		Starting
Name: _____	Sex: _____	Ethnic Group: _____	Date: _____

    Check if applicable:
    Present Employee ☐   Handicapped ☐   Minority ☐   Vietnam Veteran ☐

9. Search Committee members (if applicable)

    (1) _____   (5) _____
    (2) _____   (6) _____
    (3) _____   (7) _____
    (4) _____   (8) _____

Department/Division Head: Date: Dean or Administrative Officer: Date:

Affirmative Action Office: Date: Prepared By: Date:

Note:

    Veteran of the Vietnam era: A person who served on active duty for a period of more than 180 days, any part of which occurred between August 5, 1964, and May 7, 1975; and was honorably discharged *not more than* 48 months before applying.
    Handicapped individual: Any person who (1) has a physical or mental impairment which substantially limits one or more of such person's major life activities; (2) has a record of such impairment or (3) is regarded as having such an impairment.

Race/ethnic group definitions:
*   White (not of Hispanic origin): All persons having origins in any of the original peoples of Europe, North Africa, or the Middle East.
*   Black (not of Hispanic origin): All persons having origins in any of the black racial groups.
*   Hispanic: All persons of Mexican, Puerto Rican, Cuban, Central or South American, or other Spanish culture or origin, regardless of race.
*   Asian or Pacific Islanders: All persons having origins in any of the original peoples in the Far East, Southeast Asia, the Pacific Islands, or the Indian subcontinent. This area includes, for example, China, Japan, Korea, the Philippine Islands, and Samoa.
*   American Indian or Alaskan Native: All persons having origins in any of the original peoples of North America and who maintain cultural identification through tribal affiliation or community recognition.

Exhibit 25. Sample Applicant Documentation Form

Position title _____
Department _____
Work unit _____
Supervisor _____

Name of applicant	Interview date	Sex	Racial or Ethnic Category	Reasons for rejection after interviewing

_____
Personnel Representative   Date

_____
Interviewer (Work Unit)   Date

Exhibit 26. Sample Applicant Self-Identification Form

Name _____ Social Security Number _____

        Last   First & Middle Initial

Date _____ Sex: Male _____ Female _____ Position Applied for _____

The University's commitment to equal opportunity, nondiscrimination, and affirmative action is realized through its Affirmative Action Compliance Plan. This Plan and legal* responsibilities to equal employment opportunity require periodic reports of job applicants by race/ethnic categories, sex, handicap, and status as a disabled or Vietnam era veteran.

This information is voluntary and is for statistical purposes only. This information is kept confidential and will **not** be used in any way to evaluate your qualifications for employment. PLEASE CHECK THE APPLICABLE CATEGORIES** IN A AND B BELOW.

A.   ☐ White (Non-Hispanic)   ☐ Black (Non-Hispanic)   ☐ Hispanic   ☐ Asian or Pacific Islander
     ☐ American Indian or Alaskan Native

B.   ☐ Disabled Veteran   ☐ Handicapped   ☐ Neither (As related to Section B)

If there are any positions or types of positions for which you should not be considered, or job duties you cannot perform because of a physical or mental handicap, please describe.

_____

_____
                           Signature

*   Laws and Regulations: Civil Rights Act of 1964; Equal Pay Act; Age Discrimination Act; Rehabilitation Act; Education Amendments; Vietnam Veterans Readjustment Act; Executive Order 11246; The Pennsylvania Human Relations Act.

**   The categories are defined as follows:

A.   **White (not of Hispanic origin)**: Any person having origin in any of the original peoples of Europe, North Africa, or the Middle East.

Black (not of Hispanic origin): Any person having origin in any of the black racial groups.

Hispanic: Any person of Mexican, Puerto Rican, Cuban, Central or South American or other Spanish culture or origin, regardless of race.

Asian or Pacific Islander: Any person having origin in any of the original peoples of the Far East, Southeast Asia, or the Pacific Islands. This area includes, for example, China, Japan, Korea, the Phillipine Islands, Samoa, or the Indian Subcontinent.

American Indian or Alaskan Native: Any person having origin in any of the original peoples of North America and maintaining cultural identification through tribal affiliation or community recognition.

B.   **Disabled Veteran**: Any person entitled to disability compensation under laws administered by the Veterans Administration for disability rated at 30 per cent or more, or any person whose discharge or release from active duty was for a disability incurred or aggravated in the line of duty.

Handicapped Individual: Any person who (1) has a physical or mental impairment which substantially limits one or more of such person's major life activities, (2) has a record of such impairment, or (3) is regarded as having such an impairment.

❧ 7 ❧

Recruiting and Appointing Personnel

Most educational institutions have a centralized employment function to service most positions in the institution. However, the recruiting of candidates for faculty positions frequently is decentralized by academic discipline. Ideally, the manager of the employment function of the personnel office should be given the responsibility for the handling of all positions with the exception, perhaps, of faculty positions. In large and complex institutions, the recruitment of faculty members is usually best accomplished by academic discipline. However, central faculty recruitment authority is more common in smaller, less complex institutions.

Complexities of legal requirements such as affirmative action, equal employment opportunity, and the uniform selection guidelines dictate centralization of recruiting and initial interviewing functions. The selection of candidates can be delegated to the administrative officers with the vacancies. However, in order to assure proper techniques and adherence to affirmative action and other legal requirements, concurrence from the central employment officer is desirable.

A central employment office is essential for three reasons. First, it provides candidates with a contact point for the institution and thus saves time for campus administrators and applicants as an applicant need not visit many different offices within an institution. Second, a central office facilitates equal treatment of all candidates by providing consistently accurate basic information about employment and benefits to candidates and by screening candidates to determine their suitability for referral to departments. Third, a central employment office provides good will for the name of the institution by handling the large numbers of candidates who are turned down for employment.

A central employment office operates effectively to the extent that administrators throughout the institution understand that all employment transactions should be cleared through that office. Furthermore, the office must be easily accessible to the general public, including handicapped individuals, and should be near suitable parking and public transportation facilities.

Employment office personnel must have copies of the institution's affirmative action goals and timetables in order to be able to assist all units of the institution in meeting their goals. The employment office should be coordinated directly with the office that handles unemployment compensation for the institution. In that way, employees who have been laid off and are receiving unemployment compensation payments can be informed about appropriate job openings.

Why Are Search Committees Used?

Frequently in higher education, search committees are used for recruiting administrative personnel and faculty. Such committees serve the special function of providing maximum participation in the selection process by a variety of constituencies within the institution. Normally, the committee recruits, screens candidates, checks references, participates in preliminary interviewing, and recommends a fixed number of candidates to a designated administrator, who makes the final selection. Exhibit 27, pp. 129–130, presents a sample policy for search committees.

The membership of the committee depends on the vacancy to be filled. The committee may include faculty and staff members, administrators, and, in some cases, students. A member of the central personnel staff should be an ex-officio committee member to orient the committee to proper and legal recruiting and selection procedures. For more details on the roles and functions of search committee's, see Scigliano (1979), Kaplowitz (1973), and Huegli and Eich (1979).

How Does an Institution Recruit Candidates?

The first tenet of effective recruitment is that the position be accurately defined so that the administrator and personnel office staff know what kind of candidates they are seeking. While that sounds basic, it is a facet of employment that at times causes problems. For example, if detailed background is specified in an announcement or advertisement of a position, but the administrator later wants to employ a candidate with lesser education or experience than that advertisied, that administrator could be liable for suit by a protected-class candidate claiming that he or she would have applied and been qualified had it been known that lesser education or experience was acceptable. To avoid this problem, if the basic requirements for a position change during the campaign, the position should be readvertised as a new and different position.

The position description for a vacancy should be reread to make sure that it accurately reflects the up-to-date needs for the position. The minimum qualifications should be examined to make sure that they accurately reflect the prerequisites for the position. It is unlawful to overstate the minimum qualifications. For example, if a description states that a master's degree is required, the institution must be able to prove that this qualification is related directly to the tasks to be performed and is really necessary to the job. In most cases, allowances should be made for knowledge and skills acquired in alternate but equivalent ways. A statement might read "A bachelor's degree in accounting or equivalent," or "demonstrated ability to _____."

Exhibits 28 and 29, pp. 131–133, show sample forms for administrators to complete when requesting the personnel office to recruit candidates for an administrative professional vacancy or a clerical-service vacancy.

A second basic tenet of good employment practice is to develop a large pool of candidates for a vacancy. Many administrators do not seem to want a large number of candidates, apparently because they do not want to spend time evaluating a large pool of candidates. However, a large pool of candidates is more likely to meet affirmative action good-faith efforts and, at the same time, to result in a wider and better choice of candidates. The employment office can assist administrators by developing a large pool of candidates and then effectively screening those candidates.

What Are Effective Policies for Promotion from Within?

Good employee relations dictates that new or open positions be considered as promotional opportunities for current staff members. At the same time, an institution must be able to change the composition of its work force if the proportion of women and minorities in that group does not bear reasonable relationship to the composition of the marketplace.

Several systems can be used to provide opportunities for staff members to apply for promotional positions. A formal system for the internal announcement of vacancies communicates to all employees that the institution is concerned that they have opportunities for advancement. By granting responsibility for upward mobility to the employees, the institution reduces the likelihood that administrators and supervisors will be charged with discriminatory promotion practices.

The following procedures are essential to an effective internal vacancy-announcement program. The positions should be announced in places that are highly visible; house organs and bulletin boards are most frequently used. House newsletters should be used only if they are published weekly or biweekly. Those published less frequently do not allow employees to meet application deadlines. Announcements should follow a standard format to assure that essential position elements are used and that affirmative action commitments are met. Preferably, the announcements should be prepared by the central employment office. The announcements should state a fixed period of time during which internal applicants may bid. That time limit should represent the shortest reasonable time in which all employees have an opportunity to see the announcement and respond to it.

It may be desirable to have different procedures for different categories of positions. For example, the procedure for announcing maintenance positions may be different from the procedure for clerical vacancies. The different procedures may provide for different announcement places and deadlines. Whatever procedures are used, however, all announcements should indicate where and how internal applicants are to apply within the deadlines established. Preferably, the applicants should initially make their wishes known to the central employment office in order that all candidates be given similar treatment. Such notification can be either by telephone (a special recording telephone vacancy line can be used to record the applicants) or by a written form provided by the employment office.

The personnel office must establish priorities for the consideration of internal candidates. Should a temporary employee receive the same priority as a regular employee? Such a practice could cause strained employee relations if an administrator preselects a candidate, puts that candidate on the temporary payroll, and then selects that individual over all other regular employees who bid. Should employees within the college or department with the vacancy have priority over employees from other units of the institution? Decisions about such a policy require consideration of the autonomy of units within the institution, fairness, and feasibility.

The personnel office and the unit with the vacancy must also decide whether external recruiting should take place coincident with or only following completion of the internal bidding process. If the unit or job classification shows an underutilization of women or minorities, it may be necessary to conduct simultaneous internal and external searches. However, if underutilization is not a problem, good employee relations are fostered by giving priority to internal promotion. In any case, the central employment personnel must play an important role in such decisions.

What Are the Procedures for Promotion in Academic Rank?

Promotion in academic rank differs from promotion in staff positions in one very important aspect. Staff positions are defined and classified by pay levels based on the duties assigned and the education and experience needed to perform those duties. Thus, when promoted, a staff member assumes new or additional duties. A promoted faculty member, however, may continue to perform exactly the same duties. The faculty member's promotion is a recognition of that individual's scholarly growth and accomplishments rather than a change in assignment.

The process for the promotion of faculty is usually specified by the college or university administration with maximum participation by the faculty organization (senate). An institution's policy usually includes the following four considerations. First, a list of critical factors to be evaluated in considering a faculty member for promotion. This list may include teaching effectiveness; research or professional accomplishments resulting in publication of other public presentation; professional service to an academic discipline or field, beyond institutional boundaries; institutional service to the department or college; and community service to local, state, or national institutions or agencies.

Second, a statement on permissible nominating sources for promotion. This list may include the individual candidate, any department member, a majority of the department, the chairperson, a collegewide committee, the dean, the provost, the president or chancellor, the governing board, or student.

Third, a statement on the requirements for submitting a dossier for consideration. The dossier requirements may include biographical data, a statement of publications, student evaluations, peer evaluations, lists of courses taught, lists of funding sources, letters of references from external sources, and letters of support from the department head and dean.

Fourth, a statement about the review process. This statement may include the composition of departmental and college review committees; the department head's role; the dean's role; the membership of an institution-wide review committee; the role of the chief academic officer, the president or the chancellor, and the

governing board; the role of students in the process; and the identification of which parties are to make the final decision.

What Are Good Sources of External Candidates?

Recruiting qualified candidates is the innovative part of the
employment process. Effective recruiting results from selecting the
appropriate methods to locate qualified candidates and presenting
them with an attractive description of the position. The following
sources are generally the best.

- Employee referrals. Satisfied employees can be an effective
  source of referrals and are particularly helpful in recruiting
  minority candidates.
- Walk-Ins. Institutions that have offices that can fairly process
  walk-in candidates can fill many positions from this source.
- Newspaper advertising. Newpaper advertising is usually the
  most significant source of candidates for staff vacancies. Because this source is so significant, we discuss it separately later
  in this chapter.
- Educational institutions. The placement service of higher educational institutions is a useful source for entry-level candidates.
- State employment agencies. The effectiveness of these state
  agencies varies across the country. Some institutions work
  closely with such agencies and find them very useful. Others
  have difficulties with the services and feel that less-than-
  competent candidates are referred. The personnel office
  should attempt to develop a strong and positive relationship
  with such agencies.
- Private employment agencies. Many, but not all, private agencies
  receive their fees for services from the employers. Institutions
  unable or unwilling to pay such fees will find the usefulness
  of such agencies to be minimal.
- Professional and trade journals. Advertisements placed in professional journals reach the proper readership. However, since
  most journals are published monthly (or even less frequently)
  and since the deadlines for placing ads may be two weeks or

longer before publication, ads should be placed only for positions that do not require a quick response.

- Professional association meetings. Annual professional association meetings allow the academic community to bring together individuals seeking appointments and institutions with vacancies.

- Higher Educational Administrative Referral Service (HEARS). HEARS is an agency formed by several higher education associations to serve as a liaison for educational institutions and candidates seeking staff positions in higher education.

- Special interest publications. A number of special interest publications specialize in classified advertisements for minorities and women; for example, the *Affirmative Action Register.* Other publications serve the handicapped communities; for example, the *American Speech and Hearing Association Journal*.

- Radio and television. Radio and television are effective in serving specialized needs. For example, if an institution opens a new building and needs fifty or seventy service personnel in a short time, radio or television spots may be effective. If vacancies persist in a specialized field such as computer programming, radio spots directed to alumni and played on a home football weekend may have the desired effect. Also, radio and television spots can be used to publicize an institution's affirmative action efforts.

- Posters and brochures. Posters for high school and college bulletin boards are helpful in recruiting secretarial, clerical, and other nonprofessional candidates. Local high schools and colleges are also good sources of temporary, part-time, and on-call workers.

- Letters to incumbents. Attractively written letters to qualified administrators at other institutions who hold the job for which the vacancy exists can be helpful. A letter asking for recommended candidates may yield qualified candidates, perhaps including the administrator addressed.

- *The Chronicle of Higher Education.* The *Chronicle* is a specialized newspaper for the higher education community. Specific suggestions for newspaper advertising are discussed later in this chapter.

In order to recruit women and ethnical and racial minority candidates for faculty positions, institutions should place advertisements in minority newspapers and publications, contact the placement offices of minority colleges, and contact national professional associations such as the Association of Mexican-American Educators, the National Association of Women Deans, the National Council of Negro Women, the Society of Women Engineers, the National Association of College Women, the Association of Women in Science, the Committee on Women in Psychology, the American Library Association's Black Caucus, the Association of Women in Architecture, and the American Association of Women in Community and Junior Colleges. Other national groups that can recommend qualified candidates include the Urban League, the Association of American Indian Affairs, and the National Association of the Physically Handicapped.

How Should Classified Advertisements Be Used?

Classified advertisements are one of the most effective methods for recruiting qualified candidates. In order to be effective, however, the ads must be properly written and placed in the appropriate newspapers, journals, or specialized publications. Because such advertisements can be very costly, records of results should be kept to determine cost-effective recruitment sources.

Selecting the publications. The nature of the vacant position determines the publications in which it should be advertised. To advertise clerical or service positions, the local newspapers are probably most effective, unless it seems reasonable to assume that prospective out-of-town applicants would be willing to relocate in the institution's community. To advertise for professional nonfaculty positions, statewide newspapers and professional publications are effective. A multistate or nationwide market—including several large metropolitan newspapers and higher education journals—should be considered for top executive positions.

Advertisements in urban newspapers are usually more cost effective even though such advertisements are more expensive. However, consider that several small-town newspaper advertisements may be placed for the same cost as one ad in a metropolitan newspaper.

Consider known areas of concentration of personnel in the field of the vacancy. For example, one section of the state or region may have a concentration of computer companies. Similarly, to recruit a ferrous metallurgist, Pittsburgh, Pennsylvania, is an obvious place to advertise. Also, ask individuals currently in the position being advertised for their suggestions.

Be innovative. Where could one advertise for an executive pilot for an institution's executive airplane? The *Wall Street Journal* may be the best place to advertise. Why? Pilots spend a great deal of time waiting at airports for executives, and many of them read whatever is available, often their client's *Wall Street Journal*.

Note, too, that for a daily newspaper, Sunday is usually the best day to advertise, followed by Monday, Tuesday, Wednesday, and so forth, in that order. Saturday want ads appear to be the least read.

Writing the ad. First, select a title. Classified ads are listed alphabetically. Thus it may be necessary to use a variation of the actual job title to have the ad appear in the proper place. For example, the title "Field Accountant" would appear under the *F*'s, and an accountant is not likely to look there. The title should read "Accountant (Field)." In some case, it may be worthwhile to cross reference ads within the issue of the newspaper.

The ad should include a brief statement about what the position entails and the education and experience requirements. The ad should not overstate nor overspecify the qualifications. Consider carefully the effect of a statement like "Must be an excellent typist." Such a statement is subject to interpretation and could discourage an excellent typist who underestimates his or her abilities, while an average typist who tends to overestimate his or her abilities will apply. Statements that invite interpretation are usually ineffective.

Ads should be written to entice rather than screen out applicants. The ad should mention something positive about the institution; for example, phrases like "cultural center," "near the seashore," "excellent hunting and fishing," "extra days off at

Christmas," "educational opportunities for employees and their families."

The ad should specify how applicants are to respond. If the personnel office does not want telephone calls or drop-ins, the ad should instruct applicants to write.

The federal government and most states have laws that prohibit discriminatory advertising. These laws make it illegal for help wanted ads to specify age, race, creed, national origin, or sex (unless sex is a bona fide occupational qualification for the job advertised). The federal Equal Employment Opportunity Commission (EEOC) further urges the inclusion of the following statement at the end of the ad: "An Equal Opportunity/Affirmative Action Employer."

Designing the ad. Indicate to the publication's classified office that the heading should be in fairly bold type. A bold heading will attract the reader's attention. The body of the ad can be in regular (agate) type. An interested reader will read the ad, regardless of its size. If competition is keen for the talents being sought, consider placing a display ad. Display ads are larger and more eye-catching, and usually more expensive.

Figure 3. Sample Advertisement for a Faculty Position.

FACULTY POSITION
(Finance)

The School of Business of Anytown University is expanding its business faculty. The successful applicant would teach in a developing finance program at both the undergraduate and graduate levels. Candidate should be qualified to teach in the area of Security Analysis and Portfolio Theory, in addition to other courses in Financial Management and Investments. An earned doctorate is required.

Anytown University is located in the center of the beautiful Sunshine Mountains within easy driving distance to New York, Philadelphia, and the seashore. The institution is part of the Anystate State College System.

Send resumes to Dr. Jane Smith, 10 Campus Drive, Anytown, by January 31, 1982.

AN EQUAL OPPORTUNITY/AFFIRMATIVE ACTION
EMPLOYER

Figures 3 and 4 present examples of advertisements based on the principles just outlined. Before placing an ad, make sure it meets the following criteria: Title is accurate and clear; duties are described; necessary education and experience are specified; method of response is indicated; selling points of institution are mentioned. Then, double-check to verify that the ad complies with federal or state discrimination legislation.

What Questions Should Appear on the Application Form?

An application form is one of the tools of the employment process. The form should not ask questions that are discriminatory or that would reveal information about groups protected under the law. Questions should not be such that they have a disparate effect on various segments of the population. For example, to ask for a record of arrests might adversely affect black applicants because, historically, blacks have been arrested more readily than whites. However, it is proper to ask if the applicant has been convicted of an offense. Convictions are, in some circumstances, pertinent to specific jobs.

Figure 4. Sample Advertisement for a Nonfaculty Position.

PERSONNEL ASSISTANT
(Unemployment Compensation)

An attractive vacancy at Hometown College for an individual to handle the college's unemployment compensation program. Individual interprets the law, maintains liaison with state agencies, and represents the institution at hearings.

Bachelor's degree or equivalent with two to three years of effective experience handling unemployment compensation activities.

Educational opportunities available at reduced rates during working hours. Cultural center in an attractive campus setting. Liberal benefits program.

Write Employment Division, Old Main Building, Hometown.

AN EQUAL OPPORTUNITY/AFFIRMATIVE ACTION
EMPLOYER

Questions should be relevant to the job vacancy. Part of the application should request information about the applicant's last three employers and the employer for whom the applicant worked the longest if other than one of those three. Questions about educational background and skills that are relevant to the tasks to be performed are permissible.

While the form should not include a general question about handicaps, it may include a question about whether the applicant has a handicap that would limit or prohibit the performance of job-related tasks. However, illegal are questions on national origin, race, religion, location of relatives outside the U.S., foreign military service, and any other requests that would reveal the applicant's racial or ethnic identity (for example, a request for a photograph).

Questions about marital status are permitted, provided they are asked equally of men and women. However, since this information typically does not relate directly to tasks to be performed and is only a questionable predictor of attendance or longevity, such questions are not recommended.

A sample application form is shown in Exhibit 30, pp. 134–139. For more details and samples relative to pre-employment forms and practices, including employment applications, inquiry guides, and reference checking, see Bouchard, 1980b.

How Are Employment Interviews Conducted?

The purposes of the employment interview are to exchange information and to promote the goodwill of the institution for applicants who are not hired.

In preparing for the interview, the interviewer should:

- Provide for privacy.
- Know and understand the content of the job vacancy by reviewing the job description and any special comments made by the administrator with the vacancy.
- Plan the approximate length of the interview and decide who else will interview the candidates.
- Compose a set of questions related to the job that will be asked all applicants for the particular vacancy. The careful planning

of questions to be asked is essential. The general pattern of questions should not vary among male, female, or minority candidates.

- Study the written application presented by the applicants. The interviewer should not continually consult the application during the interview; to interview from the application form tends to limit questions to those that relate to the form. The interviewer should look for gaps in information or request expanded information.

At the beginning of the interview, the interviewer should put the applicant at ease. The interviewer should explain in detail the elements of the vacancy. This description must be honest and should indicate to the applicant both the less desirable and more desirable aspects of the position. If the interviewer overstates the case, an applicant who accepts the position may later turn into a disgruntled employee upon learning about the negative aspects of the position.

An interviewer should avoid leading statements or those that will evoke meaningless responses. Samples of such statements are: "You probably left your last position because . . ." and "I suppose you like to work with people." Rather, the interviewer should ask attitudinal questions. Motivation and a basic curiosity seem to be two characteristics of successful employees. Indeed, very few employees fail because they lack the technical knowledge or ability to do the job. They fail because of their temperaments and motivations. Therefore, attitudinal questions that evoke free responses will reveal valuable information about the applicants. Sample attitudinal questions are:

> How do you feel about your present job?
> How do you feel about the progress you've made with your present employer?
> What are the things that you particularly liked about your last job?
> What are the things that you didn't like?
> What are some of the problems you encountered with your last job?

What do you consider to be your strengths and weaknesses
related to our vacancy?

How do you think you could best help our institution?

Of your last three employers, which was the best? the worst?
Why?

Why did you apply for this position?

The interviewer should find out how the applicant fits into
the organization of his or her present employer. Sometimes titles
and relationships sound more significant than they are, and vice
versa. Ask questions such as:

What is the title of the person to whom you report?

How many people have jobs like the person to whom you
report?

How many people have jobs like yours?

To whom does your boss report? What is that person's job?

How large is the company?

This last question can elicit an answer that may reflect the applicant's curiosity. The response may be stated in gross sales, numbers
of employees, even numbers of cars in the company parking lot. In
any case, it may reflect the individual's curiosity about his or her
environment.

The interviewer should look for informational gaps by asking questions that follow the applicant's career chronologically. An
interviewer can also ask how the candidate got various jobs. The
answers may be revealing, in that if a high-sounding job title was
given by a relative of the applicant, the job may have been less
important than its title suggests.

The interviewer should avoid showing any personal feelings
about anything said during the interview. The interview should be
neither a forum for criticism nor a counseling session. However,
the interviewer should be cognizant of any contradictions voiced by
the applicant. Such situations should be explored as carefully and
as gracefully as possible. Similarly, the interviewer should note the
applicant's resistance to answer any questions. If resistance is evident and the information sought is significant, the question may
be asked again later in the interview. Or, the interviewer may ask if

the applicant has a valid reason for withholding the information. The applicant's response may yield the information sought or the reason that he or she cannot provide the information.

In sum, the interview should provide the interviewer with insight into the candidate's knowledge, personality and temperament, basic motivation, and emotional maturity.

What Information May Legally Be Sought in an Interview?

Various federal and state antidiscrimination laws and regulations govern the kinds of questions that may be asked during an interview, particularly if they are not job-related. Interviewers must be consistent in the information requested of potential employees. They must not, for example, ask a question of female applicants that they would not ask male applicants, and vice versa. Questions or inquiries about arrests, marital status, and family life tend to be prejudicial. Discretion and good judgment must always be used by each interviewer, whether a professional in the employment division, an administrator, a manager, or a supervisor. Before asking an applicant a question, the interviewer should ask "Do I absolutely need to know this information in order to make a decision on this candidate?" If not, the question should not be asked.

Any inquiry made in connection with prospective employment that expresses any limitation or specification as to race, color, religion, national origin, or age as provided by law, sex, or status as a Vietnam-era veteran, is considered discriminatory, unless that limitation or specification can be shown to be an approved bona fide occupational qualification. (Such exceptions are very unusual.) Also, questions posed to a handicapped individual or disabled veteran must relate to the performance of the duties of a specific job; general questions relative to the handicap or disability are to be avoided.

Under the law, all parts of the employment process—the application form, the interview, and any paper-and-pencil tests —must comply with antidiscrimination laws. Interviewers who wish to administer pre-employment tests should make sure that such tests measure skills relevant to the job and that such tests have been validated as nondiscriminatory. Professional help should be sought in the validation of tests.

The following list summarizes various antidiscrimination rules and regulations pertaining to employment interviewing. This is not an all-inclusive list of permissible and nonacceptable questions; however, it covers the major areas of questioning relevant to interviewing.

Permissible	*Questionable or Prohibited*
Name and Address	
One may ask the applicant his or her name and address.	One should not ask an applicant whose name has been changed for his or her original name.
Age	
One may ask the applicant if his or her age complies with applicable institutional policies, such as minimum and maximum age for employment, employment certificate, working papers, and the like. One may ask for proof-of-age card (issued by an applicant's high school) to verify minimum age requirements.	One may not ask to see a birth certificate. One should not ask questions that imply a preference for a specific age group.
Birthplace	
	One may not inquire into the birthplace of the applicant, spouse, parents, or other close relatives. One may not ask the applicant to disclose ancestry or national origin.
Height and Weight	
One may ask about an applicant's ability to perform the job requirements.	One should not ask about the height and weight of an applicant, unless they are bona fide job requirements.

Physical Disabilities

One may ask if the applicant has a physical disability that would prevent satisfactory performance on the job. One may ask about the applicant's general health.

One should not ask about a general physical disability that has no direct bearing on performance of the job in question.

Education and Experience

One may ask about schooling, both academic and vocational. One may inquire into work experience.

Military Experience

One may inquire into the applicant's experience in the U.S. armed forces or state militia.

One should not inquire into the foreign military experience of the applicant.

One should not require the applicant to produce his or her military discharge papers before employment. (Such papers show birthdate, place of birth, and the like.)

Citizenship

One may ask if the applicant is a U.S. citizen or intends to become one. One may ask an applicant who is not a U.S. citizen about the type of visa possessed.

One should not inquire whether the applicant or applicant's spouse or parents are naturalized or native-born citizens nor ask for the dates of naturalization.

One should not require the applicant to produce naturalization papers or first papers.

Marital Status

One may not ask about the applicant's marital status. Women should not be asked if their social title is Miss or Mrs.

Permissible   *Questionable or Prohibited*

Family or Relatives

One may ask for the name, address, and relationship of persons to be notified in case of accident or emergency.

One may inquire if the applicant has any relatives employed by the institution. However, such information should be used only to avoid placements in which supervisory lines or the handling of confidential information could influence rates of pay, promotions, or the granting of tenure or if an awkward work situation might result.

One should not inquire into the location outside the U.S. of places of business of the applicant's relatives.

One should not ask about the place of residence of the applicant's spouse, parents, or other close relatives.

One should not ask the applicant about the maiden name of his or her mother. Male applicants should not be asked their wife's maiden name.

One should not ask the applicant to identify dependent children. If, by chance, this information is volunteered by the applicant, one should not pursue with questions such as, "What plans can you make for childcare, if you are employed?" (Historically, questions regarding dependent children have been shown to have adverse impact on women. Thus, questioning along such lines should be avoided.)

Religion

One may not ask about the applicant's religion, church, parish, or pastor, nor about the religious holidays the applicant observes.

Language

One may ask the language(s) the

One should not ask the appli-

applicant speaks, reads, or writes, and the degree of fluency. cant's native tongue nor the language commonly used by the applicant at home. One should not ask how the applicant acquired the ability to read, write, or speak a foreign language.

Photographs

One should not require an applicant to submit a photograph before an offer of employment is made.

Memberships

One may ask the applicant about membership in organizations, the nature of which do *not* disclose race, religion, or national origin.

One may ask if the applicant belongs to an organization that advocates the violent overthrow of the U.S. government.

One should not ask the applicant to disclose memberships in organizations, the nature of which would indicate religion, race, or national origin.

Arrest and Conviction Record

One may ask if the applicant has been convicted of a crime, and the nature of the crime. (In this instance, one may inquire if conviction record is under a different name than the applicant now uses.)

One should not ask the number and kinds of arrests the applicant may have had.

How Should References Be Checked?

Prospective employers are legally permitted to check an applicant's references. However, some employers have grown cautious about asking for or providing reference information. But, since references provide useful indicators for predicting the applicant's potential for success, the interests of both the institution and the applicant are served by reference checking.

The authors have had many experiences that indicate the value of reference checking. For example, an applicant who applied for an interviewing job at a major educational institution had been an interviewer at a small company. The company president sent a letter praising the applicant's abilities, but when the company president was telephoned and the vacancy was explained in detail, he stated that the applicant was not appropriate for that particular vacancy. The particular job required an individual who could be persistently persuasive with persons of high-level authority. The president explained that the applicant had been turned down for promotion at his company precisely because of her inability to use persistent persuasion with persons in authority. In this case, the additional information reinforced and confirmed the perceptions of the interviewer who handled the case.

Since the area of reference checking is touchy at best, it should be done by a personnel professional who is trained and skilled in making such contacts. Usually, the original interviewer should make the reference check. In all probability, he or she is the most familiar with the applicant and has the necessary background to compose probing questions. The interviewer should prepare a list of questions relevant to the particular vacancy, the particular applicant, and the particular reference being checked. The applicant's present employer should not be contacted without the applicant's specific permission to do so.

The most desirable way to conduct a reference check is by personal visit. However, a telephone check serves adequately and is less expensive. But letters or form letters rarely elicit satisfactory information. People hesitate to put in writing information they would give either in person or by telephone. Too, the stylized approach of a form letter might fail to elicit the necessary information. During a telephone conversation, one can pursue different avenues to gain information, depending on the responses given.

The interviewer should call the person who had direct supervision over the applicant. Second-hand information, that is, from someone in a personnel department, should be used only if no other channel is available. The personnel office or accounting department can verify dates of employment and termination but usually do not have information regarding the job applicant's former work habits, personal habits, performance, and the like.

Usually, lists of personal references provided by a candidate are not significant points of contact. Reference checking should be limited to previous and present employers who can discuss the applicant's performance at work and experience.

In calling to check a reference, the interviewer should immediately identify him or herself (name, title, institutional affiliation) and explain the reason for calling. One should assure the contact that the conversation will be held in confidence. If the contact is not free to talk at the moment, the interviewer should arrange a time to call again. If the contact seems to doubt the legitimacy of the call, the interviewer should offer to accept a collect return call.

Once the conversation begins, the interviewer should provide background information on the vacancy to be filled. Then one can ask a general question such as, "What is your opinion of how the applicant would fit into our vacancy?" Once the contact has responded to this general question, the interviewer can ask more specific questions. The most useful questions to ask are:

> How did the applicant get along with others with whom he or she worked?
> How did the applicant get along with supervisors?
> Did the applicant have any personal habits that you consider to be negative?
> How was the applicant's attendance?
> Do you consider the applicant to be reliable?
> Did the applicant meet commitments?
> Why did the applicant leave your company?
> Do you know of any criminal record?
> Would you re-employ the applicant?
> What was the nature of the applicant's work with you?
> Was the applicant bypassed for promotions with your company? Why?
> What are the applicant's strengths and weaknesses?
> Is there anything else you'd like to tell me about the applicant?

During the conversation, the interviewer should try to establish rapport with the contact. The interviewer might try to discover if the contact has a son or daughter attending the institution, or if there are any common business acquaintances. Many times a freer exchange of information comes about if the contact identifies with the organization, the interviewer's position, or some other mutual point of interest. The interviewer should let the contact talk freely without interruption. An interruptive question at the wrong time could prevent the contact from supplying useful further information.

If the contact seems reluctant to discuss certain factors, an interviewer should politely probe. A further explanation of why the information is being requested may elicit the information sought. The interviewer should be alert for obvious pauses in answering. Often pauses indicate that further questioning may prove useful. If the answers seem ambiguous, the interviewer should try to elicit a definite opinion by summarizing the conversation in a way that urges the contact to agree or disagree with a statement like, "I take it that you don't recommend the applicant very highly for the position," or "I take it that you recommend the applicant very highly for the position." Usually, such summary statements evoke a clear-cut response.

Before concluding the call, the interviewer should make sure that all the necessary questions have been covered. The interviewer should always close the conversation by asking if the contact would re-employ the applicant? Often this question brings forth information that was not elicited by other questions. The interviewer should, of course, thank the contact for his or her help. (For further details about interviewing, see College and University Personnel Association, forthcoming.)

Who Should Make the Employment Decision and Notify the Candidates?

The hiring decision should be made by the administrator who has the vacancy. However, it should have the concurrence of a personnel professional to make sure that affirmative action, equal pay requirements, and good internal employee relation practices are met. Before the final decision is made, a final review should be made of the applicant's qualifications against the specifications for the position. If several persons interviewed the candidate, opinions should be sought from those individuals as well.

The successful candidate should, of course, be notified. Any letter of offer sent to a successful candidate can be construed as a binding legal contract. If the employee is later dismissed, and appeals that dismissal, the original letter of offer might well be used as evidence. Therefore, all letters of offer should be of a standard form that has been reviewed by legal counsel. In many institutions the letters of offer are sent by the personnel office to assure the consistency of their content.

Unsuccessful candidates should be notified that the position has been filled. There is no need to tell an unsuccessful candidate why he or she was not hired. In fact, to do so might invite litigation. What if an unsuccessful candidate asks why he or she was not hired? A suggested response is: "Your background and experience are excellent. However, we have hired (or plan to hire) someone whose background and experience relate even more closely to the vacancy than yours do."

Exhibit 27. Sample Policy on Search Procedures for Academic Administrative Positions

Policy:

It is the policy of the university to ensure the appropriate involvement of the faculty and professional staff in the search process for filling academic administrative vacancies at the department, college, campus, and central administrative levels of the university.

Responsibility:

The next-highest administrative officer will be responsible for appointing advisory search committees.

Guidelines:

The following general guidelines apply:

1. The majority of faculty members on an advisory search committee will be members of the academic unit for which leadership is sought.
2. The method for nominating faculty members to advisory search committees will be determined by procedures agreed upon by the faculty and the academic administrative officer of the appropriate academic unit.

Exhibit 27 (continued)

3. The list of faculty nominations for advisory search committees will not exceed twice the number of faculty members to be appointed by the appointing authority.
4. Faculty members from the unit appointed to the advisory search committee shall be jointly acceptable to the nominating unit and the appointing authority.
5. The appointing authority will normally designate as chairman one of the faculty members of the committee who comes from the academic unit for which leadership is sought. Exception to this guideline requires approval of the next higher level of administrative authority.
6. Faculty members from other academic units, administrators and students will be included on advisory search committees as appropriate.
7. The general charge to advisory search committees will be to identify qualified candidates. The appointing authority will provide specific charges as appropriate within the framework of this general charge applicable to all advisory search committees.

The above general guidelines apply in the search processes for filling the positions of department head, academic institute director, academic dean, academic vice presidents, senior vice president for university development and relations, and provost. In addition to these mandated positions, the guidelines may also apply to other academic administrative positions. In the case of central administrative academic officers, the committee will be appointed by the president of the university with faculty membership being representative of the total university as nominated by the appropriate senate mechanism. For academic deans, the committee will be appointed by the provost of the university, with the majority of faculty members being from the respective campus or college. In the case of academic institute directors, the appropriate vice president or provost will appoint the committee with the majority of the faculty members coming from the institute. Department head advisory search committees will be appointed by the academic dean, with the majority of the faculty members being from the department seeking a head.

In accord with the rules of the board of trustees for governance of the university, in selection of a president, the board shall consult with representatives of the faculty and the student body.

Exhibit 28. Request for Posting of Administrative
or Professional Vacancy

Date: _____

To: Department of Personnel Administration

From: _____   _____
           (Division or School)   (Department)
_____

A. If this is a new position, complete Staff Classification Exemption
    Determination Form and send with this request.
    1. Provide suggested staff classification and position title _____
    _____

B. If the position presently exists:
    1. Staff classification and position title _____
    2. Name of last incumbent? _____
    3. Item number _____

C. Please give the following information:
    1. F.T.E. _____
    2. ☐ Fiscal Year   ☐ Academic Year

    Starting Date _____

D. Do you wish the Personnel Administration to screen applicants?
    ☐ Yes   ☐ No

E. Position Description:
    1. Title of person to whom position reports _____
    2. Summary
    Brief description of duties and responsibilities (Include supervisory
    responsibilities, if applicable):
    _____
    _____
    _____

    3. Education or other qualifications desired _____
    _____

    4. Salary Range _____

F. To be interviewed by:
    Name _____ Title _____ Phone Number _____
    Building _____ Room Number _____
    Instructions on dates and times when available for interview: _____
    _____

G. Requested by: _____ Approved by: _____

Exhibit 29. Request for Clerical or Service Vacancy

Date: _____

To: Department of Personnel Administration

From: _____   _____
              (Division or School)   (Department)

Position identification
1. If this position presently exists: Job Title _____
   Position Classification ___ Replacement for Whom _____
   Account Number _____ Item Number _____
2. If this is a new position, please complete Preliminary Job Description
   for Clerical or Service Staff and submit it with this form.

   Please give the following information:
   Full time _____ Part time _____
   Regular _____ Temporary _____
   Expected duration of the position _____
   Expected Starting Date _____
   Maximum starting rate _____

Work hours
State regularly scheduled work hours:
Monday _____ to _____   Friday _____ to _____
Tuesday _____ to _____   Saturday _____ to _____
Wednesday _____ to _____   Sunday _____ to _____
Thursday _____ to _____   Total Hours: _____

Other hours scheduled (overtime, swing shift, etc.) Please explain:
_____
_____

Qualifications
Required or necessary minimum qualifications:
1. Education: _____
2. Experience: _____
3. Additional or preferred qualifications (i.e. physical exertion, driver's
   license, shorthand, etc.): _____
   _____
   _____

Clerical only

Is typing a minimum requirement for this position?　　Yes ___　No ___

If yes, what is the minimum typing speed required:　　___ W.P.M.

How many hours of typing are regularly performed?　　_____ or _____
　　　　　　　　　　　　　　　　　　　　　　　　　Per Day　　Per Week

Comments: _____

Recruitment information

Have present departmental and area employees been given the opportunity to apply for this position?　Yes ___　No ___

If yes, please attach a copy of the internal or departmental vacancy notice used.

If no, please give a brief write-up that can be used for recruiting purposes.

To be interviewed by:

Name _____ Title _____ Phone number _____

Building _____ Room Number _____

Instructions on dates and times *not* convenient for interviews: _____

Approved by _____ Date _____

Exhibit 30. Sample Employment Application Form

APPLICANT—Please complete all pages.
—Type or print, using black ink or marker.
—If you need additional space, attach a supplemental sheet.

GENERAL

NAME (LAST)	(FIRST)	(MIDDLE)	SOCIAL SECURITY NO.	DATE OF APPLICATION

PRESENT ADDRESS (STREET, CITY, STATE, ZIP CODE)			AREA CODE & PHONE NO.—DAY	AREA CODE & PHONE NO.—EVENING

ADDRESS WHERE YOU MAY BE CONTACTED IF DIFFERENT FROM PRESENT ADDRESS			ALTERNATE PHONE NO.	BIRTHDATE, IF UNDER 18 OR OVER 70

HAVE YOU WORKED FOR THIS INSTITUTION? ☐ NO ☐ YES	IF YES, INDICATE: DATES OF EMPLOYMENT	DEPARTMENT	POSITION

ARE YOU A VETERAN OF THE U.S. ARMED FORCES? ☐ NO ☐ YES	BRANCH	DATES OF ACTIVE DUTY	U.S. CITIZEN? ☐ YES ☐ NO	IF NO, INDICATE TYPE OF VISA AND ALIEN REGISTRATION NUMBER

IF THERE ARE ANY POSITIONS OR TYPES OF POSITIONS FOR WHICH YOU SHOULD NOT BE CONSIDERED, OR JOB DUTIES YOU CANNOT PERFORM BECAUSE OF A PHYSICAL, MENTAL OR MEDICAL DISABILITY, PLEASE DESCRIBE.

HAVE YOU EVER BEEN CONVICTED OF ANY CRIMINAL OFFENSE OTHER THAN MINOR TRAFFIC VIOLATIONS? _____ IF SO, PLEASE EXPLAIN. A CRIMINAL CONVICTION WILL BE CONSIDERED ONLY IN RELATION TO THE JOB FOR WHICH YOU ARE APPLYING. SERIOUSNESS AND NATURE OF THE OFFENSE, TIME ELAPSED, AND REHABILITATION WILL BE TAKEN INTO ACCOUNT.

DO YOU HAVE RELATIVES EMPLOYED AT THIS INSTITUTION?

☐ NO ☐ YES

IF YES, GIVE: NAME   DEPARTMENT   RELATIONSHIP

POSITION

TYPE OF POSITION DESIRED

SALARY EXPECTED

$

DATE AVAILABLE	ARE YOU SEEKING			SPECIFY ANTICIPATED PERIOD OF WORK AND NUMBER OF HOURS PER DAY
	FULL-TIME PERMANENT EMPLOYMENT ☐	PERMANENT PART-TIME ☐	TEMPORARY ☐	

WILL YOU WORK WEEKENDS?

☐ YES ☐ NO

PREFERRED HOURS

WILL YOU WORK IRREGULAR HOURS?

☐ YES ☐ NO

Exhibit 30 (continued)

EMPLOYMENT RECORD

LIST MOST RECENT EMPLOYMENT FIRST

EMPLOYER	START DATE	STARTING SALARY	INITIAL POSITION TITLE
STREET ADDRESS	END DATE	FINAL SALARY	PRESENT OR FINAL POSITION TITLE
CITY, STATE, ZIP CODE	LAST SUPERVISOR'S NAME		PHONE
			MAY WE CONTACT THIS EMPLOYER? ☐ YES ☐ NO
POSITION DESCRIPTION			REASON FOR LEAVING

EMPLOYER	START DATE	STARTING SALARY	INITIAL POSITION TITLE
STREET ADDRESS	END DATE	FINAL SALARY	FINAL POSITION TITLE
CITY, STATE, ZIP CODE	LAST SUPERVISOR'S NAME		PHONE
POSITION DESCRIPTION			REASON FOR LEAVING

EMPLOYER	START DATE	STARTING SALARY	INITIAL POSITION TITLE
STREET ADDRESS	END DATE	FINAL SALARY	FINAL POSITION TITLE
CITY, STATE, ZIP CODE	LAST SUPERVISOR'S NAME		PHONE
POSITION DESCRIPTION			REASON FOR LEAVING

EMPLOYER	START DATE	STARTING SALARY	INITIAL POSITION TITLE
STREET ADDRESS	END DATE	FINAL SALARY	FINAL POSITION TITLE
CITY, STATE, ZIP CODE	LAST SUPERVISOR'S NAME		PHONE
POSITION DESCRIPTION			REASON FOR LEAVING

PROFESSIONAL ORGANIZATIONS, ASSOCIATIONS, HONORS, CERTIFICATIONS, PROFESSIONAL LICENSES AND PUBLICATIONS YOU CONSIDER SIGNIFICANT. PLEASE INDICATE THE PROFESSIONAL LICENSE NUMBER AND STATE OF ISSUANCE.

(Additional sheets may be added if needed.)

Exhibit 30 (continued)

EDUCATION & TRAINING

	NAME OF SCHOOL / CITY & STATE	DATES ATTENDED FROM MO. & YR.	TO MO. & YR.	GRADUATE? YES	NO	TYPE OF DEGREE OR DIPLOMA	MAJOR SUBJECT
HIGH SCHOOL LAST ATTENDED	NAME OF SCHOOL / CITY & STATE						
COLLEGE, UNIVERSITY OR TECHNICAL SCHOOL	NAME OF SCHOOL / CITY & STATE						
COLLEGE, UNIVERSITY OR TECHNICAL SCHOOL	NAME OF SCHOOL / CITY & STATE						
COLLEGE, UNIVERSITY OR TECHNICAL SCHOOL	NAME OF SCHOOL / CITY & STATE						
OTHER	NAME OF SCHOOL / CITY & STATE						

LIST ACADEMIC HONORS, SCHOLARSHIPS, ETC., YOU CONSIDER SIGNIFICANT AND RELEVANT TO EMPLOYMENT

LANGUAGE ABILITY — LIST THOSE YOU COULD USE IN YOUR WORK

LANGUAGE	SPEAK	READ	WRITE	LANGUAGE	SPEAK	READ	WRITE
	☐	☐	☐		☐	☐	☐

	TYPING SPEED	SHORTHAND SPEED
	WPM	WPM

OTHER SKILLS, TRAINING AND HOBBIES OR AVOCATIONS THAT MIGHT BE RELEVANT TO EMPLOYMENT

REFERENCES

LIST THREE PERSONS, OTHER THAN RELATIVES OR PERSONAL FRIENDS, WHO HAVE KNOWLEDGE OF YOUR WORK EXPERIENCE OR EDUCATION

NAME	MAILING ADDRESS	PHONE

I hereby authorize investigation of all statements contained in this application. I certify that such statements are true, and understand that misrepresentation or omission of facts called for in this form is cause for termination of employment without notice. I also agree: (1) to such examination by a university designated physician as may be required, employment being contingent on the satisfactory passing thereof; (2) if employed, to enroll in the University group insurance plan; (3) if employed, to abide by all regulations of the university.

Date _____

Signature _____

No person shall be denied employment on the basis of any legally prohibited discrimination involving, but not limited to, such factors as race, color, creed, religion, national or ethnic origin, sex, age, or handicap.

❧ 8 ❧

Administering Mandated and Optional Benefits

A large percentage of the budget of any institution of higher education is expended on the salaries and benefits of faculty and staff members. A recent study, conducted by the Educational Research Group of the Teachers Insurance and Annuity Association, states that the expenditures for benefits range from 6 to over 40 percent of payroll, with the average for public universities at 19.3 percent, 19.1 percent for public four-year liberal arts colleges, 18.7 percent for private four-year liberal arts colleges, and 17.5 percent for private universities. Over 27 percent of the institutions surveyed report expenditures for benefits in excess of 20 percent of their payroll. See Cook and Zucchi (1979) for more details on this study.

Benefit programs for employees have become so commonplace that their basic purpose is sometimes forgotten. Benefit programs are intended to relieve faculty and staff of financial concern, to improve their morale, and to provide them with a tax advantage. A good benefits program enables an institution to remain competitive and thus be able to attract and retain the best possible faculty and staff.

140

Which Benefits Are Mandated by Law and Which Are Optional?

Both federal and state law mandate certain benefits coverage, including social security, unemployment compensation, workers' compensation, and in a few states, disability benefits insurance. For more details on mandated and optional benefits, see Bouchard (1980b) and Prentice-Hall (1966, 1979).

In addition to legally mandated benefits, institutions offer many optional benefits. In the area of insurance, for example, institutions may pay for, or share with the employee, the cost of

- Health care (hospital, surgical, major medical, dental, prescription drugs, X-ray and laboratory, supplemental accident, and vision care)
- Life insurance (group term insurance for employee or dependents, accidental death and dismemberment insurance, business travel insurance, or group paid-up life insurance—if the employee pays the total premium)
- Disability insurance (short-term or long-term)
- Retirement plans
- Miscellaneous coverage (legal services, group automobile and home owner's insurance, and malpractice or other liability coverage)

Some institutions purchase their insurance from an insurance company. However, larger institutions are likely to find cost savings in being self-insured for some of these programs. Such self-insurance usually requires in-house expertise in administering the plan's funding, claims payments, and design. However, there are degrees of self-insurance. An institution can purchase the necessary administrative services from an insurance firm or consultant. Such functions as paying claims, examining and pricing potential plan changes, processing unusual claims, predicting future inflationary costs, and so forth can be handled by outside consultants, with the institution paying for actual claims and for the administrative services. In most instances, a self-insurance program should include the purchase of catastrophe insurance to take care of claims above a designated limit.

The optional benefits most appropriate for a self-insurance program are health care coverage and disability insurance. Life insurance coverage is not appropriate for self-insurance under current Internal Revenue Service regulations on the tax treatment of benefits. Miscellaneous insurance coverage (legal services, malpractice, and the like) are also not appropriate for self-insurance because of their high expense and the involvement of third parties in the claims procedure. Workers' compensation and unemployment compensation, however, may be insured or self-funded. Many institutions self-fund worker's compensation coverage in those states where it is permitted. Federal law permits non-profit institutions to reimburse the state for actual claims paid instead of being taxed for unemployment compensation; that option is a form of self-funding. All larger institutions should give serious consideration to self-insurance for appropriate benefits programs.

Other optional benefits offered by higher education institutions include: (1) paid vacation, sick leave, and holidays; (2) personal leaves of absence, leaves for graduate study, and sabbatical leaves of absence; (3) time off for attending classes, voting, national guard service, jury duty, or death in the family; (4) tuition waiver or reduction, library privileges, reduced rates at artistic or athletic events, use of campus recreation facilities, faculty and staff club, or dining facilities; (5) daycare facilities; (6) and such miscellaneous benefits as uniforms, rest periods, purchasing discount plans, and professional association membership.

Although our list may seem comprehensive, it is not by any means complete. In the past decade, many institutions have expanded their benefits programs to include new elements. For example, dental care was a fledgling ten years ago. Today, many institutions have some form of dental care coverage, and many others are exploring it. Benefits that seem unusual today may well be commonplace in another ten or fifteen years.

What Does a Good Basic Plan of Benefits Entail?

A basic plan of benefits should include at least the following: a retirement plan, health care coverage, life insurance, and a disability plan. The health care coverage should include hospital, surgical, and major medical coverage. To provide less than these basic plans is to be out of step with higher education in general. Plans in addition to these basic ones should be considered based on the ability of the institution to fund and administer them. These basic programs are, of course, in addition to mandated programs like unemployment compensation, workers' compensation, and for some institutions, social security.

What Laws Affect Welfare Benefits?

Under federal law, employee welfare benefits plans are defined as plans that provide any of the following benefits: medical, surgical, hospital, sickness, accident, disability, death, supplemental unemployment benefits, scholarship fund (funded), apprenticeship or other training, prepaid legal services, and severance pay. Items such as the following are not considered to be covered employee welfare plans: overtime, shift premium, weekend premium, unfunded scholarship funds, and compensation for absences for work for reasons such as vacation, holidays, sabbatical leave, jury duty, and the like.

Various pieces of federal and state legislation affect those benefits defined as welfare benefits. These laws seek to protect the benefits of employees against underfunding, default, or financial irresponsibility on the part of the plans' sponsors. As an example of such legislation, let us consider the major federal law in this field.

In 1974, Congress passed the Employee Retirement Income Security Act (ERISA). Basically, the act applies to the nonpublic section of higher education, although it does not apply to church plans that do not elect coverage. Since it is a complex law, we will only outline the main provisions. Responsibility for implementing the law's provisions is assigned to the U.S. Department of Labor, the Internal Revenue Service of the U.S. Treasury Department, and the Pension Benefit Guaranty Corporation, a special government corporation.

ERISA is designed to protect employees and their beneficiaries in the following manner:

1. To ensure that only reasonable age and service requirements are used to determine eligibility for participation in pension programs.

2. To provide for reasonable vesting provisions in order to avoid lost years of pension participation.
3. To ensure proper funding of retirement accounts.
4. To provide for joint and survivor benefits to protect spouses.
5. To protect rights of workers in case a pension plan is terminated by an employer, through insurance provisions for plan termination.
6. To assure that employees know their rights under the plans through disclosure and reporting requirements. Descriptions of the plan in plain language are required.
7. To provide for appeal of claim denials and receipt of written explanation of the reasons for denial.
8. To provide financial penalties to employers for noncompliance.

Specific reporting and disclosure mechanisms are required. Among them are:

• A plan document that outlines how the institution's retirement and pension plan is established and maintained.
• A summary description of the terms of the plan, written in understandable language, which is used to inform the participants of the benefits provided and how to apply for them.
• A summary annual financial report, which is an abstract of the financial status of the plan, that provides participants with information about the financial condition of the plan.
• An annual report to the Internal Revenue Service that records the current year's financial data and other information about the plan.

The participation, funding, vesting, benefit accrual, and joint survivor provisions of this law apply only to pension programs, not to other employee welfare benefits plans. The law does not require an employer to provide any retirement or pension plan. However, if the employer chooses to have such a plan, the law then applies.

What Are Federally Authorized Health Maintenance Organizations (HMOs)?

The Health Maintenance Organization Act of 1973, as amended, covers all institutions that are currently offering a health benefits plan toward which financial contributions are being made, and that have twenty-five or more employees, of whom at least twenty-five live in the service area of a particular HMO. If such an HMO approaches such an institution and requests to be included in the health benefits plan the institution must offer the HMO as an alternative to the institution's health benefits plan. In addition, the institution must pay to the HMO an amount equal to the institution's cost for an employee's participation in the institution's health benefits plan. Thus, if an institution is contacted by an HMO, administrators should seek the assistance of a qualified insurance consultant. Questions about HMOs may be addressed to the Department of Health and Human Services.

The HMO Act seems to evince the Federal government's commitment to making HMOs a viable health care delivery system. Ample funds have been allocated to HMOs for their development, and rigid standards for federal approval have been established. A qualified HMO plan must offer the following prescribed set of basic health care benefits:

- Physician services (including consultant and referral)
- Inpatient and outpatient hospital services
- Emergency services, including payment for medically necessary in-area or out-of-area emergency services from providers other than the HMO.
- Short-term mental health outpatient care (up to twenty visits per member per year)
- Treatment and referral for abuse of or addiction to alcohol and drugs
- Diagnostic laboratory and diagnostic and therapeutic radiology services
- Home health services
- Preventive health services (including periodic health evaluations for adults, family planning services, services for infertility, well-child care from birth, eye examinations through age seventeen, ear examinations for children, and pediatric and adult immunizations.)

The law defines two types of HMOs and provides that an institution must offer at least one of each kind if such HMOs provide services in the employees' neighborhood and if the HMOs contact the employer. The two types of HMOs are: (1) Medical Group HMOs, an arrangement in which a group of physicians offer a health care from a central location and are paid salaries by the HMO (these salaries are not based on the specific services rendered); and (2) Individual practice association arrangements, in which the practitioners are geographically dispersed and offer a coordinated program from several locations.

An HMO's offer of services to an institution must be made at least 180 days before the expiration or renewal date of the institution's health benefits contract or at least 90 days before the expiration or renewal date of a collective bargaining agreement. If the notification deadline is missed by an HMO, the HMO is automatically eligible at the next expiration or renewal date. If the institution engages in collective bargaining, then it must offer the union an HMO alternative if an HMO has contacted the institution in a timely fashion. The institution's legal obligation is then considered satisfied, even if the union rejects the HMO option.

What Legislation Affects Social Security?

The Social Security Act became national law on August 14, 1935. The first taxes for social security (called, hereafter the Federal Insurance Contributions Act, FICA) were deducted beginning January 1, 1937, and the first benefits payable were effective January 1940. The Social Security Act has since been amended many times. In 1950, amendments provided that a nonprofit organization (including one in the private higher education sector) could obtain social security coverage beginning January 1, 1951 by filing a waiver certificate that waived the institution from the exemption. Private institutions of higher education are still exempt from coverage unless they wish to waive that exemption. The 1956 amendments and subsequent amendments authorized the participation of public employees provided the public employer specifically requested coverage. At that time, most public institutions of higher education were covered.

Both faculty and staff members and the institutions support social security equally. For example, in 1981 employees were taxed

6.65 percent of the first $29,700 of their annual earnings, and institutions had to match the employees' contributions.

The escalating cost to institutions and their employees should cause benefits plan administrators to examine all other retirement plans currently offered by their institution. The combined cost for social security and additional retirement plans can be reduced if consideration is given to reducing the benefits of the private retirement plan and coordinating that plan with social security instead of providing them as two separate benefits.

Social security covers primarily pensions, disabilities, and Medicare. Local offices of the Social Security Administration can provide information to institutions and to individual faculty and staff members about benefits. For example, all employees qualify for Medicare Part B (medical expenses) at age sixty-five whether or not they were covered under social security; there is a modest monthly premium for this coverage. Only those qualified for social security (and their spouses) qualify for free Medicare Part A (hospital coverage); others may purchase hospital coverage by paying high monthly premiums.

What Legislation Affects Unemployment Compensation?

The 1970 amendments to the Federal Unemployment Tax Act (FUTA) provide that states must extend the unemployment compensation legislation to cover employees of higher education. Although the provisions of the various state acts vary greatly, certain mandated federal principles must be incorporated. Regarding employees of higher education, the following major federal mandates apply:

- Student employee earnings are exempt from coverage provided that the student is enrolled and regularly attending classes at the institution at which he or she is an employee.
- Benefits are not available between terms, semesters, or school years for employees engaged in instructional, research, or principal administrative capacities provided such employees have a contract to resume services in the next succeeding term, semester, or school year at the same institution or another institution of higher education.

- Nonprofit institutions are given the option to pay into their state's unemployment compensation fund either by being taxed regularly or by reimbursing the fund for benefits actually paid to employees. Most institutions of higher education elect the latter.

Within these mandates, state legislatures determine the conditions under which an individual is eligible for unemployment insurance and the amount of weekly benefits payable. For more details on administering an unemployment compensation program, see Exhibit 31, pp. 153–156.

What Legislation Affects Workers' Compensation?

All states have enacted laws that provide employees protection in the event of job-related injuries. This type of protection is commonly referred to as workers' compensation. Although coverage varies from state to state, many states follow four general rules: (1) Compensation laws are compulsory for all employees; (2) there are no limits on the size of claims for medical expenses; (3) all occupations are covered; (4) and all employers, even ones employing few employees, must participate.

The funding of workers' compensation claims is also dependent on state law. A few states require employers to insure with a state fund; some permit insurance with the state fund or private insurance carriers; some states have no state fund and thus private insurance carriers must be used; and some states permit self-insurance. Because the state laws vary so greatly, details are not provided in this text. However, higher education administrators should be aware that this coverage is essential and adds to the cost of the benefits offered.

What Discrimination Legislation Affects Benefits Programs?

All forms of employee benefits plans are covered by equal pay legislation since benefits are a form of compensation. Two additional laws also affect benefits.

The Age Discrimination in Employment Act. The 1978 amendments to the Age Discrimination in Employment Act raised, from sixty-five to seventy, the maximum age of persons protected by the act. This amendment, therefore, means that mandatory retirement cannot be requested of individuals not yet seventy, with the following exceptions: (1) individuals in higher education with tenure may continue to be retired at age sixty-five until July 1, 1982, after which time the minimum age of seventy applies; and (2) bona fide executives and high policymakers may continue to be retired at age sixty-five provided they receive an annual pension of at least $27,000 from the institution itself, exclusive of contributions made by the executive, social security payments, or contributions of prior employers.

The extension of the act to cover employees until age seventy affects benefits as follows: (1) Institutions may reduce life insurance actuarially after age sixty-five (a rule-of-thumb limit for reduction of coverage is 8 percent per year); (2) institutions may discontinue employer contributions to retirement plans after an employee reaches sixty-five; and (3) health insurance coverage for employees between sixty-five and seventy may not be less (or cost employees more) than for employees under sixty-five; Medicare may be included in determining equal benefits provided the total cost of coverage does not increase for the employee.

Pregnancy Discrimination Act. The Pregnancy Discrimination Act of 1978 (Pub. L 95-555) stipulates that any health insurance coverage provided for a female employee must cover expenses for pregnancy-related conditions on the same basis as expenses for other medical conditions, and that a female employee unable to work for pregnancy-related reasons is entitled to disability benefits on the same basis as employees unable to work for other medical reasons.

Who Should Handle Benefits Matters Within the Institution?

With the installation of any individual employee plan, an institution must administer four separate and distinct functions: (1) Evaluating and recommending (after appropriate consultations) the kind and design of the plan; (2) purchasing the plan; (3) communicating the plan to the faculty and staff; and (4) funding the plan and auditing payments under the plan. These responsibilities may all be handled by the personnel staff. However, more commonly they are divided between the personnel staff and the financial office. In some situations, part of the responsibility (the purchase of the insurance) may be handled by the institution's risk management office.

It is the authors' opinion that the responsibilities may be delegated to several offices. The personnel office should have the responsibility for making effective recommendations on the kind and design of the benefits plans. However, the financing, auditing, and purchase of the plan may be handled more effectively by the fiscal or risk office. The personnel office should be responsible for dealing with faculty and staff members regarding the plan and for effectively communicating the plan. This division of responsibility requires effective cooperation between the offices involved.

The authors further recommend that institutions of higher education develop a relationship with a competent insurance consultant to assist with evaluations of existing plans and acquisitions of new coverage. The insurance field is a technical field of specialization. Thus most institutions will not have someone on the staff who is fully cognizant of this highly technical field. Furthermore, in order to secure bids for a form of insurance, the specifications must be detailed so that all bidders are bidding on the same product. Before those specifications are written, an institution must be fully aware of the various options offered by a variety of insurance carriers so that the specifications are the most appropriate for the institution. Here again, an outside consultant is almost always required.

Exhibits 32, 33, and 34, pp. 157–165, provide examples of some of the issues to be considered in planning for group life insurance, long-term disability insurance, and a tax-deferred annuity program, respectively.

What Are the Basic Principles for Operating a Benefits Program?

An institution, in planning its basic program, must consider a large number of issues. The most basic of these are discussed in this section.

Who should pay for the program? Some institutions share the cost of benefits programs with the individuals covered. Others provide the benefits at no cost to the faculty or staff members. The authors recommend shared cost to create employee vested interest. If costs are shared, employees' demands for greater and improved benefits may be more reasonable and responsible. There are two basic methods of implementing cost sharing. One is to have employees contribute to the cost of the insurance premium. The other is to have an insurance policy that states a deductible, the amount that the employee must pay for services before the plan provides benefits. Frequently, health service plans have $100 deductibles. However, that figure was introduced a number of years ago, when salaries were lower and before inflation eroded the dollar. Each year that the dollar devaluates and salaries rise, the relative value of a $100 deductible as a share of total cost decreases. Therefore, the institution assumes a greater share of the cost. Institutions could investigate policies with larger deductibles if they wish to recapture a greater sharing in the cost of the benefits.

Should all employees have the same benefits? The authors suggest that all faculty and staff should have the same benefits package with some minor differences. We see no basis for having different health insurance plans for different employees, but feel that sabbatical leaves should be restricted to faculty members and other professionals. Life insurance plans should provide insurance related to salary levels. However, if a portion of the life insurance is provided at no cost, the authors feel that that portion should apply equally to faculty and staff.

Should other than high-quality benefits plans be provided? The cost of a benefit plan is a significant portion of an institution's budget. If less-than-quality programs are installed, faculty and staff members will consistently be critical of the institution's benefits efforts. The authors believe that it is better not to introduce a particular coverage than to offer a low-quality program; an inferior plan will only be cause for complaint.

Should insurance programs be mandatory or optional? An insurance company's bid for a particular type of coverage typically is based on coverage of a large percentage of those employees eligible. To cover a lower percentage may result in coverage of only the higher-risk individuals, and thus increase the cost of coverage. One way to guarantee to participants that the cost stated will be maintained is to offer the coverage as an option to present faculty and staff and then to require coverage for employees appointed after the installation date. Although such a practice is common, it places responsibility on the institution to provide coverage that will have universal appeal. Another approach is to require all employees to participate in a certain core group of benefits programs and to have additional benefits that are optional. Under such a program, faculty and staff members may choose optional specified benefits up to a specified total dollar value. Once again, the institution must exercise care lest only high-risk individuals participate in certain programs.

What are mass-merchandised insurance programs? Mass merchandising is a specialized marketing system designed to provide certain types of insurance (liability or casualty) to large homogenous groups that have identifiable common insurance needs. Two major types of such insurance are automobile insurance and home owner's coverage. Mass-merchandized insurance may also cover valuable personal articles or personal liability insurance (usually as part of home owner's or automobile insurance). The potential advantages of such insurance programs to employees may be lower costs, monthly payroll deductions for premiums, personal contact with insurance counselors, and faster claims service.

How Should Information About Benefits Be Communicated?

Institutions covered by ERISA have a legal obligation to communicate in plain language the details of their benefits plans and their policies for participation and enrollment. Those institutions not covered by ERISA should feel an equal responsibility to do the same. Thus, updated, concise, and clearly written descriptions of the plans should be provided to each faculty and staff member. When employees sign up for a benefit plan, they should be provided with a detailed description of options available under the plan. Indeed, failure to provide an adequate explanation could subject the institution to a lawsuit by an employee for benefits not clearly excluded by a poorly written description.

Many institutions require each new employee to report to the central personnel office in order to enroll for benefits. While such a procedure is intended to ensure that new employees receive all the facts about benefits, it can be a time-consuming activity for the personnel office and for the new employees. For that reason, other institutions train individuals in each college or other administrative unit and thereby decentralize the activity. Decentralization may be a desirable, time-saving approach, as long as the training of the individuals in the various units is rigorous.

Another form of communication is the issuance of an annual or biennial statement of benefits. To prepare such statements, an institution may wish to hire a firm that specializes in this type of publication. The institution's statement should outline not only the coverage available but also the dollar value of that coverage, as few employees recognize how much their institutions contribute to such programs. Two other useful methods for communication are periodic advertised meetings on benefits and regular short articles in the house organ that cover details of the plans.

Exhibit 31. How to Administer an Unemployment Compensation Program

By Robert H. Hamill and Kimble Williams

Introduction:

An effective unemployment compensation (UC) program must be administered in a way to assure that all claimants rightfully entitled to benefits receive them without delay, while at the same time assuring that questionable claims and claims decisions are properly challenged. *Centralized control, internal and external communication,* and *financial accountability* are key points essential in the development and implementation of an effective UC program within a college or university. The results of a strong UC program will benefit the institution, since only legitimate claims will be approved. On the other hand, the cost impact of a weak program will certainly add to an institution's budget blues.

Centralized control:

Centralized control requires that the responsibility for coordinating *all* UC matters be vested with *one* office in the institution. This office preferably should be located in the personnel department for the following reasons: (1) ready access to personnel records; (2) knowledge of disciplines, dismissal, and layoff policies and activities; and (3) coordination of the employment effort, which can result in potential UC claimants being offered suitable alternate work.

Exhibit 31 (continued)

The day-to-day administration of the UC program should be assigned to a qualified specialist. This employee should develop an intimate knowledge of appropriate laws and regulations and a good working relationship with the various local and state officials responsible for handling UC matters. All data (reports, notices of determination, appeals, and the like) are then mailed to, and handled by, one institution office. This centralization is critical when deadlines must be made, as well as in controlling and assessing the total impact of UC costs.

General responsibilities of the UC specialist:

1. Establish a complete and accurate recordkeeping and statistics procedure to assess current liability, to project future liability, and to detect possible billing and bookkeeping errors by the state.
2. Receive and process all verbal and written inquiries from employees, former employees, and local and state UC offices.
3. Prepare and file all appeals to determinations or decisions which appear challengeable on the basis of fact and law.
4. Prepare for and attend all hearings.
5. Assist other employees testifying at a hearing on behalf of the institution in preparing their testimony.
6. Follow-up ongoing claims to be sure that claimants are still available in the labor market.

Internal communication:

Within the institution, the UC specialist should serve as liaison between various departments involved in hiring, firing, layoffs, and terminations and should develop internal procedures to facilitate claims handling and data verification.

Some suggested internal procedures to be established and adhered to are as follows:

1. All facts dealing with a termination should be clearly stated. If necessary, revise the institution's termination of employment forms to obtain this information. Do not hesitate to call a terminating employee's supervisor and discuss precise reasons for the termination. Always record this information. The supervisor might also be asked for a recommendation on rehiring the terminating employee. And finally, conduct exit interviews whenever possible to compare the employee's understanding of the reason for termination with that shown on the termination form.

2. The institution's employment office should be furnished with a current list (updated weekly) of UC claimants eligible for rehire to be used as a priority list of candidates for new openings.

3. The UC office and the employment office should be notified in advance of any pending layoffs or reductions in the work force. Qualified candidates from among those facing layoff can then be referred to existing vacancies. Employees forced on seasonal layoffs may be offered alternate employment in a department which is doing its essential hiring (from food service to physical plant during the summer months, for example). Document all cases where an employee on layoff refuses an offer of suitable alternate employment.

4. Department heads should be informed immediately of all claims filed by their employees or former employees to verify information needed to process the claim and to alert the department head of potential costs.

5. A good working relationship should be developed between the UC office and the accounting or payroll departments to ensure prompt forwarding of required wage information and the accuracy of the amount of UC benefits charged to the university.

6. The UC office should be authorized to secure data on students from the institution's student records section to identify claimants who may have been part-time or casual employees but whose main occupation was that of student. This is important in those states where student earnings are not covered earnings for UC purposes.

7. The institution should consider a strong follow-up program of contacting claimants who are receiving UC benefits to determine their availability to return to work. These contacts can be accomplished by mail or telephone. The letter is preferred since a copy can be mailed to the UC office where the claim was initiated. If claimants refuse to answer letters or fail to show up for scheduled appointments, the institution has established grounds to request interruption of its benefits.

Obviously if a claimant does respond but declines to accept an offer of reemployment, the results of that interview should also be documented and forwarded to the appropriate UC office with a request for interruption of benefits.

External communication:

1. The UC specialist should attend all hearings.·

2. The UC specialist should make the state aware of questions about interpretations of the law or UC procedures.

3. The UC specialist should keep abreast of pending legislation and be prepared to cause pressure to be brought to bear against unfavorable legislation.

Exhibit 31 (continued)

Financial accountability:

Educational institutions may choose one of two methods available to them to reimburse their state for the cost of their incurred compensation claims.

The first method is a payroll tax where costs are determined on a percentage of payroll basis. As a general rule, this method seems to work best with small institutions with relatively small payrolls.

The second method is the reimbursement in which the state bills the institution, quarterly, on a dollar-to-dollar basis according to the amount of benefits paid to claimants. Larger institutions using this system who have conducted cost studies generally acknowledge that the reimbursement method represents substantial cost savings over the payroll tax method. A particularly effective control under the reimbursement method is for the institution to charge each operating college, school, or administrative department for the cost incurred claims for employees from their unit. This discourages indiscriminate hiring of part-time or short-term employees and helps the employment office in its effort to re-employ former employees who are receiving UC benefits.

An institution should carefully review its payroll, attrition (turnover), and employment and layoff patterns to determine which option would be most economical for its own operations.

Summary:

Unemployment compensation is the law of the land and is now applicable to nonprofit educational institutions. Institutions, therefore, should recognize the need for effective policies and procedures in implementing and administering their UC program. Naturally, individual state laws may dictate certain policies and procedures. The result, however, should be the same guaranteed prompt payment to qualified claimants and nonpayment to unqualified claimants. That should be your goal.

Source: College and University Personnel Association, in press.

Exhibit 32. How to Set Up a Group Life Insurance Program

Harvey Randall—New York State Department of Civil Service

Although most employees of colleges and universities are covered under group life insurance programs established by their employers, some are not covered. Group insurance is relatively inexpensive, and the cost can be shared between the employee and the employer. Any institution not providing some form of life insurance is subject to faculty and staff criticism; not providing such coverage could also affect the recruitment of new employees.

In establishing group life insurance programs, consideration should be given to the following:

1. Classes of employees to be covered

It is desirable to provide life insurance for all classes of employees, even though there may be variances, such as amounts of insurance, employee premiums, and the like. It should also be determined if the insurance will cover only full-time employees or if part-time employees may also participate. There should be no doubt about which employee categories are eligible. In addition, questions concerning service requirements for eligibility for participation, age at which insurance levels might be reduced, required participation or voluntary participation, and related matters must be raised by the institution with the insurance companies who might be interested in submitting proposals.

2. Contributory or noncontributory plan

Many state laws require that there be a minimum contribution by the employer with respect to the purchase of a group life insurance contract. The question of employee contribution is undoubtedly negotiable under labor-management agreements where such agreements exist.

3. Type of plan

The institution has a number of options available with respect to the type of plan it offers. Undoubtedly, the institution would wish to consult with employee representatives to obtain their views as to the type of coverage most desired by employees. In the last analysis, however, the institution as the purchaser, must make the determination. The following types of insurance are commonly provided in group plans:

Plan 1. A plan providing for an amount of insurance based on annual earnings, usually described as a ratio, such as 1.5 times salary or 2-times salary.

Exhibit 32 (continued)

Plan 2. A level coverage plan, providing the same amount of insurance for each employee, regardless of age, sex, or length of service.

Plan 3. A decreasing term plan, providing an amount based on the participant's entering age and decreasing in amount each year thereafter until a level amount is reached at a later age, such as sixty or sixty-five. Of course, such a plan would need to be checked against age legislation.

Plan 4. A modification of decreasing term insurance could be designed to provide level-type protection until a certain age and thereafter decrease slowly until another age is reached. Once again, such a plan would need to be checked against age legislation.

Plan 5. A plan to provide minimum coverage and thereafter increasing coverage for each year of service.

Before any plan is finalized, it is extremely important to determine if all provisions comply with the statutes of your state's insurance code. The following illustrates the relationship among the types of plans described above.

If Plan 1 would provide for life insurance in the amount of three times the annual salary, not to exceed $50,000, *the same premium could provide for:*

$23,000 face value policy in Plan 2; or

$85,000 policy at age twenty-five decreasing to $4,200 at age sixty-five in Plan 3; or

Under Plan 4, $27,000 policy to age fifty reduced to $2,750 at age sixty-five; or

Under Plan 4, $10,000 policy at employment, with $1,800 of insurance added for each year of service thereafter.

(Note: Plans providing for benefits based on age may be challenged as unlawful discrimination because of age. A legal opinion should be sought.)

4.   Optional provisions

Another consideration would be an option which would permit the employee to purchase, at favorable rates, additional insurance coverage above the amount purchased by the employer without cost to the employer. Several alternatives are available and could be designed to meet the special needs of the institution. Other basic provisions which should be considered are: (1) disability benefits (payout or waiver of premium), (2) coverage at retirement, (3) insuring the lives of dependents, and (4) accidental death or dismemberment coverage.

5.   Conversion privileges

Many states require that group term insurance policies provide for a conversion to ordinary life policies upon separation from service, with the institution being required to make a sometimes substantial contribution to the insurance carrier in the event the employee exercises that option. This might be a substantial hidden expense and should be investigated thoroughly by the employer.

6. Selecting the underwriter

The institution should solicit proposals from insurance companies interested in underwriting such insurance contracts by submitting specifications for consideration by the companies. Only by specifying the program to be offered can realistic comparisons be made. Too often, if companies come forward with their own unique proposal, there is no clear way of trying to evaluate the offerings between and among the various companies because they are not using the same common base for the purpose of establishing a program.

7. Information for a proposal

The following information is usually required by an insurance company to prepare a proposal: (1) a listing of the employees to be covered giving age and, where required, date of appointment; (2) a breakdown of the various benefits to be provided under the coverage to be offered; (3) an indication of whether the program is to be self-accounting or insurance-company services; and (4) other terms and conditions which the institution would wish to have considered in the development of the proposal.

Upon the receipt of the various proposals pursuant to the specifications, the institution should consider each proposal and then select the one which seems to be offered by the lowest responsible bidder. Thereafter, appropriate administrative action should be taken to enter into an agreement with that insurer. However, before making final commitments, the institution's legal counsel should be consulted with respect to assuring the officials concerned that the proposed contract would be able to meet the statutory requirements of the state and would provide the benefits sought. It might also be suggested that counsel be invited to participate in the preparation of the specifications and in the consideration of the various proposals submitted by the insurance carriers so that his or her expertise in this technical area could be utilized more effectively.

Wherever possible, the contract should also provide for the administrative guidelines with respect to the implementation of the insurance coverage and the procedures to be followed in protecting the employees of the purchasing institution.

Source: College and University Personnel Association; forthcoming.

Exhibit 33. How to Set Up a Long-Term Disability Insurance Program

By Harvey Randall
New York State Department of Civil Service

What is disability insurance?

An increasingly large number of colleges and universities offer group long-term disability benefits to protect employees from the economic consequences of total disability because of the employee's inability, by reason of sickness or bodily injury, to engage in any occupation for which he is reasonably fitted by education, training, or experience.

Eligibility for coverage and the extent of coverage varies from campus to campus, but generally employees are covered after completing a fixed minimum period of service (one to three years) and receive benefits payable until they are no longer disabled, reach a specified age or die, whichever event occurs first.

Although premiums will vary, depending upon the size of the group, and the age, and salary of participants, the average cost is usually less than 1 percent of covered payroll for the plan described below.

Establishing the program:

To establish the program, the institution should decide the types of benefits it wishes to provide and then seek competitive bids from insurance carriers qualified in their state to issue such insurance. Before determining the type of plan which would best suit the institution, a study should be made of disability benefits which may be available already under social security benefits, the life insurance program, the pension plan, the institution's sick leave policy, and worker's compensation.

The specifications for coverage might include such items as:

1. *A Waiting Period.* In order to reduce the costs of the program, most plans provide for a waiting period of six months before benefits become payable by the insurance carrier.
2. *Income Protection.* A typical plan might provide for 60 percent of covered monthly salary up to $1,000 per month and 40 percent of covered monthly salary up to a benefit of $2,000 per month. Most contracts provide that this monthly income is reduced by any income benefits payable from social security, worker's compensation, sick leave programs, and pension benefits payable by the institution's retirement program. The amount of protection provided by the insurance program, plus other benefits available, should be less than the

employee would receive if he were at work. Otherwise, he may not be encouraged to return to work.

3. *Retirement Provision.* A number of plans provide for the protection of the individual for the period during which disability benefits are payable by continuing to have contributions made to the employee's normal retirement program. This provision permits the individual to continue to accrue benefits which would become payable upon retirement, at which time the benefits under the disability insurance would normally cease.

For example, an employee with a base annual salary of $15,000 would have a covered monthly salary of $1,250. The monthly income benefit payable would be $750 per month, assuming a 10 percent contribution for retirement, $125 would be paid toward the purchase of annuity benefits on behalf of the employee.

Each insurance contract should be tailored to the needs of the institution and should consider the other benefit programs made available to its employees. Standard contracts should be avoided, unless the institution satisfies itself that the provisions of the contract meet the needs of the institution's operation. Also, many institutions share the cost of the disability insurance with the employee.

Granting a leave of absence for disability:

The institution's program should permit disability leaves of absence for persons receiving benefits. The leave of absence should provide for reinstatement to employment when the employee is able to resume the duties for which he is, by reason of education and training, qualified. Such reemployment might be assured for the disabled employee, if he is able to return within a certain period of time, such as one or two years after the onset of the disability.

Note: Such leave status would not automatically extend a temporary appointment which would otherwise expire during the period of disability, and this limitation should be clearly indicated when granting such leave.

Who makes application for disability insurance:

In most instances, the disabled employee applies for benefits under the insurance program on his or her own initiative. However, from time to time, an employee cannot, or will not, recognize that he or she is, in fact, disabled and unable to perform the assigned duties, even after the condition is called to his or her attention. Two approaches can be taken in the latter case. If the employee refuses to apply for disability, the employee may be placed either on an extended leave of absence without pay or informed that it will be necessary to terminate his or her employment for

Exhibit 33 (continued)

poor work performance. Often this action will encourage the employee to take the initiative in filing for benefits.

The institution may use a special committee on disability made up of physicians and other staff members to review each case and make recommendations. If the committee approach is used, the committee will need to proceed in some cases, whether or not it has the cooperation of the employee. The committee should understand that it is only required to determine whether or not there is sufficient evidence to warrant a conclusion that the employee would be eligible for disability benefits if the application for such benefits was submitted to the insurance carrier.

The institution's policies should provide that (1) the employee is discontinued from service pending the outcome; (2) when a determination is made, that it is probable that a disability benefit would be payable upon timely application; and (3) the employer files an application for such benefits on behalf of the employee.

Dispute over determination of disability:

Of special note in the disability situation where the employer files the application on behalf of the employee alleged to be disabled is the fact that it is the insurance carrier who makes the final determination as to whether or not a disability benefit is payable under the insurance contract. If the insurance carrier finds that the employee is not disabled, under the definition of disability in the insurance contract, the institution will be obligated to handle the case in another way. Either the institution will have an obligation to restore the employee to service, or it may be necessary to take other steps to separate the employee for failure to perform his duties satisfactorily. The employee relations aspect of such a termination of employment must be given consideration before such an action is taken.

Discrimination aspects:

It is unlawful under federal law (and many state laws) to deny continuation of employment because of a disability. Clearly, this is so with respect to a disability unrelated to the duties to be performed. With respect to disabilities which obviously affect job performance, it is necessary to determine if any reasonable accommodation can be made so as to permit the staff member to be continued in service or whether the disability is such that discontinuation of service (temporary or otherwise) is required. Rehabilitation must also be considered as a possible method of accommodating the disabled individual.

Source: College and University Personnel Association, in press.

Exhibit 34. How to Set Up a Tax-Deferred Annuity Program

By Harvey Randall
New York State Department of Civil Service

Purpose:

The tax-deferred annuity program provides an opportunity for employees of educational institutions to supplement retirement income on a more favorable basis than they could do on their own. (See Section 403(b), Internal Revenue Code.) Through an agreement with the institution, employees may request a reduction in salary. The institution contributes the amount of this reduction to an annuity contract for the employee. This amount is not taxed to the employee currently. Federal income tax is deducted from the current reduced salary. The same provision may apply to state and local taxes. The proceeds of a tax-deferred annuity are taxable as income when received as part of an annuity income after retirement, at which time the employee will presumably be in a lower bracket and may also qualify for the double personal exemption. This, of course, assumes that tax rates will not increase to the point where the rate during retirement is greater than the current rates. Tax-deferred annuities, therefore, reduce current taxes, increase current spendable income, and provide a future retirement income. (The Tax Reform Act of 1978 permits *deferred compensation plans,* which should not be confused with tax-deferred annuity plans.)

Considerations in developing a program:

When a college or university decides to offer a tax-deferred annuity program, the first decision is the number of carriers to be selected. If more than a single carrier is selected, the program will be more difficult to explain and administer. A determination should be made as to whether or not the contracts for the annuity should be on an "individual" or on a "group" basis. The Internal Revenue Code permits life insurance features as part of the annuity contract, and it should be decided whether or not the program is to include such life insurance features.

Preparing specifications of your plan for bids:

The institution should establish contract specifications to be met by the interested insurance companies. Professional help may be sought at this stage. If it is determined that only a single carrier is to be selected, the specifications should indicate that fact. If more than a single carrier is to be selected, the carriers should be advised as to whether every acceptable

Exhibit 34 (continued)

bidder will be permitted contracts, or whether there will be some fixed limit as to the number of insurance companies authorized to participate.

Prepare a set of specifications for the plan and get bids. Insurance companies will use different assumptions and plan designs to explain their programs; therefore, only by requiring that your own hypothetical problem be used for analysis can you achieve a valid basis for comparison. Such a hypothetical problem could be stated as follows: "The specimen contract is to be issued on the life of an annuitant assuming, that the entering age of the annuitant is forty-five, and further assuming that the maturity date of each contract will be at the annuitant's age sixty-five (twenty contract years)."

The company should be asked to make its calculations based upon an annual premium of $1,000 payable annually for the twenty-year period and asked to supply the following information:

1. Amount of annuity payment under each settlement option, including a settlement option on two lives. (For the options on two lives, the company should be asked to assume that the beneficiary is age sixty-five at the maturity date.);
2. Cash surrender value at the end of each contract year;
3. Amount of death benefit payable in the event of death of the annuitant prior to the contract date of maturity (if there is an insurance feature provided);
4. If the company provides for applying all, or a portion, of the premiums to a variable annuity, the company should be asked to ignore this contingency and base all computations on a fixed-dollar annuity basis.

Factors in selection:

1. Which contract(s) offers the greatest annuity return for the premium dollar expended;
2. Which contract(s) offers the greatest flexibility of participation. Within reasonable limitations, the employee should be able to participate and then temporarily to withdraw, or increase or decrease the amount of the "reduction" without surcharge or loss of benefits;
3. Type and frequency of service provided by the company. Is there a local agent to provide advisory service, or will everything be handled by mail?;
4. Are annual statements of account provided? Does this statement include a computation of the maximum exclusion allowance for the following tax year based on current year's salary?;
5. Is the plan portable, or will termination require the participant to take up a paid-up annuity?

Final selection and implementation:

A report by the chief personnel officer, including an analysis of the bids received and his or her recommendations as to the selection of the carrier(s), should be submitted to the administration of the institution for consideration and action. The administration should authorize the program and select the insurer or insurers. All agreements should first be reviewed by the institution's legal counsel, including the "reduction" contracts.

After the insurer(s) has been selected, meetings should be arranged to explain the program to interested faculty and staff members. Booklets explaining the features of the tax-deferred annuity program should be distributed. Employees should also be urged to discuss the matter with their legal or tax adviser.

Special considerations:

State-operated colleges and universities may face special problems with respect to public retirement programs, and legislation may be required to continue the "normal" employer contribution for retirement and related programs, as well as making certain that such benefits would be payable without regard to the "reduction" of salary.

Source: College and University Personnel Association, in press.

❦ 9 ❧

Planning and Implementing Tenure Policies

Current tenure policies for many higher education faculty have evolved from statements produced by the American Association of University Professors (AAUP). In 1915, the AAUP issued an initial general report on tenure, and their subsequent statements outline specific standards for tenure regulations. Prior to the issuance of those statements, faculty members served more or less at the will of administrators and could be dismissed for teaching, researching, or publishing in unpopular subject areas. Thus, faculty members banded together to form the AAUP in order to safeguard the right of scholars to have academic freedom and to research and profess in new, controversial, and unpopular subject areas without fear of loss of employment.

Initially, the AAUP's activities consisted of assisting dismissed faculty members in fighting their cases and in calling public attention to such dismissals. The AAUP issued its standards regarding tenure in 1940 (American Association of University Professors,

1941). These principles, which have been adopted in some form by the higher education community include the following principles: (1) the probationary period should not exceed seven years; (2) adequate prior notice should be given before termination during probation; (3) tenured faculty may be dismissed only for cause, including financial exigency; and (4) hearings on dismissals of tenured faculty should be based on court practices.

What Do Statements of Academic Freedom Include?

Policies concerning academic freedom are based on the principle that a free society is free only if its educational professionals are free to study, publish, discuss, and teach issues in a manner uninhibited by censure from without or within. Faculty must be free to study unpopular issues without fear of reprisal. A typical institutional statement assuring academic freedom follows:

> All faculty members are entitled to full freedom in research and in the publication of the results, subject to the adequate performance of other academic duties; but research for pecuniary return should be based on an understanding with the authorities of the institution.
>
> All faculty members are entitled to freedom in the classroom in discussing their subject, but they should be careful not to introduce controversial matter that has no relation to that subject.
>
> Every college or university faculty member is a citizen, a member of a learned profession, and an officer of an educational institution. When he or she speaks or writes as a citizen, those statements should be free from institutional censorship or discipline, but the special position of educational officer imposes special obligations. As professional educators affiliated with an institution, faculty members should remember that the public may judge an academic profession and an institution by an individual scholar's public utterances. Hence faculty members should at all times be accurate, exercise appropriate restraint,

show respect for the opinion of others, and make
every effort to indicate that they are not speaking as
representatives of their institution.

Although historically tenure and academic freedom have
been linked, all faculty, tenured or not, should have the freedom
to study, publish, discuss, and teach unpopular issues without
censure.

What Is the Meaning of Tenure?

Tenure is the status granted faculty members who successfully complete a probationary period of employment. Once
granted tenure, a faculty member may be dismissed only for a bona
fide reason and only after an institutional hearing on the dismissal
action. Thus the award of tenure is a form of granting a permanent
appointment and is the single most significant decision made by the
institution in the life of a faculty member. The granting of tenure is
usually based on conjectures about the faculty member's future
professional contributions and such decisions are necessarily judgmental. The granting of tenure is necessarily based on predictions
for the future productivity of a particular faculty member relative
to other faculty members within the discipline.

The specific policies of institutions differ. For example, tenure is usually available at the ranks of professor, associate professor, and assistant professor, but a few institutions grant tenure at
the instructor rank. At most institutions the probationary period is
seven years; however, shorter periods are used by some institutions. Institutions may interpret the seven-year period in two ways.
If an individual is *not* to be awarded tenure, some institutions send
a one-year notice of termination at the end of the sixth year; others,
at the end of the seventh year.

Newly appointed faculty members are usually not immediately granted tenure. Instead, faculty members appointed to
tenure-eligible ranks are appointed with a specified number of
years of probationary credit for years taught at another institution
or at the same institution in a non-tenure-eligible rank. Most institutions specify a maximum number of years of probationary

credit that may be granted upon appointment in order to allow the institution ample time for evaluation prior to the award of tenure. A faculty member who is promoted to the rank of assistant professor or research associate (or above) may, with his or her concurrence, and at the discretion of the appropriate administrative officer, be given up to four years maximum probationary status credit for time spent as an instructor, research assistant, or assistant librarian at this university.

Upon appointment, a faculty member usually signs a contract signed by an officer of the institution that outlines the conditions of appointment. A typical contract includes the following items:

1. Name of faculty member, college or department, and rank and title
2. Effective date of appointment, length of appointment, and annual salary
3. Statement of present tenure status; for example, "Probationary tenure status with zero years of academic tenure credit" or "This position is not eligible for tenure"
4. An agreement to accept certain conditions such as benefits plans, patent and copyright regulations, tenure regulations, and the like

Exhibits 35 and 36, pp. 174–175, present sample contracts for a tenure-eligible position and one not eligible for tenure. Exhibit 37, p. 176, shows a sample contract used to designate tenure eligibility upon promotion to a tenure-eligible rank. Of course, such contracts are binding legal documents and acquire paramount importance in legal disputes over the denial of tenure.

What Constitutes Reason for Dismissal of a Faculty Member?

Probationary faculty members have provisional status. A probationary faculty member may be dismissed without recourse to a grievance process (unless the faculty member claims discrimination under civil rights legislation). Most institutions regularly evaluate a faculty member's performance during the probationary period. However, just cause is not needed to terminate a probationary appointment. An institution is obligated to provide a timely notice of termination unless the dismissal is for a major cause such as theft. Some institutions inform a faculty member of the general reasons for termination, but such information need not be required. See Chapter Eleven for additional information on probationary periods.

It is good human relations to avoid the situation of carrying a faculty member through the entire probationary period if it is obvious that he or she would never qualify for tenure. Indeed early reviews should be used to counsel faculty members about the actions they need to take to meet tenure requirements. In some cases, the reviews serve the purpose of recommending that the faculty member seek employment elsewhere.

As noted, tenured faculty members may be dismissed only for the causes stipulated in the institution's tenure policy. Many institutions, however, devote too little attention to the definitions of the bases for dismissal of tenured faculty members. Many policies include causes such as moral turpitude and financial exigency, but fail to explicitly define these terms. For example, what is meant by financial exigency? Does it mean that one program must be curtailed or that the entire institution must be in dire fiscal straits? It may be interpreted in the courts to mean the latter and thus may be an inadequate policy should an institution want to discontinue a particular discipline.

In these days of frequent litigation, an institution's policy should state the causes for dismissal quite specifically. Typical causes for the termination of appointment of a tenured faculty member include:

Voluntary resignation
Mandatory retirement age
Death
Incapacity due to disability
Neglect of obligations
Breach of the canons of ethics prescribed for the particular
    discipline

Reduction in or discontinuance of a program
Redirection of a program
Dishonesty
Insubordination
Immorality or sexual harassment
Incompetence
Conviction for a crime
Enrollment decline
Reduction by legislative mandate

What Additional Stipulations Should Be Included in a Tenure Policy?

An institution's tenure policy, of course, covers a variety of issues in addition to the causes for dismissal of tenured faculty. In writing or reviewing its tenure policy, an institution must consider the following issues and questions.

Alternates to tenure-eligible appointments. Under what conditions can individuals be appointed in other than tenure-eligible appointments? What types of appointments are to be used?

Conditions of the probationary period. How long is the probationary period? At which points are performance reviews held? What notice of termination of appointment must be given? Does the probationary faculty member who is informed that tenure will not be awarded have the right to appeal that decision? If so, is the appeal limited to procedural fairness or is the institution required to give reasons for the denial of tenure? How much prior service at the institution or at other institutions may be counted toward probationary time? May the probationary period be accelerated? If so, how? If the probationary faculty member is absent for illness or other reasons, is such time counted? If so, under what conditions?

Notice of conditions of appointment. What information should the notice of appointment include? Which representatives of the institution must approve or sign it?

Rank. At which ranks is tenure awarded? Is tenure granted automatically upon promotion to certain ranks? What procedure applies to individuals who are actively seeking a degree at the institution? Should the tenure apply to individuals at ranks other than academic ranks such as librarians, student counselors, coaches, physical education instructors, and so forth?

Part-time appointees. Should continuing part-time faculty be eligible for tenure?

Funding sources. Is tenure granted to all faculty members, regardless of source of funds? Or, should it be granted only to those paid on continuing funds controlled by the institution?

Evaluation procedures. What process is to be used to evaluate faculty members prior to the granting of tenure? Who will be involved? Who has the authority to deny review to the next level in the review process? Who has the ultimate authority to grant or deny tenure? What factors will be evaluated? Will the same factors be used for every faculty member or will the list of factors be tailored to the particular charge of a faculty member? If so, who makes that decision? Who writes the letters denying tenure? Who writes the letters granting tenure?

Locus of the award of tenure. When tenure is awarded, does it provide the faculty member rights within the discipline, the college, the entire institution, or on the several campuses of a multicampus institution?

Dismissal and appeals. On what basis may a tenured faculty member be dismissed? What rights of appeal does the faculty member have? Is a hearing required in every case? Who makes the final judgment in such cases? How much severance pay does a dismissed tenured faculty member receive? Under what conditions is there no terminal pay?

Retraining. Will the institution commit itself to retraining in the event of cutbacks? If so, under what circumstances and for how long?

A study of tenure policies by the College and University Personnel Association (1980c) includes survey responses from over 1,000 institutions about their tenure policies and their practices regarding many of the issues noted in this chapter. For more information regarding tenure, see AAUP/AAC Commission on Academic Tenure (1973).

Each institution must decide what type of tenure policy it wishes to have. Administrators should carefully consider all the issues raised in this chapter to ensure that their institution's policy is complete. Exhibit 38, pp. 176–182, presents a sample tenure policy.

Are There Alternatives to Tenure?

Institutions that have a high percentage of tenured faculty must face the probability of declining enrollment during the 1980s and the probability of needed changes in curricular emphasis. These institutions are seeking alternatives to tenure and ways to diversify the current faculty by appointing new members. Such institutions should consider four approaches to this problem. First, appointing new faculty members on fixed-term appointments not eligible for tenure. Second, appointing part-time faculty. Third, developing early retirement plans to counter the change in the minimum mandatory retirement age to seventy (see Chapter Eight for information on early retirement plans). Fourth, initiating a program of evaluation for tenured faculty members and providing for the termination of faculty members who do not successfully follow a prescribed developmental program following a poor evaluation.

Exhibit 35. Sample Contract for a Tenure-Eligible Appointment

The president of Anytown University has approved your appointment to the faculty of the university as follows:

Name   _____

College or department   _____

Rank and title   _____

Effective date of

appointment   _____

Annual salary and service $ _____ for forty-eight weeks'
                                 service, payable in equal monthly
                                 installments.

Present tenure status   ☐   Permanent tenure.
                             ☐   Provisional status with _____ years of
                                 academic service credit.
                             ☐   Ranks of assistant, instructor, research
                                 assistant, lecturer, and assistant librarian are
                                 not eligible for tenure.
                             ☐   This appointment is not subject to tenure
                                 because it is not under the purview of a
                                 college dean or the dean of libraries.

In accepting this appointment, you are entitled to the benefits of, and agree to abide by, the regulations in force throughout your employment at the university with respect to:

1. the employee benefit plans (medical insurance, group life insurance, and retirement plans);
2. academic tenure (if applicable), academic freedom, patent and copyright policies, and resignation; and
3. the procedure whereby you refund to the university any part of your annual salary not earned as of the date your service with this university terminates.

If you agree to these terms of your appointment, please sign below and return the original as specified in the letter of offer.

_____
(Signature of provost)

Accepted _____   Date _____
                 (Signature)

Exhibit 36. Sample Contract for a Non-Tenure-Eligible Appointment

The president of Anytown University has approved your appointment to
the faculty of the university as follows:

Name	_____
College or department	_____
Rank and title	_____
Period of appointment	_____
Salary for period of appointment	_____

This appointment is not subject to the terms of the university tenure
policy.

In accepting this appointment, you are entitled to the benefits of, and
agree to abide by, the regulations in force during your employment at the
university with respect to:

1. the employee benefit plans (medical insurance, group life
   insurance, and retirement plans);
2. the patenting of discoveries or inventions resulting from
   research, copyright policies; and
3. the procedure whereby you refund to the university any part of
   your annual salary not earned as of the date your service with
   this university terminates.

If you agree to these terms of your appointment, please sign below and
return the original as specified in the letter of offer.

_____
(Signature of provost)

Accepted _____   Date _____
             (Signature)

Exhibit 37. Sample Memorandum of Tenure Status

Under the terms of the university policy on tenure, you became subject to the provisions of the tenure policy effective with your promotion to a rank eligible for tenure.

Name _____

College or department _____

Rank and/title _____

Tenure status effective _____

       ☐ Permanent tenure
       ☐ Provisional status with _____ years of academic service
       credit

_____   _____
      (Signature of dean)   (Date)

If you agree with this tenure status, please sign below and send the original to the Personnel Procedures Division.

Accepted _____   Date _____
            (Signature)

Exhibit 38. Sample Tenure Policy

Faculty tenure:

Tenure implies a mutual responsibility on the part of the university and the tenured faculty member. In granting tenure to a faculty member, the university makes a commitment to his or her continued employment, subject to certain qualifications. The university expects that tenured faculty members will maintain the level of performance by which they initially earned tenure.

Definitions:

1. The term *tenure* means continuous reappointment to an achieved academic rank. It is hereinafter understood that tenure must be granted or denied by specific action of the university regents.

Tenure is designed as a means to protect the academic freedom of faculty members. This is to say, tenure is a means to assure unfettered, unbiased, unencumbered search, verification, and communication of truth by professional scholars and teachers.

Tenure is designed to provide faculty members with freedom from political, doctrinaire, and other pressures, restraints, and reprisals which would otherwise inhibit their independent thought and actions in their professional responsibility of search, verification, and communication of truths.

2.   The term *probationary period* refers to the period of employment in an academic rank prior to the time tenure is granted. Notwithstanding different uses of the term elsewhere, the probationary period does not include any period of employment following the awarding of tenure.

3.   The term *prior service* means academic employment at an institution of higher education before the first appointment in the effective probationary period at the university.

Eligibility for tenure:

1.   All employees of the university who hold a regular full-time academic rank of assistant professor or above are eligible for tenure.

2.   It is understood that a faculty member who has been granted tenure by the university, and thereafter accepts an administrative post within the university, retains tenured status as a member of the faculty.

3.   When an initial appointment is made to a position which is primarily administrative, but carries with it academic rank of assistant professor or above, specific understanding should be reached at the time of offer with the individual concerned and agreed to in writing by the provost, the dean, and the academic unit as to whether the individual will be reviewed for tenure at the proper time and what conditions must be met before there is tenure eligibility.

Whenever a regular faculty member during the probationary period assumes primary administrative responsibilities, agreement should be reached in the same manner. Likewise, whenever an administrator is given academic rank at any time following the initial appointment, the same would apply.

4.   It is understood that a faculty member who has been granted tenure by the university and thereafter changes from a full-time appointment to a volunteer or part-time faculty appointment on other than a temporary basis forfeits tenured status.

Probationary periods:

1.   The contract of employment furnished to a candidate for appointment to the faculty shall specify, in addition to the rank and salary, the length of the probationary period entailed in the appointment and any special conditions pertaining to the appointment. All such conditions must be set forth in writing by the provost whenever any faculty appointment is offered.

Exhibit 38 (continued)

2.　The probationary period for a faculty member whose effective date of appointment is later than the start of the academic year but no later than the first day of the second semester will be considered as dating from the beginning of the first semester, provided that the department or division in question records in writing its prior agreement to such an arrangement. If the effective date of appointment is later than the first day of the second semester, the probationary period shall begin with the first semester of the next academic year.

3.　For a faculty member who is eligible for tenure and whose initial appointment is at the rank of assistant professor or associate professor, the probationary period shall be six academic years of twelve regular semesters, except in cases noted in the paragraph following. Included in the probationary period is prior full-time service (up to a maximum of three years) in professorial ranks at other institutions of higher education unless the faculty member requests in writing at the time of the first regular appointment that such service should not be included and the academic unit, the dean, and the provost approve. Included also is prior regular, full-time service (up to a maximum of three years) which the appointee may have performed in the past at the university in the rank of instructor or above unless the faculty member requests in writing at the time the faculty member is most recently appointed to a tenure-track position that such service should not be included and the academic unit, the dean, and the provost approve. Prior full-time service as instructor or in a comparable nonprofessorial rank at other institutions of higher education and prior full-time service on temporary appointments at the university will be counted as part of the probationary period if this arrangement is agreed upon in writing at the time of the first regular appointment. The parties to such an agreement are the appointee, the academic unit, the dean, and the provost.

4.　In certain unusual cases tenure may be awarded to faculty members of extraordinarily high merit prior to the end of the sixth probationary year. Any academic unit's recommendation to award tenure before the end of the usual probationary period should be accompanied by an accounting of compelling reasons for this action. If the university's decision at that time is not to confer tenure, however, the faculty member in question may, subject to continuation or renewal of contract, continue to serve in the probationary period, and be considered for tenure again without prejudice.

5.　A new faculty member appointed at the rank of professor or associate professor may be given tenure from the date of appointment, or the probationary period may be set at two, three, or four years, when prior service in a professorial rank at another institution is less than three years. Persons with three or more years of such prior service may have a probationary period of no more than three years. The probationary period's length shall be set by the tenured members of the appointee's academic unit, subject to agreement by the dean and provost at the time of offer. If a majority of the unit's tenured faculty members favor tenure upon appointment, the determination of tenure shall be made in the regular fashion.

6. Whenever an untenured part-time faculty member converts from part-time to full-time, with the rank of assistant professor or above, specific written understanding must be approved by the provost as to how the period of part-time service will be counted toward satisfying the probationary period for tenure.

7. A maximum of one year of leave of absence without pay may be counted as part of the probationary period, provided the department or division in question records in writing its prior agreement and secures administrative approval. Leaves of absence without pay counted as part of the probationary period must entail appropriate evaluation of professional activities carried out during the leave.

8. During the probationary period, a faculty member will be provided by the chair of the academic unit with an annual, written evaluation of performance. Such annual evaluation shall be provided prior to the applicable notification deadline for reappointment, with a copy sent to the dean.

9. A faculty member at any rank who is denied tenure shall be retained on the faculty until the end of the academic year following that in which notified of the denial, unless there are reasons to the contrary.

10. Faculty members accorded tenure will normally commence their continuous appointments in the academic year immediately following the regents' action.

Criteria for the tenure decision:

The choices that the university makes in granting tenure are crucial to its endeavors toward academic excellence. A decision to grant tenure must reflect an assessment of high professional competence and performance measured against national standards. Tenure should never be regarded as a routine award.

The tenure decision shall be based on a thorough evaluation of the candidate's total contribution to the mission of the university. While specific responsibilities of faculty members may vary because of special assignments or because of the particular mission of an academic unit, all evaluations for tenure shall address the manner in which each candidate has performed in: teaching, research or creative achievement, professional service, and university service.

Exhibit 38 (continued)

Above all else, it is essential to any recommendation that tenure be granted that the faculty member has clearly demonstrated scholarly attainment, primarily but not exclusively through teaching and research or creative achievement.

Each academic unit, with the participation and approval of the dean and the provost, shall establish and publish specific criteria for evaluating faculty performance in that unit, so long as those criteria are in accord with this policy.

In those cases in which specific assignments might limit the faculty member's involvement in any area of faculty responsibility, a written understanding to this effect should be filed with the provost, approved by the dean and the chair of the academic unit at the time the assignment is made.

The award of tenure carries with it the expectation that the university shall continue to need the services the faculty member is capable of performing and that the financial resources are expected to be available for continuous employment. It also carries the expectation that the faculty member will maintain or improve upon the level of attainment which characterized the qualifications for tenure.

Procedures for the tenure decision:

1.   A faculty member who is eligible for tenure consideration should be notified by the chair of the academic unit at least five weeks before the initial vote by the faculty member's colleagues.

2.   At the time of notification, the candidate for tenure shall be requested to submit material that will be helpful to an adequate consideration of the faculty member's performance or professional activities in relationship to the tenure criteria. The candidate should be advised to consult with the chair or any other senior colleagues concerning the materials to include. However, the responsibility for the contents resides with the candidate.

3.   The chair should be responsible for providing copies of the candidate's material to each of the voting members of the academic unit and to the provost. Copies of the candidate's material should be distributed to the faculty of the academic unit at least two weeks prior to the vote. The provost's copy should be forwarded through the deans with the academic unit's recommendation forms.

4.   Preceding the vote, all tenured faculty voters who are available shall meet for a discussion of the candidate's qualifications for tenure. It is assumed that the eligible voters will have studied the candidate's materials prior to the meeting.

5.   The candidate should not be present during the discussion of his or her qualifications. The candidate should be available, however, to enter the meeting on invitation to answer questions or clarify circumstances relevant to the qualifications.

6.   Formal consideration for tenure shall originate with the polling by secret ballot of all tenured members of the candidate's academic unit, including when possible those who are on leave of absence. If it is proposed to consider a tenure recommendation prior to the candidate's sixth probationary year, the tenured members of the unit shall hold a preliminary vote on whether or not to do so, and consideration of early tenure will proceed only if a majority of tenured faculty members favor such consideration. Subsequently, in any formal poll of tenured faculty taken prior to the candidate's sixth probationary year, no tenure recommendation will be forwarded unless a majority of those polled favor granting tenure. Whatever the result of the faculty poll taken during the sixth probationary year, it will be forwarded. In all cases, the result of the vote must accompany the recommendations.

7.   The chair shall submit a separate recommendation with supporting reasons.

8.   While primary responsibility for gathering complete information on professional activity rests with the individual faculty member, the chair should assume a share of this responsibility to be certain that all tenure recommendations are initiated on the basis of full documentation, which must be considered by any person or group making a recommendation.

9.   All recommendations shall be in writing and, with the exception of the faculty recommendation resulting from the secret poll, reasons for the recommendations must be stated. When recommendations are made, at any stage of the review process, notification of such recommendations must be provided the chair and the individual candidate. It shall be the responsibility of the chair to inform the faculty of the unit about recommendations made at the various stages of the review process.

10.   Copies of the academic unit recommendation will be forwarded separately to the appropriate dean and to the Campus Tenure Committee. The Campus Tenure Committee and the dean will attach their recommendations to the tenure materials and separately forward all materials to the provost.

11.   The main purpose of the Campus Tenure Committee is to provide faculty advice on whether or not the academic unit's recommendation with regard to both substance and process is sustained by the accompanying documentation and is consistent with the approved tenure criteria. If defects are found in either of these particulars, the recommendation will be returned to the academic unit for remedy or correction.

Exhibit 38 (continued)

12.   The Campus Tenure Committee will be composed of nine tenured faculty members on staggered three-year terms selected by the president from nominations from the Faculty Senate.

13.   In determining its recommendation, the Campus Tenure Committee may request information or advice from any person. Committee members from the originating academic unit of a case under consideration will absent themselves from discussions regarding that case.

14.   The existence of the Campus Tenure Committee in no way limits the right of administrative officers to solicit advice from faculty members in determining their recommendations.

15.   In any tenure case in which the president plans to submit to the regents a recommendation contrary to that of the Campus Tenure Committee, the president shall so notify the committee, allowing sufficient time and opportunity for the president and the committee to conduct a thorough discussion of the case before the president presents a final recommendation to the regents.

16.   At any stage of the tenure review process, the concerned faculty member may appeal to the Faculty Appeals Board if it is believed that procedural violations have occurred in the case or that violations of academic freedom have occurred. If it is believed that there has been discrimination on the basis of race, sex, age, creed, or ethnic or national origin, the faculty member may appeal to the Committee on Discrimination. Such appeals must be made within thirty calendar days after discovery of the alleged violation, and the review process will be suspended until a resolution is effected. Such an appeal shall not have the effect of extending the faculty member's terminal year, should tenure be denied.

17.   The president will notify each faculty member by May 31 of whether or not tenure has been granted, except when appeals make this impossible.

Source: Adapted from the University of Oklahoma's policy on tenure as of March 1979. As such, this statement does not represent that university's complete policy.

❧ 10 ❧

Promoting Human Resources Development

In this decade, we are witnessing a decline in the number of individuals in the traditional college-age group and a decline in the percentage of those individuals who enroll at higher educational institutions. To adjust to these social changes, institutions must help their faculty, staff, and administrators prepare to meet changing needs. Decreasing enrollments and the resulting reductions in staff also make improved management of time and resources a necessity.

Among other major changes that are affecting the administration of higher education are:

- Advances in technology. New communication technologies require the training of teams of workers and the development of new procedures for acquiring, organizing, storing, and retrieving new forms of information.

- Employees' demands for greater autonomy. Employees are demanding greater individual freedom and initiative under less autocratic leadership.
- Reductions in resources. Institutions are expected to continue to accomplish their missions despite reductions in funding and staffing.
- Accountability. Many institutions now use a general systems approach to improve total organizational productivity. This approach emphasizes interrelationships among operating departments and requires organizational development through training and development programs.

Such changes compel administrators in higher education institutions to seek management strategies that will function effectively in this relatively new environment. Some institutions have responded by introducing such methods as management by objectives (MBO) and time management. Others have redefined the traditional personnel function to include academic personnel administration and have introduced total compensation (reward) systems. New administrative strategies also include organizational development, creative risk taking, team building, shared decision making, and conflict resolution.

For a detailed discussion of the changes facing higher educational administrators, see Castetter (1976). Eiben and Milliren (1976) discuss a variety of strategic responses to such changes.

What Are Organizational Development and Human Resources Development Programs?

Organizational development is planned, organized change that is institutionwide and is managed by the top administrators in order to increase organizational effectiveness. An organizational development plan uses knowledge and research provided by behavioral science researchers to devise appropriate changes in such institutional processes as decision making, problem solving, policy making, and communication. For details on organizational and staff development, see Richardson (1975), Claxton (1976), Craig and Bittel (1967), and Schmuck and Runkel (1972).

From the point of view of personnel professionals, organizational development is best achieved by improving the faculty and staff's capabilities for discharging new, changing, and continuing responsibilities through effective human resources development programs. Effective human resources development programs have the following objectives:

- To create an on-campus environment conducive to enhancing professional growth for faculty, staff, and administrators
- To improve instructional methods and delivery
- To assess the organizational climate and the effectiveness of the organizational structure
- To establish specific goals for individuals and administrative units
- To streamline procedures that tend to inhibit individuals in their employment
- To assess changes as they occur and develop plans to meet the changes
- To clarify communication channels and networks
- To uncover conflicts among individuals and administrative units
- To encourage institutionwide unity in purpose

Obviously such programs cannot be implemented by the personnel officer alone. They require action by the chief administrative officer as well as by key faculty, administrators, and support staff members. However, the personnel officer, by integrating faculty and staff development with organizational development efforts, can create a climate that will (1) enable administrators at all levels to understand the need for change, (2) simplify the chief administrative officer's task when decisions for change need to be made, and (3) initiate effective means for facilitating and coping with change.

For example, one objective of a development program is to improve teaching methods and delivery. Although academic department heads are responsible for all activities within their departments, many of them are not chosen for their managerial skills.

Most department heads would welcome a series of workshops on how to plan, manage people, or work within a budget. The agenda of such a series could also include information about improving instructional methods and delivery, and how to overcome anticipated faculty resistance to such changes. For more details on college teaching methods and delivery, see Eiben and Milliren (1976), Hoover (1980), and Thayer (1976).

How Are Human Resources Needs Determined and Assessed?

A successful program of human resources development must begin with a needs assessment, that is, the specification of the types of training and development needed in the organization. Then priorities among the needs should be established. The priorities are determined by a combination of factors including the pressing need for the item, a recognition by all parties of that need, and the ability to produce an effective program in that area. For a sample instrument for assessing higher educational needs, see Exhibit 39, p. 192.

A list of needs can be assembled by the personnel officer using many sources that are readily available. The best sources of information are:

- *Personal observations.* The personnel officer should note questions being asked that suggest faculty and staff's needs for information. What mistakes are being made that suggest a need for improved methods? What complaints are being made about teaching? What new programs are being introduced that require new skills of faculty and staff? What misunderstandings are evident that suggest a need for information?
- *Meetings.* Discussions with faculty, staff, administrators, students, and student employees will elicit development needs and may uncover areas in which improved communication is necessary.
- *Study of grievances.* A study of the kinds of grievances being submitted may reveal gaps in knowledge on the part of employees and supervisors. Such a study should also reveal how

well the supervisory staff is prepared to handle such grievances. The frequency of grievances in specific areas may suggest a need for management development.

- *Accident reports.* A study of the frequency, severity, and types of accidents will reveal employees' needs for safety training and information.
- *Exit interviews.* An examination of the remarks made in exit interviews may reveal development needs within various departments.
- *Staff attitude surveys.* The process of asking all faculty or staff members to respond to a formal attitude survey may disclose needs. However, attitude surveys should not be undertaken unless the institution is prepared administratively and financially to respond in a timely manner to the facts uncovered by the survey.
- *Position descriptions and analysis.* A comparison of the educational and experience prerequisites outlined in the position descriptions with the available talent in the work force will disclose needs for basic skills and training, and perhaps lead to the establishment of a formal apprenticeship program. Similarly, position analysis of the design of positions will uncover needs.
- *Performance evaluation.* The evaluation of faculty, staff, and administrators' performance may uncover skills and informational needs that suggest development programs.

For more details on needs determination and assessment, see Craig and Bittel (1967).

Some institutions have formal development committees to assist the personnel officer in identifying needs, developing programs, setting priorities in the programs, selecting instructors, publicizing programs, and evaluating programs.

The composition of such a committee varies, of course, among institutions. However, the following principles of operation for the committee are recommended. The committee should be created and named by the chief executive officer of the institution. The regular members of the committee should represent areas of influence in both the academic and nonacademic segments of the institution. A representative of the personnel office should be a continuing, ex-officio member of the committee. If the institution has a continuing education program, a representative of that program may serve as a continuing, ex-officio member. Committee members should be appointed for terms of no less than three years. In order to assure continuity, their terms should be staggered.

How Is a Human Resources Development Program Staffed and Funded?

Ideally, the institution should recognize the importance of human resources development and provide at least one professional staff member and some support staff for this function. A large staff and a large financial commitment are not necessary to initiate programs of training and development. Fortunately, most institutions have faculty and staff members with relevant expertise who can be engaged as instructors in the development programs. The services of these faculty and staff members can be used effectively to institute programs of training and development. Institutions with limited funds may begin their development programs with ready-made or in-house models built on this resource. For more details on staffing, see Nadler (1979).

Institutions that do not have training and development programs because the central budget does not include such programs should start slowly with a few successful programs in order to create the awareness for the necessity of funding. Necessary funding might be obtained by charging departmental budgets a fee for faculty, administrators, and staff members who attend sessions. Such fees can be more modest than the cost of sending those same personnel to off-campus training programs. The fees can also be used to finance the development of future courses. There are two advantages to directly charging departmental budgets for participation. First, attendance at the sessions is usually greater than if the cost is paid from central funds. Second, the evaluation of the worth of the courses is usually more critical if departments are charged directly.

Where Should Human Resources Development Efforts Begin?

Ideally, training and development should begin at the top. Deans and other principal administrators should go through programs first, and then programs should be addressed to personnel down through the organization. In that way, the principles learned in the development program can be more readily implemented and applied. This ideal plan may, however, be impractical for some institutions if deans and other top administrators do not place a high priority on their personal participation. In this case, a program should start by addressing middle management and individual faculty and staff members. If top administrators are reluctant to participate, it is better to start with a group of faculty or staff who are enthusiastic about the program. The enthusiasm of the participants will afford the program a better chance of succeeding, and a successful program may then encourage principal administrators to participate. For example, middle managers participating in a management development session may encourage their supervisors to attend the same program. Thus success at the middle-management level may well lead to requests for similar programs at higher levels. One need not wait for the ideal conditions to initiate a development program, as long as the organizational climate is conducive to learning and some prospective participants are ready.

There are two approaches to the process of selecting participants for development sessions. One suggests that individuals volunteer themselves as participants; the other, that administrators select the individuals to attend. Whatever approach is used, participation should be voluntary; no employee should be forced to attend. Participation in programs that provide skills for upward mobility should be coordinated with the institution's affirmative action program. Such development programs can provide opportunities for advancement to protected classes of faculty and staff.

Human resources development is the responsibility of every effective administrator. Every administrator should regularly assess the development and training needs of his or her staff and should encourage staff to participate in development programs, within and outside the institution, that will meet the changing needs of the institution. Indeed, administrators should be evaluated on their effectiveness in promoting staff development.

What Are Examples of Training and Development Programs?

Some higher education institutions have developed sophisticated training and development programs. Examples of specific programs currently in use in higher education institutions include:

1. Tuition reimbursement for faculty, staff, and administrators for courses taken at the home institution or other institutions
2. Paid leave and expenses to attend professional meetings
3. Sabbatical leave programs for personal development
4. In-house training programs in such subjects as:
    a. Supervisory techniques, leadership styles, and time management
    b. Oral communication, writing skills, report writing, and reading enhancement
    c. Public relations
    d. New teaching techniques
    e. Preretirement counseling
    f. Selection and interviewing techniques, and affirmative action procedures
    g. Handling gripes and grievances, supervising unsatisfactory employees, and collective bargaining
    h. Performance evaluation, position analysis, and position evaluation
    i. Transactional analysis
    j. Problem solving, decision making, and team building
    k. Stress management and prevention of employee burnout
5. Formal apprenticeships
6. Skills training (for example, typing, shorthand, word processing, first aid, and safety.

When Should Program Evaluation Techniques Be Determined?

Evaluation techniques and criteria for each development program must be determined during the beginning stages of program design. Use of more than one evaluation technique and measurement is encouraged. Exhibit 40, p. 194, presents a sample questionnaire for assessing the response of participants to a program.

In order to be effective, human resources development programs should be directed at solving institutional problems, meeting faculty and staff members' needs, and planning for organizational change. For example, an institution's five- or ten-year plan may outline new directions required to meet new goals. Those goals must be studied by the institution's human resources development professionals who, in turn, should develop programs that provide faculty and staff with a means to meet both their and the organization's needs by developing their abilities. In Chapter Eleven, we describe some of the tools commonly used to determine human resources development needs—performance standards and performance evaluations.

Exhibit 39. Sample Questionnaire for Assessing Developmental Needs

I. Please indicate the degree of need you think exists on the campus for training and development by checking each item below.

		Level of Need		
		Great	Some	Little
A.	*Support staff*			
	1. Communication (including interviewing skills)	___	___	___
	2. Safety	___	___	___
	3. Office skills	___	___	___
	4. Data processing	___	___	___
	5. Word processing	___	___	___
	6. Dealing with students	___	___	___
	7. Report writing	___	___	___
	8. First aid	___	___	___
	9. _____ (Other: Specify)	___	___	___
	10. _____			
B.	*First-line supervisors*			
	1. Interviewing skills	___	___	___
	2. Disciplining employees	___	___	___
	3. Motivating employees	___	___	___
	4. Handling complaints and grievances	___	___	___
	5. Planning and organizing	___	___	___
	6. Decision making	___	___	___
	7. Time management	___	___	___
	8. Stress management	___	___	___
	9. _____ (Other: Specify)	___	___	___
	10. _____	___	___	___
C.	*Administrators*			
	1. Leadership and delegating responsibility	___	___	___
	2. Conducting meetings	___	___	___
	3. Planning and organizing	___	___	___
	4. Controlling work	___	___	___
	5. Team building	___	___	___
	6. Finance, accounting, and budgeting	___	___	___
	7. Use of computers	___	___	___
	8. Communication	___	___	___
	9. _____ (Other: Specify)	___	___	___
	10. _____	___	___	___
D.	*Full-time faculty*			
	1. Academic advising skills	___	___	___
	2. Counselling and coaching techniques	___	___	___

     3. Verbal communication   ____ ____ ____

     4. Written communication   ____ ____ ____

     5. College procedural matters   ____ ____ ____

     6. Adult learning strategies   ____ ____ ____

     7. Chairing committees and
         meetings   ____ ____ ____

     8. Budgeting   ____ ____ ____

     9. _____ (Other: Specify)   ____ ____ ____

    10. _____

  E. *Part-time faculty*

     1. Teaching and learning
         strategies   ____ ____ ____

     2. Planning course content   ____ ____ ____

     3. Counselling and coaching
         skills   ____ ____ ____

     4. College procedural
         matters   ____ ____ ____

     5. Orientation to the
         college   ____ ____ ____

     6. Motivating students   ____ ____ ____

     7. Use of audiovisual aids   ____ ____ ____

     8. Knowledge of available
         resources   ____ ____ ____

     9. _____ (Other: Specify)   ____ ____ ____

    10. _____   ____ ____ ____

II. Please list the three needs that you feel are most important to meet in the coming fiscal year.

     1. _____

     2. _____

     3. _____

III. Please list the three needs that you feel are the most important to meet in the next five years.

     1. _____

     2. _____

     3. _____

IV. Please check your current status: _____ staff, _____ administrator, _____ full-time faculty, _____ part-time faculty

Thank you.

Exhibit 40. Sample Form for Assessing Reaction to a Training Program

Please circle the rating on the scale which best reflects your reaction.

1. Rate the overall presentation in terms of clarity and understandability.

1	2	3	4	5	6	7	8	9	10

Not at all   Very good   Excellent

2. To what degree will the information obtained in this session be useful to you in your daily work?

1	2	3	4	5	6	7	8	9	10

Very little   Satisfactorily   To a large extent

3. Do you feel that this program met your needs?

1	2	3	4	5	6	7	8	9	10

Not at all   To some extent   To a large extent

4. Rate the subject content in terms of your expectations of this program.

1	2	3	4	5	6	7	8	9	10

Poor   Very good   Excellent

5. Rate the presenter's ability to effectively demonstrate the subject content.

1	2	3	4	5	6	7	8	9	10

Poor   Very good   Excellent

6. Would you recommend this program to other employees?
Yes _____ No _____

7. Check the following categories as appropriate:
   ☐ Presented new ideas and approaches
   ☐ Made me cognizant of similar problems that other employees are facing
   ☐ Provided solutions for some problems
   ☐ Provided an opportunity to look objectively at myself and my job

8. List any questions that were not answered in this session.

_____

_____

_____

9. Comments:

_____

_____

_____

_____

❦ 11 ❧

Setting Standards and Evaluating Performance

Evaluation of the performance of employees is an essential activity because the lifeblood of a successful university flows in a competent faculty and staff. To maintain competence, an institution must select, orient, and motivate effective individuals for specific assignments. Essential for success are techniques for dismissing ineffective faculty and staff members and for rewarding productive performers equitably. To be equitable performance evaluation must be based on prescribed performance expectations and standards.

To be most effective, performance evaluation must be a continuous process that involves frequent communication. The purpose of the evaluation must be clearly documented and communicated to those involved.

While there is little disagreement concerning the need for evaluating work performance, there is widespread disagreement concerning the methodology and purpose of performance evaluation. In this chapter, we highlight the key elements of performance

195

evaluation programs and methodology, and we provide some examples of performance standards.

The purposes of performance evaluation are many:

- to improve employees' performance
- to ensure that duties performed are consistent with institutional objectives
- to counsel employees in regard to personal and professional development
- to identify employees deserving of promotion
- to assist in disciplinary action or discharge
- to identify areas for training and development
- to determine eligibility for salary increases
- to provide supervisors with information regarding their supervisory effectiveness
- to provide recognition of good performance
- to minimize potential legal action relative to equal employment opportunity and upward mobility

Is Performance Evaluation a New Concept?

In examining purposes, we find it useful to briefly summarize the history of performance evaluation programs in colleges and universities. The impetus to define performance standards for employees resulted from industry's drive for efficiency in the early part of this century. Efficiency experts sought to measure the most time-efficient ways in which to perform tasks, and employers naturally sought to evaluate individuals against these new standards of performance. Industry's efforts to systematize evaluation led to criticism of the casual, haphazard, and unsystematic approaches to performance evaluation in government agencies and in publicly funded colleges and universities. Many such agencies and institutions, therefore, initiated a variety of efforts to reform their performance evaluation programs. Legislative efforts for reform included such acts as the Federal Civil Service Classification Act of 1923, the Taft-Hartley Labor Act of 1947, the Fair Labor Standards Act of 1963, the Civil Rights Act of 1964, and the Civil Service Reform Act. State legislatures passed companion bills.

In higher education, the advent of the American Association of University Professors (AAUP) increased educators' awareness of the need for faculties to evaluate the effectiveness of their peers in order to ensure high levels of professionalism and to affirm the faculty's professional right to self-regulation. Many institutions, in response, instituted student and peer evaluations of faculty performance. For details about student and peer evaluations, see Marsh and others (1975), Rodin and Rodin (1972), and Seldin (1980).

Historically, the use of ineffective performance evaluation methods for determining merit increases for nonacademic personnel has led to unionization. Many unions of blue-collar employees negotiate for single-rate plans and automatic pay progression plans, rather than for plans dependent on merit rating. This "cure" has caused renewed management interest in finding performance evaluation systems that are fair and equitable and that are acceptable to employees and their unions.

Our review of the history of performance evaluation in colleges and universities leads us to three general observations. First, we note an increased use of performance evaluation programs for purposes of personnel development in higher education. Second, we find that many programs have been ineffective because they are not systematic and they fail to relate the evaluative procedures to organizational purposes, unit objectives, and position goals. Third, very few institutions have set expected standards against which to measure employees' performance. Therefore, in many cases, factors other than task-related factors have been measured.

What Is Performance Evaluation?

Performance evaluation is the appraisal of an employee's performance against the performance requirements for his or her position. It represents the supervisor's best judgment as to how well the individual fulfills the specified requirements of the position, and what possibilities the individual has for improvement and advancement. It describes the quantity, quality, timeliness, and manner of performance necessary to accomplish satisfactorily the duties and responsibilities of the position. Performance requirements establish *how* the principal work activities should be accomplished, *how much* work must be done within a given amount of time, and *how well* it must be done.

Castetter (1976) offers the following general principles for performance evaluation:

- The evaluation program should be formalized, especially for supporting decisions on salary and wage increases, transfers, and promotions.
- The primary purpose of performance evaluation is to facilitate change in individual behavior in order to achieve personal and organizational goals.
- The methodology should place emphasis on collecting factual information about specific achievements as they relate to established goals.
- Both supervisors and subordinates should participate in determining performance expectations.
- The foundation of performance evaluation is the list of standards or goals established for various positions in the institution.
- Results of performance evaluations should be used to discuss performance and progress of personnel in relation to specific goals.
- Performance strengths should be recognized and weaknesses identified so that individual action plans can be developed to make the needed corrections.
- Supervisors should be thoroughly trained in the purpose and use of the performance evaluation program.

How Is a Performance Evaluation Program Implemented?

To plan, develop, and maintain a performance evaluation program in institutions of higher education generally requires the institution to have first drawn up the following documents: a statement of the institution's purposes and mission, policies on performance evaluation, a list of objectives for each unit and position, a set of performance standards and goals, and individual position control guides. These last guides include position specifications, personnel qualifications, areas of authority, and position relationships. The administrators can then develop a performance evaluation process and a performance evaluation training program.

The performance standards for faculty members should differ from those for other staff members *only* in their degree of specificity. The performance standards are written descriptions, established by administrators and communicated to faculty and staff members, that define satisfactory performance for all assigned tasks. They represent specific criteria of performance, understood and accepted by both parties, that are deemed to be desirable, achievable, and measurable (to whatever extent is possible and appropriate).

Standards may be expressed in either nonnumerical or numerical form. Nonnumerical standards are less specific and are usually stated in terms of activities required to meet a particular outcome. An example of a nonnumerical standard is "Resolves priority problems in a timely manner." Numerical standards are stated in terms of costs, savings, percentage gain or loss, and time factors. A combination of both nonnumerical and numerical standards may be used.

While it may be difficult to establish performance standards that specify the results expected of instructional personnel, it is possible to establish standards for the actions to be taken in an effort to accomplish results. For example, if one cannot specify what an instructor should accomplish, one can specify the kinds of instructional activities that should be undertaken. Similarly, if one cannot measure the quantity of results produced by an instructor, one can measure how that individual goes about fulfilling the responsibilities of the position. For discussions of result-oriented performance evaluation, see Pajer (1972), and American Association of University Professors (1979).

How Are Performance Standards Established and Used?

An administrator who wants to set standards for his or her subordinates should first examine formal and informal statements of the responsibilities assigned to those subordinates. For a department head seeking to set standards for faculty, this preliminary examination will include an annual meeting with each faculty member to jointly determine what each faculty member will do during the next year. At that meeting, they should discuss courses to be taught, faculty service assignments (department and senate committees), publications in process, and other scholarly work. The percentage of time to be devoted to each activity should also be discussed. For example, they will agree that during the next year the faculty member will devote 75 percent of the time to teaching, 10 percent to faculty service, 10 percent to publications in progress, and 5 percent to other specific scholarly activities.

During that meeting, the department head and faculty member should reach an understanding about expectations (standards) for each of the major position elements. For example, they may agree that the faculty member is expected to:

> meet all scheduled classes on time
>
> hold regularly scheduled office hours for student conferences
>
> give effective lectures and update lecture information regularly
>
> assure that all tests are learning experiences for students
>
> give timely and constructive critical responses to students about their work
>
> make maximum use of a variety of instructional approaches to generate and maintain student interest

Obviously this list is only a sample, but it serves to outline the kinds of understandings that should exist between the faculty member and the department head. Such a list of expectations should serve as the basis of understanding for future performance reviews.

For administrators who seek to establish standards for non-faculty employees, the first step is a review of the position description and less formal specifications of the positions, such as daily task sheets or lists based on a management by objectives system. From an accurate position description, an administrator should be able to establish performance standards for most positions. If standards cannot be established, the administrator should consider whether the position is needed and whether it has been properly described.

Setting staff performance standards can be accomplished with or without professional assistance. A professional consultant would probably divide the position into its component parts and examine each component to determine whether it is a necessary task, the best method for accomplishing the component task, the appropriate duration of the task, and the cost effectiveness of the task. The results of this thorough examination should enable an administrator to eliminate unnecessary tasks and to identify inefficient work methods and impediments to productivity. The administrator can then construct an effective assignment of tasks and establish standards of performance for each component task. Administrators and supervisors whose department has many employees, such as a maintenance office, can use computers to organize the job components into efficient work schedules. Computer simulations can also identify potential savings that would result from reducing some standards and redesigning schedules to eliminate some positions. For example, administrators could assess the potential savings from reducing the frequency with which offices are cleaned or wastebaskets emptied.

Administrators working without professional assistance should list each duty or responsibility of a position and, in consultation with the employee, develop written expectations of performance. Expectations should specify one or more of the following:

> quality of results (completeness, accuracy, or format)
> quantity of results to be achieved in given time
> adherence to legal or policy requirements
> adaptability to change and flexibility in thinking
> ability to work with others as needed
> care of equipment, materials, and work space
> ability to plan ahead

Such specification should be relatively easy to accomplish for clerical or blue-collar positions. Administrative and faculty positions are more difficult and require broader scope and less specificity. However, if there is a need for the position, there is a way to specify the extent to which it is to be performed. Standards need not be elaborate for most positions. Exhibit 41, p. 211, presents sample performance standards for a faculty member; Exhibit 42, p. 212, sample performance standards for a clerical position, and Exhibit 43, p. 213, sample performance standards for a supervisory position.

Once the performance standards have been established, the administrator or supervisor can evaluate an employee's work performance by deciding whether the standards were met, not met, or exceeded. If the employee did not meet the standards, the evaluator must ask, What training is needed to improve performance? Is discipline or discharge called for? If the employee exceeded the standards, the evaluator should ask, Is this a promotable employee? To what kinds of position? When? Is the individual eligible for a merit increase? For every employee, the evaluator should assess strengths and weaknesses and should consider what kind of supervisorial direction might help the employee. Evaluators should, finally, determine the type of information they need to evaluate their own supervisory techniques.

Should Employees Serve Probationary Periods?

Every faculty or staff member should serve (and should understand the purpose of) a probationary period of employment. This probationary period—also called a provisional period, trial period, or introductory period—is the time immediately following appointment during which the employee may be disciplined or dismissed without recourse to a grievance procedure unless the employee claims discrimination under civil rights legislation.

The institution's policy on probationary periods should be stated in writing and given to a new faculty or staff member during the final pre-employment interview. Faculty probationary periods are usually longer than those for other categories of personnel. Under many tenure policies, faculty members serve up to seven years in such a status. (For more information about faculty probationary periods, see Chapter Nine.) Probationary periods for other personnel are usually much shorter—three, six, or twelve calendar months, or a designated number of workdays or calendar days. The institution's benefits apply to probationary employees in most cases. Frequently, however, seniority systems do not apply during this period. In such cases, seniority usually is made retroactive to the date of hire following the satisfactory completion of the probationary period.

Usually, only one probationary period is served unless the employee changes positions within the institution during the initial probationary period. In such cases, a new probationary period may be needed. Some institutions require a formal performance evaluation prior to completion of the probationary period. All supervisors should conduct a formal or informal performance evaluation at this time. Once an employee's probationary period is over, dismissal for poor performance may be difficult because the employee may use the institution's grievance procedure.

Probationary policies for faculty usually provide for notice if reappointment is not to take place during the probationary period. For example, notice of nonreappointment during the probationary period is given (1) not later than March 1 of the first academic year of service; (2) not later than December 15 of the second academic year of service; and (3) twelve months before the end of the academic year after two or more years of service. Such notice is usually not specified for employees other than faculty. However, a short period of notice may be given in some cases to facilitate good employee relations.

The following is a sample policy on the probationary period for staff employees:

> An employee's period of probation starts on the employee's first day of regular employment and lasts until the employee has completed six consecutive months of regular employment. During this probationary period an employee cannot use the grievance procedure. The employee's employment may be terminated for any reason at any time during the probationary period. If a probationary employee bids on and is hired for a new job with a different job title, the employee will serve a new probationary period of six consecutive months.

For guidelines for a complete policy on the probationary period, see Exhibit 44, pp. 214–216.

What Is the Job Ownership Phenomenon?

As we have noted, the initial orientation of a new faculty or staff member is very significant. However, in higher education, too often new faculty and staff are left to their own devices. When expectations are vague and standards of performance are nonexistent, an individual can only perform the job as he or she perceives it. In a matter of four or five years, that individual will have what is called "job ownership," that is, the individual's perception of the job's duties are so deeply entrenched that change is difficult. To dismiss an employee at this stage can be very difficult since the individual is performing the job in the same way as he or she previously performed it. Therefore, the individual has done no wrong.

Unfortunately, employee job ownership abounds in higher education. Good personnel administration should strive for its elimination. Administrators can eliminate it by setting performance standards, orienting the new faculty or staff member to the responsibilities of the position and the performance standards to be met, and reviewing the performance against those criteria on a regular basis.

What Are the Procedures for Faculty Promotion Reviews?

Many institutions have comprehensive procedures to evaluate probationary faculty members in their final review prior to the granting or denial of tenure (see Chapter Nine). Similar procedures may be used for faculty promotion reviews. The faculty member should be asked to submit a dossier to the appropriate department, college, and institution review committees. To ensure the equitability of the review process, the department should specify the format and content of the dossier. Usually, a dossier will contain:

1. A promotion (and/or tenure) recommendation form, which provides pertinent data about the candidate and outlines the actions taken at the various review levels (see Exhibit 45, p. 217, for a sample form).

2. A biographical data form, which provides up-to-date biographical data (see Exhibit 46, p. 218, for a sample form).

3. A work assignment sheet, which provides information on the particular work assignments of the faculty member during each quarter or semester of employment.

4. A section on teaching ability and effectiveness, which might contain a list of courses taught for each semester and their enrollment, a summary of student evaluations, statements from other faculty regarding the candidate's teaching effectiveness, and statements of administrators that attest to the candidate's teaching and advising effectiveness.

5. A section on research competence, which might include a list of publications in standard bibliographical form (including articles published in refereed journals, books or parts of books, articles published in nonrefereed journals, research reports, papers accepted for publication, and manuscripts in progress). This section might also include information on research projects, grants and contracts, graduate theses supervised, membership on graduate degree candidates' committees, creative accomplishments (such as sculpture, paintings, musical compositions, or films), patents, and so forth.

6. A section on scholarship and mastery of subject matter, which might report on progress toward advanced degrees, participation in seminars or workshops, papers presented at technical and professional meetings, speaking engagements, courses developed, new teaching methods developed, honors or awards for scholarship or professional activity, and so forth.

7. A section on service to the institution and the public, which might include a record of committee work at all levels, participation in governance, administrative support work, service to governmental agencies, service to industry, service to public and private organizations, and so forth.

8. Letters of evaluation and reference, to which may be appended a description of how the letters were solicited (including a sample letter of request) and identification of those who submitted letters.

9. Statements of evaluation of the candidate by review committees and administrators at each level of review. This section

might outline the relative emphasis given to each of the facets of work assignment, statements regarding reasons for differences of opinion if they exist within a review committee, a summary of the results of earlier promotion and tenure reviews of the candidate, and so forth.

While much has been written about the inherent permanency that follows the granting of tenure for faculty members, little has been said about a similar feeling of permanency that is rather traditional for long-term staff employees. It's a form of job ownership. The longer the service, the more pronounced the inadequacies in performance must be before dismissal is likely to take place. Arbitrators tend to be extremely sympathetic to long-term employees facing dismissal.

What Are the Approaches to Performance Evaluation?

Selection of an approach for evaluating work performance must be based on the institution's needs and the category of employees to be evaluated. The most commonly used approaches are the following:

Approach	*Notes*
Informal	Opinions on performance are given from random observations. This approach is the most subjective and works best in a small department.
Rating scale	This traditional approach requires the evaluator to rate the employee on various performance characteristics. The characteristics may be stated in one-word descriptions, short descriptive phrases, or long descriptions.
Essays	This is the simplest of the formalized approaches to implement. However, the evaluator must have good writing skills and must keep the narrative job-related.
Critical incident	The supervisor writes up each performance incident (good or bad) as it occurs, and the

	write-ups thus present specifics rather than generalities. This approach requires that the evaluators have good writing skills.
Checklist	The evaluator is given a choice among weighted performance related statements. This approach is perhaps the easiest to use.
Ranking	This method requires each evaluator to compare each employee's total job performance with the total work performance of co-workers.
Forced distribution	The evaluator groups employees into categories of average, above average, and the like, with limits on the number of employees to be assigned to each category.
Management by objectives	The supervisor and employee agree at the beginning of the evaluation period about fixed objectives for the next month, quarter, or year. At the end of that period, the supervisor measures the extent to which the objectives are met. This system allows the employee to participate in the definition of performance standards.

Faculty and administrative evaluations often also include a self-evaluation segment, which allows the employee to examine and evaluate his or her performance on the job. (For details on self-evaluation, see Herman, 1973; Baird, 1979; and Millman, 1981.) The evaluation of faculty performance may also include student evaluations. There exists considerable disagreement, however, regarding the weight to be placed on student evaluations. Similarly, the evaluation of supervisory employees may include an evaluation by their subordinates. This approach can both encourage communication and improve supervisory skills.

How Important Is the Performance Evaluation Form?

Although considerable attention needs to be given to preparation of a performance evaluation form, the form itself is probably the least significant part of the total performance evaluation process. The form should be designed to facilitate the purposes of the performance evaluation program and the institutional objectives.

In designing a performance evaluation form, one should seek contributions and suggestions from all sections of the institution and perhaps examine a number of forms used by other institutions with similar missions and objectives. Exhibits 47, 48, and 49, pp. 220–232, present sample performance evaluation instruments for faculty, managerial and professional, and secretarial-clerical employees, respectively. For more details on performance evaluation forms, see Bouchard (1980b).

How Should the Performance Evaluation Be Conducted?

The most important aspect of the performance evaluation process is the evaluator's interview with the faculty or staff member who has been evaluated. One of the ultimate goals of performance evaluation is that the employee understand the ways in which he or she can improve his or her performance. In order to achieve this goal, the evaluator needs to be well prepared and should try to have documented evidence of the items to be covered during the interview. Prior to the interview, the evaluator must have decided what the interview is to accomplish. In addition to reviewing the employee's performance history, the evaluator should have suggestions for improving any evident deficiencies in performance. The evaluator should be able to outline a suggested developmental plan that represents the first step toward improving deficiencies.

The interview should be focused on the employee's performance, not on personal traits. For example, to inform an employee that he is inclined to be stubborn may only evoke a defensive response, such as "I am not stubborn." However, to explain incidents wherein the employee's resistant behavior affected performance, for example, by alienating colleagues and causing disharmony, is to indicate specific ways in which certain behavior is counterproductive.

The interview should be a conversation rather than a lecture. The evaluator should listen to the employee and not argue. The interview provides an occasion for the employee to point out that the supervisor may be ineffective in creating an atmosphere in which excellent work can be accomplished. The evaluator should inform the faculty or staff member of the expectations of the position and how well he or she meets these expectations. If improvements are called for, the faculty or staff member should be encouraged to follow suggested programs for improvement.

If these items are covered, if the interview is uninterrupted by other extraneous business, if cool heads prevailed, and if good relationships are built between the evaluator and the employee, the interview should have positive results. Exhibit 50, p. 233, presents a list of do's and don'ts for performance evaluation interviews.

What Are the Pitfalls of Performance Evaluation?

Objectivity is the goal of most approaches to performance evaluation. To maintain a high degree of objectivity, the evaluator must try to control certain subjective responses that may induce errors. Let us consider each of six subjective responses that threaten objectivity.

The error of the "halo effect." Supervisors often appraise an employee in terms of their own attitude toward the employee rather than by careful attention to the individual factors of work performance. Supervisors should try to put their feelings about the employee aside to notice that the employee who is a nice person may still do poor work. The opposite of the "halo effect"— downgrading an employee one does not like but whose work is good—is also an error.

The error of prejudice and partiality. To consider race, creed, color, religion, politics, nationality, or sex in appraising work performance is not only an error of judgment but also a violation of the employee's constitutional rights.

The error of leniency. Supervisors are often too lenient; indeed leniency is probably the most common error in performance evaluation. Leniency usually results from a supervisor's unwillingness to face the unpleasantness that might arise from an unfavorable appraisal. But leniency toward poor employees is unfair to good employees, as the clustering of ratings at the top of the scale renders a top rating valueless. Supervisorial leniency also gives poor employees an unearned feeling of success and thus hinders their improvement in performance. Many supervisors believe that low ratings reflect poorly on their supervision; thus, above standard ratings may become defenses for the supervisor.

The error of the central tendency. On a normal distribution curve, more scores are near the mean than any other point on the scale. To give a rating that is near the norm is an error if it does not reflect true performance. The error is most likely to occur when a supervisor is careless about the rating or does not know the employee well. A standard rating for unusually good or poor performance is unfair to the employee and to coworkers.

The error of employee potential. The performance evaluation should measure the employee's accomplishments in relation to the position and not reflect a subjective judgment of the employee's potential.

The error of association. In the process of rating, busy supervisors may rate an employee's performance as uniform in all ways rather than differentiating those qualities that are unusually good or poor. Although an overall evaluation is required, supervisors should independently evaluate various aspects of the employee's performance and specify these aspects to the employee.

Exhibit 41. Sample Performance Standards for a Faculty Member

Responsibility (percentage of assignment)	*Standards*
Teach three sections of History 10 and 14 (75 percent).	• Meet all class sections on time. • Advise and assist students during regularly scheduled office hours. • Update lecture materials regularly. • Develop, administer, and score examinations focused on learning experiences. • Provide timely and constructive feedback to students about examination results. • Lecture effectively. • Facilitate class discussions and self-directed learning. • Cover the course material as outlined in the syllabus and catalogue. • Effectively use a variety of media and instructional methods for clarity of presentation and to generate and maintain student interest.

Note: A full statement of performance standards would follow this format for each responsibility or duty assigned to the faculty member.

Exhibit 42. Sample Performance Standards for a Clerical Position

Duties	*Standards*
1. Type letters, memos, reports, manuals, and the like from handwritten drafts and machine dictation.	• Less than 5 percent of work is returned because of typing, spelling, or punctuation errors. • Erasures are clean without smudges. Copy is neatly arranged on page. Insertions and deletions are accurate. • Correct number of copies are made. • Less than 5 percent of work is returned because of poor proofreading. • Attachments called for are present. • Work is completed within one day.
2. Handle telephone reception.	• Answer telephone within three rings. • Record messages accurately. • Deliver messages on time. • Treat callers courteously and provide accurate information.

Note: A full statement of performance standards would follow this format for each responsibility or duty assigned to the clerical employee.

**Exhibit 43. Sample Performance Standards for a Supervisor of
Building Maintenance**

Duties	*Standards*
1. Supervise labor details in construction, maintenance, and repair work.	• See that correct work methods are used. • See that impartial and fair discipline is maintained over employees. • See that proper safety measures are followed (evidence: good safety record). • See that tools and equipment receive correct care (evidence: infrequent replacements).
2. Plan and lay out work to be done.	• Resolve priority problems with care. • Lay out work, materials, and tools so that employees have minimal lost time. • Complete jobs within deadlines.

Note: A full statement of performance standards would follow this format for each responsibility or duty assigned to the supervisory employee.

Exhibit 44. Guidelines for Policy on Probationary Periods

Simply stated, the probationary or provisional period of employment is the initial period following appointment during which a disciplinary or dismissal action may take place without the faculty or staff member having recourse to a grievance procedure. An exception to this restriction would be an employee's claim of discrimination under civil rights legislation.

Although an employee is learning the job during the probationary period, the learning process may take longer than the probationary period specified in the policy. Therefore, a learning period is different from and may rightfully exceed a probationary period.

The probationary period is an important time in the relationship between the employee and the supervisor and thus becomes an important institutional policy. It is a period of adjustment between an employee and the employer.

Policy items and sample policy language:

The period may be called by several different names: probationary status, provisional appointment, trial period of employment, introductory period, probationary period.

The purpose of a probationary period is usually defined: "The probationary period shall be utilized by the department head for observing closely the employee's work, for securing the most effective adjustment of the new employee to his or her position, to the persons with whom he or she comes in contact, and to unfamiliar surroundings. It serves as a means of rejecting an employee whose performance does not meet required standards. This is the period in which a new employee tries the job and is in turn tried in its performance." "The first three calendar months of employment will be considered as temporary for the purpose of performance evaluation of classified employees." "All classified employees are required to serve on a provisional basis to provide the employer an opportunity to evaluate the employee's performance." "This period provides for job adjustment and an opportunity for both the employee and the university to determine whether or not to continue the relationship." "Continued employment of new staff employees is contingent upon satisfactory completion of an initial trial period of employment." "This period is used for observation of one's work by his or her supervisors and to permit one to adjust to his or her job and working conditions."

The length of the period can be expressed in months, days, workdays, and the like: "An employee is a probationary employee for the first three months of employment." "All new employees are considered to be in a probationary status for ninety days from date of employment or transfer." "The trial period normally is six months." "The first three calendar months of employment will be considered as temporary." "Newly hired employees shall be considered on a probationary status for a period of forty-five working days from the date of employment."

Normally only one probationary period is worked for an institution; however, some institutions require more than one: "If a probationary employee bids and is accepted on a new job with a different job title, the employee will serve on a new probationary period." "Employees promoted to a higher-rated position shall serve a probationary period in the new position. (This policy provides the right to the former job if the employee fails on the new job during the probationary period.)" "At any time during employment, an employee may be placed on probation up to a maximum of thirty days for unsatisfactory conduct or service, upon written approval of the area head."

The original probationary period may be lengthened under certain conditions: "One calendar day will be added to the probationary period for each scheduled day not worked. The probationary period may not be extended except as a result of absence from work." "The original probationary period may be extended an additional ninety days upon approval of the area head." " . . . a probationary period of thirty working days exclusive of vacations, leaves of absence and sick leave." "With approval of the personnel office, this trial period can be extended for an additional period not to exceed thirty days, and written notice of such extension will be given to the employee."

The employer usually may dismiss an employee during the probationary period without restriction from other procedures, such as a formal disciplinary procedure or a grievance procedure: "During the period, the university may discharge the probationary employee without being subject to the grievance procedure." "The employee's employment may be terminated for any reason at any time during the probationary period." "A probationary employee may not use the grievance procedure." "There is no obligation to continue employment through the probationary period. Supervisors are responsible for initiating termination or transfer if a staff member's performance is not acceptable." "At any time during the probationary period one may resign without prejudice, or the university may terminate the services without the usual two weeks' notice." "Should the work not be satisfactory, the employee will be notified in writing by his or her supervisor prior to the completion of the six months' provisional period, and the employee may be terminated at such time without right of appeal."

Some procedures require a formal performance evaluation prior to the end of a probationary period: "The supervisor receives a probationary review form from the personnel department, discusses the performance with the employee, completes the review form indicating whether performance is satisfactory. The completed form is returned to the personnel depart-

Exhibit 44 (continued)

ment." "During the trial period and three or four weeks before the end of the trial period, the new employee's immediate supervisor arranges evaluation conferences to review the quality and quantity of work performed and the employee's working habits. A record of the final evaluation conference is prepared by the supervisor. One copy is reviewed by the department head and retained in the department file. One copy is given to the employee, and one is sent to the personnel office." "Probationary employees are evaluated by the immediate supervisor at regular intervals." "These evaluations will be in writing and discussed with the employee."

Some procedures mention performance evaluation, but not in a formal manner: "Prior to the end of the probationary period, a determination should be made whether to retain the employee." "Prior to the end of this probationary period, the employee must be evaluated by his or her supervisor and a specific recommendation made for his or her continued employment beyond the probationary period."

The subject of benefits received by employees during the probationary period is sometimes covered: "Participation in fringe benefits starts in accordance with the sections pertaining to each benefit even though the probationary period has not expired." "Probationary staff members may utilize all staff benefits with the exception of vacation which may not be utilized until the completion of three months of service." "All university policies and conditions of employment except the use of the grievance procedure shall be applicable during the probationary period."

Some policies include a statement about seniority: "After the completion of the probationary period, seniority shall be effective as of the original date of employment." "A probationary employee shall have no seniority (except as otherwise provided in this agreement) until he or she has completed the probationary period. Upon the completion of the probationary period, he or she will acquire seniority from the date of hire."

Source: College and University Personnel Association (1980b, pp. 1–5).

Exhibit 45. Sample Promotion/Tenure Recommendation Form

Recommendation form for promotion to the ranks of professor, librarian, associate professor, associate librarian, and senior research associate.

Date _____

Name	Social Security No.	Promotion ☐	Tenure ☐
Present rank and title	College	Department	

Graduate faculty status	Rank and date of initial appointment to the university	
☐ Senior member	Rank and date of appointment to tenure eligible position	
☐ Associate member	Years of credit granted toward tenure at appointment to tenure eligible position	
	Previous promotions	
☐ Nonmember		
	Rank	Date
Proposed rank and title	Tenure status as of effective date of promotion	

Unit	Recommended	Not Recommended	Signature	Date
Check One				
Department	☐	☐	Chairperson—Department review committee	
	☐	☐	Department head	
College	☐	☐	Chairperson—College review committee	
	☐	☐	Dean	
University	☐	☐	Chairperson—university promotion and tenure review committee.	
	☐	☐	University provost	
	Approved ☐	Disapproved ☐	University president	

Exhibit 46. Biographical Data for Promotion/Tenure Review

I.

Last Name	First name and initial	
Exact title of position	College	Work location
	Department	

II. Academic Training

Name and address of institution	Major subjects	Minor subjects	Degrees—Dates
Under-graduate			
Under-graduate			
Graduate school			
Other			

Professional status—Law, CPA, other degrees or licenses held   Honorary degree(s)—Institution

III. Occupational Record

Previous employers with addresses, including U.S. military (most recent first)	Work Performed; if teacher, list subjects taught	Rank or title	Dates
			From / To
			From / To
			From / To
			From / To

IV. Previous sabbaticals

Activity or Project	*Results*; Publications, Reports, and the like	Dates

_____   _____

(Signature)   Date

Exhibit 47. Faculty Performance Evaluation Form

Department _____

Faculty member's name _____

Rank _____

Please check the appropriate block to reflect your objective opinion of the faculty member's performance in carrying out responsibilities. The evaluation should reflect performance for the past year. Refer to the instructions for use of this Form before making your evaluations. Answer each evaluation criterion independently.

Criteria   *Evaluation*

(See instructions for   (Mark an *X* below the appropriate evaluation
description of criteria.)   in accordance with the descriptions of the
                                 evaluations presented in the instructions.
                                 Mark only those that apply.)

Teaching effectiveness

1.0	1.5	2.0	2.5	3.0	3.5	4.0

Research contribution

1.0	1.5	2.0	2.5	3.0	3.5	4.0

Continuing education
contribution

1.0	1.5	2.0	2.5	3.0	3.5	4.0

Service contribution

1.0	1.5	2.0	2.5	3.0	3.5	4.0

Scholarship and
professional growth

1.0	1.5	2.0	2.5	3.0	3.5	4.0

Overall Evaluation _____

The overall evaluation is determined by reviewing each of the evaluations assigned and making a subjective judgment as to the appropriate overall evaluation. Care should be exercised in relating the applicability of each evaluation criterion to the individual being evaluated in relation to approximate time spent on that activity. The result should give emphasis to the activity on which most time is spent. For consistency, the overall evaluation should be on the same scale of 1.0 to 4.0.

Date _____

_____

(Signature of the evaluator)

INSTRUCTIONS:

The performance of each faculty member is evaluated on a scale from 1.0 to 4.0 on five criteria on a form provided for the purpose.

The evaluation form is designed to evaluate the faculty member's performance giving emphasis to major assignments. For example, if the faculty member is primarily a teacher, teaching should receive the most weight. If a particular criterion does not apply, it should be omitted in the evaluation.

To facilitate consistency in interpreting the criteria and evaluations, the following definitions are provided:

Evaluations:

Indication of level of performance on a scale from 1.0 to 4.0 using the academic unit as the reference group.

3.5 or 4.0	Superior performance of assigned duties
2.0, 2.5, or 3.0	Average performance of assigned duties
1.0 or 1.5	Below average performance of assigned duties

Criteria:

Teaching Effectiveness. The ability to make students think critically and purposefully. The ability to interest students in the problems of the course, the ability to construct effective instruments of evaluation and to interpret the results impartially, the ability to maintain sound academic standards, and the ability to lead students in the development of research models and the conduct of research. Consider activities such as modification of courses or syllabi and consider effectiveness in the academic advising of students.

Research Contribution. The creativity and originality of research contributions together with an evaluative judgment relating to the general importance of the contribution and the potential basis for future work in the same or related fields. Consider the publications of the findings of research efforts. Consideration should be given, also, to patents, works of art, performances, scientific achievements, and the like, together with an

Exhibit 47 (continued)

evaluation of how the contributions are received by peers in the professional field. Consideration may be given to the number and amount of grants obtained.

Continuing Education Contribution. The leadership exercised in bringing the forefronts of knowledge to the practitioners through such means as short courses, special seminars, in-plant training, and participation in other continuing education activities such as corresponding courses, unit courses, and the like.

Service Contribution. The contributions of the faculty member to students, the university, and the community. Consider activities such as committee work, community and government service, professional society activities, and administrative duties performed for the department or the university. Evaluate the influence on students through activities such as counseling, work with student organizations, and the like.

Scholarship and Professional Growth. Academic preparation together with evidence of continuing scholarly growth from courses or seminars attended, written works both published and unpublished (such as texts, monographs, articles, creative works), participation in professional organizations. Consider the individual's relationship with the current state of knowledge in his or her professional field.

In evaluating the individual's performance against the criteria, consider accomplishments over the last year. Consider each of the criterion independently.

Exhibit 48. Performance Evaluation for Managerial and Professional Employees

Name _____ Soc. Sec. No. _____ Position no. _____
Agency name _____ Sub. division _____ Agency code _____
Class title _____ Class code _____ Date entered present position _____
Date of evaluation _____
Describe briefly the principal duties in present job _____

The following performance evaluation is designed to measure the performance of managerial and professional employees. Where management by objectives is established in an agency, the employee should be evaluated on those predetermined and predefined goals or objectives. These goals or objectives should be approved in advance and identified in writing. In cases where management by objectives is not established, the supervisor should identify the major duties and responsibilities of the job and evaluate the employee accordingly. In still other cases, there may be special assignments performed by the employee as assigned by the supervisor. When evaluating such an employee, the supervisor should identify on the performance evaluation form those major projects, job duties, and special assignments that are important to the overall performance of the operation and the employee.

PART I: List five major predetermined goals or objectives on which the employee is to be evaluated. Where predetermined goals and objectives are not used, the employee should be evaluated on projects, job duties, and special assignments. Circle the appropriate performance level.

1. Goal/objective/project/major job duty/special assignment _____   4   3   2   1

2. Goal/objective/project/major job duty/special assignment _____   4   3   2   1

Exhibit 48 (continued)

3. Goal/objective/project/major job duty/special assignment _____

     4   3   2   1

4. Goal/objective/project/major job duty/special assignment _____

     4   3   2   1

5. Goal/objective/project/major job duty/special assignment _____

     4   3   2   1

PART II: Performance Factors—The following performance factors tend to reinforce the performance levels identified in Part I. *The supervisor in completing Part II should indicate the employee's performance level by circling the appropriate level of performance.* Use the remarks section to record your comments.

1. *WORK HABITS.* To what extent does the employee demonstrate adaptability and a sense of priorities?

     4   3   2   1

Remarks _____

2. *PLANNING AND ANALYTICAL ABILITY.* To what extent does the employee demonstrate the skills to analyze and solve problems?

4 3 2 1

Remarks

3. *MANAGERIAL SKILLS.* To what extent does the employee effectively work well with and through others to complete assignments in a timely and productive manner?

4 3 2 1

Remarks

4. *COMMUNICATIONS SKILLS.* To what extent can the employee effectively express himself or herself orally and in writing including correspondence and reports and presentations at conferences, seminars, workshops, as required by the job?

4 3 2 1

Exhibit 48 (continued)

Remarks _____

	4	3	2	1

5. *DEVELOPMENT OF OTHERS*. To what extent does the employee develop others to become more effective in work assignments and better prepared for future job opportunities?

Remarks _____

Determining the Overall Evaluation: Add the numbers circled in Parts I and II. Divide the total by ten to determine the overall evaluation. Indicate the overall evaluation score by circling, or inserting and circling, the overall evaluation score on the scale provided.

Performance Levels

		Scale
		4.00
Employee's performance regularly exceeds the job requirements.	(3.50 and above)	3.75
		3.50
		3.25
Employee's performance meets normal job requirements on a sustained basis.	(2.75 to 3.49)	3.00
		2.75
		2.50

Employee's performance reflects that there is a need for improvement on a sustained basis. (2.00 to 2.74)

2.25
2.00

Employee's performance fails to meet the job requirements. (1.99 and below)

1.75
1.50
1.25

Supervisor's comments concerning the overall evaluation:

PART III—Developmental Trends:

1. *Significant changes.* Indicate any significant changes in performance since the employee's last evaluation.

2. *Development and training.* Indicate recommendations for further development and training for purposes of preparing the employee for additional responsibilities or for the improvement of current job performance.

Identify any training or developmental activities the employee has completed since his or her last performance evaluation. Such training was (*check one*) taken as a result of the supervisor's recommendation _____ , or the employee's initiative _____ .

Exhibit 48 (continued)

Evaluated by ———————————————— Title ————

Reviewed by ———————————————— Title ————

To the employee:
You are requested to sign on the line provided below to indicate only that you have had an opportunity to review and discuss your performance evaluation with your supervisor. *Your signature does not indicate that you agree with the evaluation.*

Employee's comments:

Employee's Signature ———————————————————— Date ————

Note: Performance Levels: 4 = exceeds normal job requirements, 3 = meets normal job requirements, 2 = improvement is needed to meet job requirements, 1 = fails to meet job requirements. Acceptable satisfactory performance requires an average rating of 2.75, when rated goals, objectives, and performance factors are combined.

Exhibit. 49. Performance Evaluation for Secretarial-Clerical Employees

College or administrative unit _____ Date started at university _____

Title and code number _____ Date started this position _____

Reason for evaluation:

☐ Probationary period _____ step increase movement from _____ step to _____ step

☐ Interim evaluation (first year following C or B step)

☐ Other _____

Appraisal Factors

A. Quality of work—Neatness, accuracy, thoroughness.

☐ Performs poorly. Makes frequent mistakes. Generally unsatisfactory.

☐ Does minimally acceptable work. Accuracy and finish of final product often need revision or correction.

☐ Work meets acceptable standards. Makes only occasional mistakes.

☐ Work is above average. Seldom makes errors.

☐ Work is of exceptionally high quality. Consistently thorough and accurate.

Comments: _____

B. Quantity of work—Volume of work regularly produced; consistency of output and speed.

☐ Produces consistently high volume of work. Extremely productive and fast.

☐ Volume of work frequently above expected level.

☐ Does normal amount of work. Volume is satisfactory. When situation requires, production increases markedly.

☐ Volume is generally below what is expected. Does just enough to get by.

☐ Does not meet minimum requirements. Volume of work generally unsatisfactory.

Comments: _____

Exhibit 49 (continued)

C. Job knowledge and learning ability—Degree of understanding of the job and related functions. Rapidity with which the employee has developed.

☐ Complete mastery of all phases of job and related functions. Grasps new methods and procedures immediately. Extremely rapid learner.
☐ Excellent understanding of job and related work. Well informed. Learns quickly.
☐ Adequate knowledge of the job. Can answer most questions. Able to learn new aspects of job.
☐ Lacks knowledge of some phases of work. Experiences difficulty in grasping new ideas.
☐ Poor understanding of job. Fails to grasp new ideas.
Comments: _____

D. Judgment and initiative—Problem-solving capabilities. Ability to analyze facts and circumstances, recognize need for action, and take constructive steps to resolve problems within the limits of established boundaries. Degree of supervision required.

☐ Misinterprets the facts. Fails to take independent action. Makes decisions without regard for consequences. Requires very close supervision.
☐ Recognizes facts only partially. Makes errors in judgment. Seldom acts independently. Requires fairly close supervision.
☐ Good common sense. Generally makes sound decisions. Able to act independently. Moderate degree of supervision required.
☐ Decisions are logical and sound. Frequently takes independent action. Requires only occasional supervision.
☐ Exceptional problem-solving ability. Highly logical. A real self-starter. Minimal supervision required.
Comments: _____

E. Dependability and reliability—Ability to meet deadlines. Punctuality and attendance.

☐ Unreliable. Rarely meets deadlines. Often absent or late.
☐ Sometimes requires prompting. Frequently fails to meet deadlines. Occasionally absent or late.
☐ Takes care of necessary tasks and completes with reasonable promptness. Usually present and punctual.
☐ Exceeds normal work demands. Almost always present and punctual.
☐ Exceptionally dependable. Carries out assignments promptly and efficiently. Always present and punctual.
Comments: _____

F. Attitude and cooperation—Effect upon and willingness to work with and for others. Flexibility, courtesy.

☐ Exceptionally courteous and cooperative. Consistently striving for higher level of achievement.
☐ Above average degree of courtesy. Highly cooperative. Shows high level of interest.
☐ Interested in work. Demonstrates desire to improve. Courteous and cooperative.
☐ Lacks courtesy. Shows limited or sporadic interest in work.
☐ Discourteous and uncooperative. Exhibits disinterest in work.
Comments: _____

G. Supervisory ability—COMPLETE ONLY FOR INDIVIDUALS WITH SUPERVISORY RESPONSIBILITY—Leadership, ability to train and motivate. Ability to communicate.

☐ Exhibits little supervisory capabilities. Inadequately trains and motivates employees. Unable to obtain cooperation or desired results.
☐ Has some difficulty in training and motivating employees. Needs additional development in this area.
☐ Adequately trains and motivates subordinates. Exhibits leadership capabilities.
☐ Generates good work climate. Recognizes and develops individual potential in employees.
☐ Exceptional ability to train, develop and motivate subordinates. Maximizes employee potential.
Comments: _____

Exhibit 49 (continued)

H. Overall evaluation—Composite appraisal of employee's total performance of duties.

☐ Exceptional.
☐ Exceeds requirements.
☐ Meets requirements.
☐ Minimally meets requirements.
☐ Inadequate.
Comments: _____

Summary statement: _____
_____
_____
_____
_____

Employee's comments: _____
_____
_____
_____

Supervisor's signature _____ Date _____
Reviewed by _____ Date _____
*Employee's signature _____ Date _____

*My signature indicates only that the evaluation has been reviewed with me. It does not necessarily signify my concurrence.

Exhibit 50. Performance Evaluation Interview: Do's and Don'ts

Do's

Do maintain ongoing (year round) communication with employees that provides specific performance standards and both positive and negative feedback.

Do establish an appointment time with employee several days in advance of the interview.

Do provide the employee with an explanation of performance evaluation procedures at the beginning of employment and at the time the interview is established.

Do arrange for a private meeting place to reduce or eliminate interruptions.

Do be prepared to devote an adequate period of time (twenty minutes to one hour) to the interview.

Do begin the interview by establishing a friendly rapport with the employee.

Do encourage two-way communication during the interview.

Do discuss past performance.

Do discuss the employee's strengths and weaknesses and possible areas for improvements.

Do allow the employee to voice feelings about the strengths and weaknesses of the supervision he or she receives.

Do determine how the employee feels about his or her work assignment and work load.

Do be open to changing the ratings on the evaluation form if the employee presents evidence that warrants doing so.

Do develop mutually agreeable action plans to increase the employee's knowledge and skills and improve performance.

Don'ts

Don't rate all employees identically.

Don't use the evaluation interview as an opportunity to provide an entire year's worth of negative feedback.

Don't wait until the time of the interview to complete the evaluation form.

Don't allow interruptions from others during the interview.

Don't dominate the conversation.

Don't discuss salary increases during the evaluation interview.

Don't let the interview deteriorate into an argument.

Don't neglect to discuss the employee's perceptions of the organization's and department's goals.

Don't forget to obtain the employee's signature on the evaluation form at the conclusion of the interview, even if he or she disagrees with its content.

Don't change ratings on the form in order to appease an employee.

Don't change ratings on the evaluation form after employee has signed it.

❦ 12 ❦

Formulating Retirement, Resignation, Retrenchment, and Disability Policies

Personnel policies are needed to govern the severance of employment. Severance occurs as a result of retirement, voluntary termination, dismissal for cause, retrenchment, death, illness leading to disability, and layoff. Policies are needed for each of these situations, particularly for those in which severance results from an employee's inadequate performance or disability. In the absence of a clear policy, any inconsistencies that occur may lead to grievances and litigation. Dismissal for cause is discussed in Chapter Thirteen. This chapter is devoted to retirement, resignation, retrenchment, and disability.

234

What Should a Retirement Policy Include?

An institution's retirement policy must comply with the Age Discrimination in Employment Act of 1967, as amended in 1978 (see Chapters Six and Eight). Prior to the 1978 amendments, most institutions stipulated mandatory retirement at age sixty-five or sixty-eight. In response to the new laws, some institutions offer enticements for early retirement. Academic administrators may favor early retirement for faculty in order to facilitate the flow of new ideas in their disciplines. Nonacademic administrators may favor it so that they need not retain modest producers who are past their prime.

Three incentive plans for early retirement are:

1. Pension supplements. In return for a faculty member's agreement to retire early, the institution agrees to make additional payments to or on behalf of the faculty member. These additional payments may include severance pay, the payment of a percentage of the individual's salary for a fixed period of time, or the purchase of a supplemental annuity plan for the individual.
2. Phased retirement. The individual is offered a reduction to less than full-time employment at a reduced salary for a fixed period of time. The employer's pension contributions may be continued at the rate appropriate to the former full-time salary and may be escalated annually to adjust for estimated salary increases.
3. Reemployment on a consulting basis. In return for an individual's agreement to retire early, the institution agrees to hire the individual on a consulting basis for fixed periods of time.

Institutions are now developing other incentive plans. One common theme is the continuance of faculty and staff benefits during the period of early retirement.

Most of the plans are too new to be judged as effective or ineffective in accomplishing their goals. Some institutions have discovered that some excellent senior faculty members have chosen early retirement, and thus these institutions lost faculty members whom they did not want to lose. Careful evaluation of that possibility must be explored before initiating such a program. Of course, these institutions were able to retire some nonproductive faculty as well.

Institutions should undertake a cost study to determine the cost of offering the incentive and the savings realized by retiring a highly paid professor and hiring a lower-paid assistant professor as a replacement. Institutions should also study the ages at which faculty and staff members retire voluntarily. Such a study may offer some surprises and guidance about the advisability of introducing incentives for early retirement. An institution that has excellent retirement plans and other benefits for retirees may find that many faculty and staff members retire considerably before the mandatory retirement age, and thus there is no need to provide incentives.

Many institutions award emeritus rank to designate an honorary position for distinguished faculty members upon their retirement. Institutions should have a written policy that specifies who is eligible for the emeritus rank, who grants emeritus rank, and what privileges are granted to recipients. Exhibit 51, p. 241 presents a sample policy for the emeritus rank. For more details on emeritus rank and retirement see Dorfman (1979).

When Should Preretirement Counseling Begin?

Individuals in their fifties should begin planning for their retirement. Institutions should consider offering a series of preretirement counseling sessions for such individuals. These counseling sessions should cover both the financial and psychological aspects of retirement, since retirement can be traumatic for most people. Questions such as the following are on the minds of potential retirees: Will I have enough money on which to live? How should I handle a will? Should I establish a trust fund? If so, what kind? What health care benefits will I have? How does Medicare work? What will my pension be? What will Social Security provide? Should I sell my home or stay where I am? How will my dependents be cared for if something happens to me? What will my tax situation be? How am I going to spend my time on a day-to-day basis after retirement?

While individuals have to answer many of these questions on their own, personnel departments should provide faculty and staff members with the means to consider various alternatives. Meetings with small groups of faculty and staff members who are similarly situated are usually most effective. The questions raised by members of the group add to the knowledge of the total group. For details on retirement planning, see Garrison and England (1979).

What Notice Should Be Required Prior to Resignation?

Statistics show that most faculty and staff members voluntarily leave an institution for employment elsewhere prior to retirement age. An institution should develop and disseminate a resignation policy so that faculty and staff members who are contemplating leaving will know what is expected of them. The policy should stipulate the amount of notice required and the manner in which such notice is to be given.

The amount of notice required should depend on the category and occupational field of the employee. The higher the level of the position, the longer the notice should be. For example, the policy for faculty and senior officers might require four months' notice, whereas that for clerical employees might require two weeks' notice. Administrative employees might be required to give one month's notice. Of course, if a faculty or staff member does not give timely notice of resignation, the institution has no recourse. However, in order to maintain a good relationship for the future, most faculty and staff members will try to provide the required notice.

Written notice should be required from faculty, senior staff officers, and administrative personnel, but not necessarily from service employees or clerical employees. A letter should be required at the higher levels to avoid misunderstandings, changes of intentions, and possible litigation. Exhibit 52, p. 242, offers a sample policy on resignation.

What Should a Policy Regarding Retrenchment Include?

Most institutions have policies that govern retrenchment of nonfaculty employees. Such policies, usually called layoff policies, specify (1) a definition of a layoff; (2) the amount of notice required; and (3) priority for selection of employees for layoff. Normally, length of service plays a major role in selection of employees for layoff. Length of service may be defined to include only employment in the particular unit in which retrenchment occurs or institutionwide service. Layoff policies sometimes describe bumping systems and may include a statement about alternate employment. Such policies also discuss benefits eligibility and provisions for recall. Most layoff policies cover temporary and recurring layoffs, such as summer layoffs for food service employees, as well as permanent reduction in the staff. Exhibit 53, pp. 242–244 presents a sample policy on reduction in force.

In contrast, little has been done in higher education in regard to addressing the prospect of faculty retrenchment. Most institutions do not have policies for faculty retrenchment other than the statement about financial exigency contained in their tenure regulations. All institutions should develop contingent plans for faculty retrenchment, for in the absence of a policy, how would dismissals proceed? Should it be assumed that the first to be fired would be part-time faculty, followed by nontenured full-time faculty, followed by tenured faculty? Would such a plan provide proper and cost-effective course coverage?

A retrenchment policy should also answer the following questions: What rights do those dismissed during retrenchment have? Do they have the right to retraining? For how long are their positions held for them? Are all their benefits cut immediately upon their dismissal? Should length of service be a controlling factor in deciding which faculty members are dismissed? What effect will retrenchment have on the institution's affirmative action policy?

A retrenchment policy should speak to those issues and perhaps to the criteria to be used in considering which units will be cut. Reductions in a given academic unit range from reduction in the numbers of sections of a course offered to reduction in the number of elective courses or in the number of subdisciplines or disciplines to elimination of the entire academic unit. Some institutions find that eliminating an entire field causes fewer personnel problems than cutting subdisciplines or courses in many departments. For detailed discussions of faculty retrenchment, see College and University Personnel Association (1980c), Pondrum (1980), Johnstone (1980), and Bouchard (1980a).

What Policies Are Needed for Absences
Due to Accident or Illness?

In the absence of specific policies covering absences for accident or illness, individual administrators and supervisors will make decisions that may be inconsistent and unfair. An institutional policy should stipulate: (1) how long an individual will be paid during an absence; (2) following paid time off, how long an individual will be granted official leave without pay; (3) how long the institution's benefits plan will be available to individuals on leave without pay and whether additional charges will be made; and (4) how long the individual will have to reclaim his or her position.

Some institutions provide insurance plans that cover absence due to illness. However, most institutions grant employees time off with pay for illness. The amount of paid sick leave may be a set annual amount (for example, employees with up to five years of service receive twenty days in a calendar year) or it may be earned and accumulated monthly (for example, for each full month of employment, an employee accumulates one day of sick leave which may be accumulated indefinitely if not used).

Sick leave policies should stipulate that the time be used for illness of the faculty or staff member. (Some few institutions allow usage for illness in the immediate family.) Accumulated sick leave is a form of insurance to be used only if needed. Some institutions pay employees for unused sick leave as an incentive against the abuse of sick leave. However, the authors are not aware of instances in which such payoffs have changed appreciably the habits of abusers of sick leave. Employees should be encouraged through supervision to save their sick leave for the times of serious illness. Close supervisory attention to the problems of abuse is usually the most effective deterrent. Heavy usage of sick leave in a particular unit deserves special attention. It may be a symptom of morale problems or overstaffing. It is easy to be absent if the work lacks challenge, the human relations climate is unhealthy, or the employee feels that he or she will not really be missed. Sick leave usage studies should be made by unit for comparative purposes.

For terminally ill or seriously injured faculty or staff members, disability retirement should be considered. Some institutions have long-term disability insurance programs, and disability provisions may be found under federal social security, retirement plan provisions, and within the institution's life insurance program as well.

Should Exit Interviews Be Held?

As employees leave, they should be asked about their reasons for leaving and for information about the institution as an employer. Obviously, a personal interview is most beneficial, but an exit interview form or questionnaire is satisfactory. Exhibit 54, pp. 245–248, presents a sample exit questionnaire.

By collecting information from departing employees, the institution will acquire information useful in improving the institution's human relations environment; for example, training needs, inadequate physical facilities, poor supervision, lack of attention to institutional policies, lack of a competitive pay structure, lack of opportunity for advancement, needs for additional faculty and staff benefits, and areas with too heavy or too light a workload.

Exhibit 51. Policy on Emeritus Rank

Normal eligibility:

Emeritus rank is granted in recognition of meritorious service to the university. It may be granted upon retirement to those holding the rank of full professor, to those university personnel classified as executives, to associate deans, or to directors of academic units. To be eligible, individuals in the above ranks or positions must have held the title at the university for a period of at least five years prior to retirement from the university.

Procedure for granting emeritus rank:

During the first week of April each year, a memorandum concerning recommendations for emeritus rank is distributed by the Office of Personnel Administration to the deans and the appropriate members of the president's staff. On May 1 each year, a summary of the responses is provided to the president. Prior to submitting the summary to the president, reviews are conducted by the Office of Personnel Administration to insure that each individual appearing on the list is eligible for emeritus consideration. Recommendations made at other times of the year should be forwarded to the Office of Personnel Administration for action. The same review procedures described herein shall apply.

Approval of emeritus rank:

Emeritus rank may be granted by the president to individuals who are eligible upon the recommendation of the appropriate officer. Emeritus rank may be granted to the president by the Board of Trustees.

Notification of approval of emeritus rank:

Notifications of approval are submitted to the Board of Trustees for information purposes. Simultaneous with the material being sent to the Board of Trustees, a letter and a certificate is sent by the president to each retiree being named to an emeritus rank. Copies of these letters are sent to the appropriate administrative officers who originated the requests for emeritus rank and to the Office of Personnel Administration. Public news releases will be made announcing the names of retirees who have been granted emeritus rank after the names are presented to the Board of Trustees for its information.

Privileges of emeritus rank:

The following privileges are available to a retiree of emeritus rank in addition to those privileges normally available to the retired faculty member: (1) listing in the faculty directory, (2) receipt of the university weekly newsletter, (3) registration of a vehicle for parking on campus, and (4) use of appropriate university facilities.

Exhibit 52. Policy on Resignation from University Employment

For faculty members:

Notification of resignation by a university faculty member is expected to be early enough to obviate serious embarrassment to the institution. The faculty member shall, therefore, give not less than four months' notice of resignation. For faculty members who teach, it is expected that such resignation from employment shall be effective at the end of a fiscal year. Thus, in any particular year, the final date for tendering a resignation for a faculty member who teaches is March 1 to be effective June 30.

A faculty member on the staff of this university may inquire into and consider the acceptance of an appointment elsewhere at any time and without previous consultation with his or her superiors. It is agreed, however, that if a definite offer follows he or she shall not accept it without giving such notice as is indicated in the preceding provision. The faculty member is at liberty to ask superior officers to reduce, or waive, the notification requirements there specified, but he or she is expected to conform to their decision on these points.

For clerical or service employees:

Under normal circumstances, an employee is expected to give two calendar weeks' notice of termination of employment.

For other employees:

An employee should give adequate notice prior to the effective date of his or her resignation. Ordinarily, this should be at least one month.

Exhibit 53. Policy on Reduction in Force

In the event the university reduces the number of employees in a work area, temporary and probationary employees in the work area shall be released first in that order. Any additional reduction in the work area shall be in inverse order of unit seniority, provided the employees remaining in service have the required qualifications and are able to perform the work that remains to be done. If an employee is to be retained who has less seniority than one who is to be laid off, the university shall state the reason therefore in a notice to the employee retained and the employee laid off; as soon as the reason ceases to exist, the exception will be ended.

It is recognized that an employee may be capable of functioning in work areas other than the work area to which the employee is regularly assigned. An employee who is to be laid off shall be assigned to a vacant position if one exists, provided the employee has the required qualifications and is able to perform the work. If more than one such vacancy exists, the employee may express his or her preference. If no such vacancy exists, the employee may elect to replace the least senior employee in the unit, starting, if applicable, with temporary and probationary employees, in that order; provided the employee remaining has the required qualifications and is able to perform the work. In the event the employee is not qualified or able to perform the work of the least senior employee, the employee may replace the next least senior employee, provided the employee remaining has more unit seniority than the next least senior employee and is qualified and able to perform the work. If not qualified or able to perform that work, the employee may proceed to the next person up the unit seniority list, and so on, provided that to replace any employee, the employee remaining must have more unit seniority than the employee replaced and be qualified and able to perform the work.

If a temporary employee is replaced who was assigned to a position held by an employee on leave of absence, the employee on leave shall assume his or her position at the end of the leave if he or she has unit seniority greater than that of the employee then holding the position. An employee replaced who is not a temporary or probationary employee also shall have replacement elections as enumerated earlier. The university is not obligated to provide additional training to an employee who does not qualify to make a replacement election.

The university shall endeavor through advance planning to make any reduction in force through attrition. In the event any reduction in force should result in a layoff from the university, the university shall notify the employee at least fifteen calendar days in advance of the layoff, provided that lesser notice may be given in the event of unforeseen, nonprocedural circumstances.

Any layoff of an employee shall be considered to begin at the end of the last shift for which work was available for that employee.

Whenever a vacancy occurs, employees who are on layoff shall be recalled in accordance with their unit seniority in the reverse order in which they were laid off, provided they have the requisite skill and ability to perform the job in the judgment of the university. A regular employee on layoff shall:

1. Maintain the university's hospital expense plan, including surgical and major medical benefits; the university's dental plan; the university's vision care plan; and the university's accidental death and dismemberment insurance plan (if enrolled) for the first 120 calendar days of the employee's layoff by payment on return to work by biweekly payroll deductions of an amount twice the employee's normal payroll deductions for insurance until the amount of the normal

Exhibit 53 (continued)

contributions due during the layoff is paid, unless the employee notifies the university in writing prior to the date of the layoff that she or he does not wish to continue such coverage, which notice of termination shall terminate all insurance coverage as of the end of her or his final pay period. If an employee ceases employment prior to paying for the amount of normal contributions due during the layoff, such amount remaining due shall be reimbursed by lump-sum payment by the employee to the university.

2.   Be eligible for participation under the then existing university's policy governing educational privileges for the first 120 calendar days of the employee's layoff.

3.   Accumulate unit seniority.

4.   Not contribute to retirement unless paid for days during the layoff, unless he or she makes private arrangements to contribute.

5.   Receive the cash equivalent of accumulated vacation, compensatory time and unused service days, if recall to regular employment is not anticipated within 120 calendar days from the date of layoff. If recall is anticipated within 120 calendar days from the date of layoff, the following contributions apply:

   a.   At the option of the employee all or part of accumulated vacation, compensatory time, and unused service days may be carried over to the return to regular employment.

   b.   If the employee elects to receive payment of the cash equivalent of accumulated vacation, compensatory time, and unused service days for all or part of her or his work days included in the layoff, and such work days extend into more than one pay period, the cash equivalent paid shall be distributed over the appropriate work days of the employee's regular work schedule as though the employee were not on layoff. Accumulated vacation, compensatory time and unused service days paid under this section shall not be credited toward accumulating additional vacation, service day, or sick leave time off.

6.   Not accumulate vacation, sick leave, and service days and may not use previously accumulated sick leave.

A part-time employee (half-time or more) on layoff shall accumulate unit seniority and receive the cash equivalent of accumulated and unused service days and vacation which the employee is eligible to use if recall to employment is not anticipated within 120 calendar days from the date of layoff. If recall is anticipated within 120 calendar days from the date of layoff, at the option of the employee all or part of accumulated and unused service days and vacation which the employee is eligible to use may be carried over to the return to employment.

Exhibit 54. Exit Questionnaire

Department name _____ Departmental number _____

Exiting employee's class title _____

Length of employment in current position _____ Last date of employment _____

1. Sex: ☐ Male   ☐ Female

2. Race and Ethnicity

☐ Black non-Hispanic   ☐ Hispanic
☐ American Indian or Alaskan Native   ☐ White non-Hispanic
☐ Asian or Pacific Islander

3. Please check reason for leaving your current position:

☐ Promotion   ☐ Resignation
☐ Transfer   ☐ Leave without pay
☐ Retirement   ☐ Demotion
☐ Dismissal

4. Please check any of the following which contributed to your decision to leave your current position:

☐ Better job opportunity   ☐ Family circumstances
☐ Working conditions   ☐ Health
☐ Content of work   ☐ Going to school
☐ Salary   ☐ Military service
☐ Supervision   ☐ Self-Employment
☐ Commuting distance   ☐ Moving from area
☐ Lack of opportunity for advancement   ☐ Better fringe benefit package
☐ Other (Explain) _____

Exhibit 54 (continued)

5.   Please rate each of the following benefits:

	Excellent	Good	Fair	Poor	No opinion
Rate of pay	☐	☐	☐	☐	☐
Paid holidays	☐	☐	☐	☐	☐
Retirement plan	☐	☐	☐	☐	☐
Tuition waiver	☐	☐	☐	☐	☐
Life insurance	☐	☐	☐	☐	☐
Health insurance	☐	☐	☐	☐	☐
Sick leave	☐	☐	☐	☐	☐
Annual leave	☐	☐	☐	☐	☐

6.   Please rate communication in the following areas:

	Excellent	Good	Fair	Poor	No opinion
Policies, procedures, and guidelines	☐	☐	☐	☐	☐
General orientation to the department	☐	☐	☐	☐	☐
Specific knowledge of your job	☐	☐	☐	☐	☐
Between you and your supervisor	☐	☐	☐	☐	☐

7.   a) Did you receive a current job description for your position when you were employed? ☐ Yes ☐ No

     b) Were your job duties and responsibilities fully and correctly explained to you when you were employed?

     ☐ Yes ☐ No   If no, explain: _____

8. Please rate the following in your job or department:

	Excellent	Good	Fair	Poor	No opinion
Friendliness and cooperation of fellow employees	☐	☐	☐	☐	☐
Cooperation within the department	☐	☐	☐	☐	☐
Cooperation with other departments	☐	☐	☐	☐	☐
On-the-job training	☐	☐	☐	☐	☐
Equipment provided	☐	☐	☐	☐	☐
Classroom training	☐	☐	☐	☐	☐
Orientation to the job	☐	☐	☐	☐	☐
Physical working conditions	☐	☐	☐	☐	☐

9. Was your work load usually: ☐ Too great   ☐ Too light   ☐ About right   ☐ Varies

10. Please check supervisory action on each of the following points:

	Almost always	Usually	Sometimes	Never
Follows policies and practices	☐	☐	☐	☐
Demonstrates fair and equal treatment	☐	☐	☐	☐
Provides recognition on the job	☐	☐	☐	☐
Communicates well with subordinates	☐	☐	☐	☐
Develops cooperation	☐	☐	☐	☐
Resolves complaints, grievances, and problems	☐	☐	☐	☐

Exhibit 54 (continued)

11. Did you experience any of the following while working in this department?

	Yes	No
Harassment	☐	☐
Favoritism of other employees	☐	☐
Unfair promotional practices	☐	☐
Unfair treatment	☐	☐
Threats for filing a grievance	☐	☐

Comments: _____

12. Are you leaving for any reason which would appear to reflect discrimination on the basis of race, color, sex, religion, national origin, age, handicap, or status as a Vietnam-era veteran? ☐ Yes ☐ No   If yes, explain: _____

Did you attempt to seek remedy of the situation? ☐ Yes ☐ No

13. What suggestions would you make for improving the following: working conditions, employee relations, supervision of the office, productivity, and efficiency?

_____

_____

_____

14. Would you recommend this department to a friend as a place of work? ☐ Yes ☐ No

❧ 13 ❧

Improving Faculty and Staff Relations, Communications, and Grievance Procedures

The broad policies promulgated by top administration play a part in forming the attitudes of the faculty and staff toward the institution. But employees' basic attitudes toward the institution are formed usually at the first level of contact, during contacts between a department chairperson and a faculty member, or a supervisor and a janitorial worker. In general, the way problems are handled at that level reflects the attitude of the institution as a whole.

Faculty and staff relations professionals can facilitate an institutionwide attitude toward effective employee relations. By monitoring personnel policies and communications to faculty and staff members, faculty and staff relations professionals can create awareness among administrators of techniques for developing positive attitudes. By monitoring disciplinary actions and dismissals, faculty and staff relations professionals can assist administrators in accomplishing their purposes without creating fear among those faculty and staff members who are effectively discharging their responsibilities.

While positive attitudes and communication of those attitudes are essential to successful management and the achievement of the institution's mission, problems relating to individual faculty and staff members are still likely to occur. Effective and equitable performance evaluation (see Chapter Eleven) is one element of a good employee relations program, for high performers are rewarded and constructive criticism is given to less-than-acceptable performers. In this chapter, we discuss other elements of an employee relations program.

What Causes Conflicts in the Workplace?

Four major entities interrelate in the higher education workplace: faculty and staff members, institutions, unions, and government. Each of these entities has a different perspective even though all are interested in the production of services. An exploration of the needs and desires of each of these four entities reveals the source of various conflicts.

The needs and desires of faculty and staff members include recognition, security, adequate pay (not necessarily top pay), reasonable working conditions, fair treatment, and opportunities for advancement. The basic needs of institutions include quality and productivity, minimized costs, autonomy (freedom from outside rules, regulations, or interference), and a peaceful and stable work force (no work stoppages, low turnover).

In defining the needs of the unions, we can consider both the needs of the individual union locals and those of the union headquarters. Their goals include increasing their membership, a measure of a union's success and the source of a union's fiscal base; acquiring power to influence government and employers; achieving internal solidarity; and gaining a voice in management's affairs.

Finally, the government's goals include achieving low rates of unemployment, maintaining labor-management peace, preventing severe inflation or depression, encouraging the continued growth of the gross national product, and protecting both democracy and free enterprise.

Several conflicts are readily apparent among these different needs. The government wants full employment and faculty and staff want security, while institutions want minimized costs (hiring the fewest number of employees needed). The unions want a voice in the institutions' affairs, while the institutions want autonomy. By understanding the conflicting needs of these four major parties, we begin to understand the conflicts that confront the personnel administration.

What Factors Motivate Employees?

At General Electric several years ago, a number of successful middle-management personnel were asked what factor or factors had contributed most to their success. About 10 percent responded that they had gained knowledge and development through education, special training, seminars, and other miscellaneous stimuli. However, about 90 percent credited a former mentor or supervisor as the major reason for their success. They all had worked, at one time early in their careers, for individuals who cared enough to teach and develop them. Such early caring for new employees seems all important in their development.

In contrast, work-related factors that are perceived to be negative by employees block their motivation. Examples of such demotivators include the following situations:

- An employee learns from an outside source about a proposed reorganization in his department
- An employee is told that effective immediately she will work at a different location. She was not consulted nor forewarned.
- An employee asks to schedule time off, but his administrator gives him an indirect put-off.
- An employee feels she is never asked for her opinion or when asked, the question is only perfunctory.

- An employee feels he is not allowed to use initiative.
- An employee finds that her written proposals go unanswered.
- The organization has too many forms and too much red tape.

Generally speaking, actions taken by the institution or its representatives that ignore the questions, feelings, and aspirations of employees, cause those employees to be resentful toward the institution and thus be less motivated to want to further the goals of the organization. Administrators must eliminate demotivators and enhance employees' motivation. Effective administrators let subordinates know that they are important to the total work effort. Aware of the needs of their subordinates, effective administrators encourage them to seek ways to improve skills and be effective, provide for training for upgrading, and maintain a productive working atmosphere. Effective administrators emphasize increased productivity, work simplification, effective management of time, and improved understanding of people. Thus, they are able to solicit and receive maximum productivity with no reduction in quality. Effective administrators assist their employees in understanding the work situation more clearly by raising questions and probing the employees for their own answers. Effective administrators are able to sell goals to subordinates and in turn teach them to sell their ideas to others. They view work as a communication process in which creativity is encouraged.

Administrators need to recognize the differences in the behavior patterns of individuals. While administrators need not be experts on human behavior, they should be able to recognize basic differences among the people they supervise. For example:

- Some individuals need security, whereas others thrive on risk taking.
- Some individuals seek promotion, whereas others are content with the security of a known situation.
- Ambitious new staff members may feel status and recognition of progress to be more important than money, whereas older employees with children in college may have a stronger interest in salary and benefits.

- Some employees need to move around or they feel caged; others feel comfortable only in a known routine and have a higher degree of "sitability."
- Some individuals are encouraged by flattery, while others are suspicious of flattery and are more receptive to sympathetic understanding.

Effective administrators are those who are able to recognize these differences and use them in a positive way. Personnel officers should help the institution's administrative staff to understand these principles.

As a specific example of such differences, administrators should realize that younger staff members are apt to look at their relationships with administrators quite differently than older colleagues. While generalizations can be misleading, certain traits of younger staff members are significant and worthy of mention. Most younger staff members are interested in personalizing their relationships with their administrators. They are motivated by organizational activities that are personalized for them, such as specialized training and development programs. They want to be part of small units so that their contributions will be recognized more readily. They cherish personalized communication and minimal organizational formality. They value time for themselves and, therefore, may be motivated by schedules that include such options as flextime, rewards of extra time off, the option to work at home, and so forth.

How Can Positive Attitudes Be Generated?

Faculty and staff members need to have a regular flow of information about institutional policies, plans, benefits, problems, and so forth. An informed staff is frequently an effective staff. Institutions should use several communication devices to present such information to the faculty and staff.

House organ. Most institutions issue some sort of regular paper or magazine to faculty and staff members. A house organ should create positive employee relations and should be the institution's most effective communications device. A house organ is a useful tool only if readers regard it as the place they are most likely to find timely announcements by the administration. In addition, it must be issued frequently enough that administrators regard it as an effective communications tool. (We recommend a weekly publication to meet these criteria.) The house organ should provide information about (1) new or revised policies and presidential pronouncements; (2) vacancy announcements for effective internal promotion programs; (3) personnel actions (promotions, tenure grants, retirements, deaths, and the like); (4) the institution's benefits plans; (5) events on campus; and (6) events of human interest about individual faculty and staff members. (Note: While human interest items provide a form of recognition to individuals, too many such items in an issue of the house organ can create passive interest and may destroy its effectiveness as a basic communication instrument.)

Benefits statements. Each faculty and staff member should receive a printed statement on each insurance benefit provided. Although the notice should be written in plain language, it should give a detailed account of all facets of the particular benefit program since it has a contractual connotation. Most faculty and staff members will not read the benefits booklet when they receive it; rather, they will set it aside as a reference document for use when a need arises. Therefore, short articles about special and positive facets of the benefits programs should be printed in the house organ in order to call attention to such facets. A benefits document that is most likely to be read by each faculty and staff member is an individually tailored benefits summary statement. Companies such as BENEFACTS (Hampton Plaza, 300 E. Joppa Rd., Baltimore, MD 21204) produce such statements at relatively reasonable rates. The statements usually inform the faculty and staff members about the contributions made by the institution on their behalf.

Policy manuals and handbooks. A policy manual (normally loose-leaf for ease of making changes) is a necessity. It should contain the official institutional policies. Since policy manuals must be updated, their distribution needs to be controlled, perhaps one manual for each major administrative officer. In addition, each faculty and staff member should receive a handbook that contains brief statements about major policies relevant to employment. Each brief statement about a policy should be followed by a reference to the official policy in the policy manual. Although changes in policy and procedure cause handbooks to become outdated rather quickly, references to the complete policy manual will increase their life. A brief handbook is more likely to be read by new faculty or staff members, whose newness may provide the incentive to seek such information. For details about policy manuals, see College and University Personnel Association (1980b).

Announcement letters. Executive officers of the institution may write letters to faculty and staff to announce a new policy or organizational change. Relatively brief letters are most likely to be read. Such letters or statements in the weekly house organ are good means to ensure that all segments of the institution are aware of a policy change. If announcements of a policy change are sent only to those persons having formal policy manuals, there is a strong possibility that the policy will be inserted into the manual without being read by anyone other than the employee who files the policy in the manual.

Group meetings. Two general types of meetings may be held: those called for a specific purpose and regular, recurring meetings. Special group meetings are excellent for such purposes as explaining a new benefits program, holding preretirement counseling sessions, or introducing a new salary plan. Such meetings should provide employees with the opportunity to ask questions for clarity. However, not all persons readily accept group meetings. For example, some faculty members prefer to receive information in written form. Too, audiences at group meetings may have a variety of levels of understanding about the subject matter being presented. The presenter has to decide whether to assume a certain level of knowledge or to risk boring some members by being very basic. A final precaution is that misunderstandings can arise from group meetings, since not all listeners interpret answers to questions in the same way.

Regular, recurring meetings provide a greater chance for good communication because repeated contact enables the presenters and listeners to understand each other better and because there is usually more time to discuss misunderstandings. Regular, recurring meetings require an agenda in order to be efficient and effective. Ideally, such meetings should provide for presentations by a variety of individuals. The meetings should reflect effective long-range planning and should provide listeners with time to digest new ideas. Such meetings should decrease an institution's need to rely on crisis management.

Regular, recurring meetings should take place between the personnel officer and his or her staff and the personnel officer and the person to whom she or he reports. Such regular meetings create opportunities to provide for systematic planning and to discuss issues that are not crises. The administrator who says, "I don't believe in regular meetings. I'm available whenever a subordinate wants to see me," probably lives by crisis management. For a detailed discussion of leading such meetings, see Professional Development, Inc. (Guyon, 1979).

One-on-one meetings. Unfortunately, most administrators tend not to think of one-on-one contacts as the formal meetings they are. They are the daily communication devices that can build good employee relations. Some may be rather formal, such as the annual performance evaluation meeting, or a meeting to attend to a gripe or grievance. However, most are routine and can be ineffective if not handled properly. A hastily given order that produces an improper result and causes the subordinate to have to do something over is an example of poor communication. Frequent improper directions can soon cause discontentment and be a demotivator for that faculty or staff member.

Formal training and development sessions. The long-range mission of the institution can be communicated effectively in sessions in which staff members are brought together for professional development. Those selected to instruct such sessions must, of course, not be counterproductive by their subject matter, lack of understanding about the institution's philosophies, or their off-hand innuendos. For details on development sessions, see Solomon and Berzon (1976), and CBI Publishing (1978).

What Elements Should a Policy on Discipline Contain?

Although a positive communication program will facilitate better understanding among employees, it will not obviate the need to evaluate and discipline faculty or staff members who do not produce, nor will it necessarily eliminate fear of mistreatment. Ideally, poor performance should be addressed during the employee's probationary period. However, poor performance and other acts of commission or omission that occur after the probationary period require institutional policies and programs for discipline and dismissal. Faculty and staff members should be informed of the terms of the institution's policies on discipline and dismissal, probationary period, and rights appeal. Dismissal procedures for faculty are usually found in the institution's tenure regulations. Similar policies for staff members need to be adopted and disseminated.

The main principles of a discipline and dismissal policy are the following:

1. Discipline procedures usually do not apply to persons on provisional tenure, other probationary employees, or to casual employees. An administrator can usually take action without faculty or staff having recourse to a grievance procedure unless that action is perceived to be discriminatory under civil rights legislation.
2. Disciplinary actions are usually described as corrective rather than punitive.
3. Causes for disciplinary actions are usually stated in general terms rather than specific terms. However, some institutions publish lists of offenses with specific disciplinary actions indicated for each, and frequently unions try to bargain for such a list. Lists have their dangers, because it is impossible to devise an all-purpose list. If a faculty or staff member perpetrates a strong breach of conduct that is not specifically listed, an appeal of the action taken against that individual might cause the disciplinary action to be overturned simply because it is not on the list.
4. Usually, discipline is progressive and starts with an oral warning. Usually a written summary of the oral warning is prepared for the employee's file. Subsequent discipline is usually in the form of written warnings sent to the staff member. In some cases, the employee is required to sign the warning letter as evidence of having received it. The signature does not indicate concurrence with the content of the letter.

5. Usually, warning letters are considered inactive after a passage of time. For example, a policy might state that if following the issuance of a warning letter, a twelve-month period passes without incident, the letter may no longer be used toward future progressive discipline. However, such inactive written warnings should not be destroyed. If, at some future date, that employee is dismissed for cause, such letters may be used to counter the employee's argument to an arbitrator that he or she has had an exemplary record up until the recent incident. The institution may have to show evidence of prior problems with the employee.

6. Some policies specify that the result of a disciplinary action might include suspension without pay for a short period of time.

7. Termination of employment is usually a final step taken if the progressive discipline of oral and written warnings does not solve the problem. Usually, a set number of progressive disciplinary actions results in termination of employment. For example, discipline follows if a staff member receives three valid warning letters. However, dismissal may be immediate without progressive discipline for major acts of misconduct or serious dereliction of duty. Examples of causes for immediate dismissal are theft, immorality, and the like.

8. Most policies require an administrator to discuss the dismissal of a staff member with the personnel officer before action is taken in order to ensure that the institution's philosophy and policy are adhered to.

Exhibit 55, pp. 267–272, presents guidelines on policy for disciplinary procedures including termination of employment. Exhibit 56, pp. 273–274, offers a sample policy on failure to meet acceptable standards of performance.

What Is Due Process?

The Fourteenth Amendment of the U.S. Constitution forbids any state to "deprive any person of life, liberty, or property, without due process of law." Various court decisions have interpreted this amendment to mean that public institutions cannot take any action that causes a negative material change to an employee without due process. For example, due process is required if a faculty member's status is changed or an employee is to be dismissed. Due process means that the employee must receive notice of the reason for the action and must be given the opportunity to relate his or her side of the situation.

The exact nature of the process required in any given circumstance may vary. However, the courts have generally accepted a procedure whereby the faculty member is allowed to relate his or her side of the situation to either the administrator taking the action or to a committee established to hear such testimony. If a faculty or staff member disagrees with the action taken, appeals may typically be made through the institution's structure for making such appeals. If the faculty member appeals through the courts and if due process has not taken place, the institution's action may be negated by the court.

How Should Gripes and Grievances Be Handled?

When an institution takes the necessary steps to reward producers and discipline nonproducers, it should expect some gripes and grievances on the part of disgruntled faculty and staff members. Indeed, an institution that has no evidence that some employees are disgruntled should review its performance evaluation processes to see whether corrective improvement is being promulgated or whether the evaluation is simply a paper exercise.

Most people find the handling of complaints a distasteful process, and many administrators quite naturally try to avoid it. Although one may view a grievance as an interruption of one's work, actually grievances and their resolution are an important part of administrative work. True, a grievance might make an administrator look bad; no one likes to have to admit that he or she was wrong, just as no one likes to see mistakes disclosed publicly. And tempers sometimes flare during the grievance process, which aggravates an already uncomfortable situation. But administrators must set aside such attitudes and, instead, view the handling of a gripe or grievance as an opportunity for effective communication.

To help administrators develop positive attitudes, the institution could initiate a program that would nurture positive faculty and staff relations.

The first step in handling a gripe or complaint is to recognize that one exists. Gripes that are ignored may soon become formal complaints or grievances. In most cases, a formal grievance is nothing more than a developed gripe that the administrator failed to recognize and handle at an earlier time. Administrators must listen to what faculty and staff members say and be alert for indirect messages. People issue indirect messages to avoid the conflict a direct message might provoke. However, if the indirectives go unheeded and if the issue is of enough significance, conflict is inevitable. If an employee makes casual comments about additional work that has been assigned and the difficulty of getting it done, the issue may not be workload but proper remuneration. If a faculty member comments that another department seems to have an inordinate number of faculty members on sabbatical leaves of absence, that faculty member may be saying that the administrative attitude in his or her department stifles requests for such leaves. Administrators should develop the attitude that gripes and indirectives represent real problems.

An administrator who hears the indirect message will not allow the issue to fester. By paying attention to the issue, the administrator may be able to prevent serious problems. By considering the message as an opportunity for communication, the administrator can explain the reason for the present policy and correct any misinformation that underlies the complaint. If the administrator does not follow up with discussion, the discontented employee may look to colleagues for communication. The issue may soon be blown out of proportion as groups of employees become excited about the issue. At that point, resolving the issue is usually difficult.

Ideally, there should be no difference in the way that the grievances of nonunion employees and those of union employees are handled. However, it takes administrative zeal to ensure an effective grievance procedure for nonunion employees. Administrators must exercise self-discipline and a dedication to fair play to properly handle grievances of nonunion employees. If the administrator does not exercise such administrative zeal, faculty and staff members will realize the hollowness and ineffectiveness of the published grievance procedure. In fact, unless the administration is dedicated to effective faculty and staff relations it is questionable whether a formal grievance procedure should be developed.

A formal grievance should be based on an administrative action or inaction rather than on a clash of attitudes. But, it is frequently difficult to find the real basis for the grievance, given the rhetoric of the debate. An administrator must look for the hidden problem. A faculty or staff member who is upset may become inarticulate and may have difficulty in explaining the basis of the upset. The irrational nature of some complaints contributes to poor communications. The administrator must have an open mind and is obligated to look for the real problem.

Let us consider a sample case: Henry McCloud refused to teach an assigned section of English which was scheduled for 4 P.M. on Monday, Wednesday, and Friday during the fall semester. His department head felt that her authority was being questioned so she made an ultimatum that he teach the section or "start looking for some other university that may want your services." McCloud filed a grievance.

This confrontation was actually based on past perceptions rather than the case at hand, and normal, cordial communications had broken down between the participants. McCloud had been ill during the past spring semester, and the department head had to use funds intended for another purpose to pay a substitute to teach McCloud's classes. In addition, McCloud had served on a faculty committee that made recommendations, which the department head opposed, for substantial changes in the department. Finally, McCloud did not want to accept that particular section assignment because, having been told by the department head to complete the work on his doctorate, he had scheduled the last phase of it for the fall semester. The only time that his dissertation committee could meet with him would have conflicted with a large number of the late Friday afternoon classes in the English section assigned. Had the department head created an atmosphere of open communication, the conflict could have been minimized, the threat and the grievance avoided. There were other class sections that could have been assigned to McCloud.

A second example of a breakdown in communication which led to a grievance is the case of George Rogers, a janitorial worker who refused to be reassigned from the building in which he was working to the building next door. The relevant facts are these: By campus policy, janitorial workers are employed to work in any building but are usually assigned to one building, and management rarely moves the janitorial workers. But, because of a change in standards, the size of the janitorial crew was reduced and janitorial workers were reassigned to new buildings. Rogers' response was: "You can't do this to me. You don't have the right." The supervisor felt that Rogers' response threatened his management's rights and responded by defending his rights, "We'll see who has the right after you've moved."

Rogers filed a grievance, but the supervisor claimed that Rogers did not have a valid grievance. Thus, the two parties were at an impasse and could reach no solution. The supervisor was right in saying he did have the right to move Rogers; however, additional facts in the case were not brought out in their discussion. Rogers knew that management had the right to move him, but he had a minor disability that made climbing stairs difficult for him. His present building had an elevator, but the newly assigned building did not. He perceived the possibility of failure in the new building. He was self-conscious about his disability and did not like to discuss it. The supervisor, unaware of this, chose to argue on the basis of his rights. Had the supervisor made an attempt to determine *why* Rogers did not want to move, the impasse might have been avoided.

Both of the preceding examples illustrate the importance of communication in the resolution of gripes and grievances. The administrator should ask the employee, What do you see as a solution to your problem? Why? Questions like these enable the administrator to identify the real problem and to devise a solution to that problem. Some administrators, however, take a legalistic approach toward the definition of a legitimate grievance. They ask the employee to point out the clause in the contract or in the policies that support the employee's complaint. Such an approach can eliminate grievances, but it does not eliminate problems. A gripe must be discussed, and if an employee feels aggrieved, that is sufficient reason to probe into the problem. In contrast, the legalistic approach almost guarantees an adversarial relationship.

Gripes and grievances are best solved by administrators who try to understand the viewpoint of the aggrieved. Empathy enables one to better understand the problem and propose an adequate solution. If, after discussion and thought, the administrator feels that a gripe does not constitute a grievance, a hearing should be held if for no other reason than to hear the discussion and dismiss the grievance as unfounded, a process similar to that used in our judiciary system.

Do Ombudsmen Help?

To assist faculty and staff members in determining whether they have a legitimate grievance worthy of pursuit, some institutions have an ombudsman or a number of ombudsmen located throughout the institution. Faculty or staff members who feel that they may be aggrieved are encouraged to discuss their gripes with the ombudsmen. While an ombudsman has no authority to make a decision in the case, he or she may intercede to seek a solution or to point out to the aggrieved individual that the grievance is not legitimate. Ombudsmen can help avoid adversarial relationships between a faculty member and a department chairperson, or a staff employee and a supervisor.

Ombudsmen may be selected in a variety of ways. They may be appointed by groups like a faculty senate or by administrators, or they may be elected by faculty or staff groups.

Are Formal Grievance Procedures Recommended?

Effective faculty and staff relations include the publishing of formal grievance procedures for all segments of the university community. Faculty and staff members need to know that, should a problem arise, there is a fair procedure for resolution.

Appeal procedures for faculty members regarding dismissal usually are included within the tenure regulations (see Chapter Nine). Typically, the appeal procedure is used in cases of the termination of employment of a tenured faculty member, a probationary faculty member released during the probationary period with less advance notice than that specified, and a faculty member appointed on a fixed-term contract who is dismissed during that term. Standing committees made up of faculty members elected by the faculty senate and representatives of the administration are appointed to hear such appeals. Usually, the committee makes a recommendation to the chief executive officer who takes final action. For complaints by faculty members on situations other than dismissal, other procedures may be established. Exhibit 57, pp. 274–278, outlines additional procedures for faculty members.

Following are the major elements of a policy on staff grievance procedures. Similar procedures are used for faculty under some union contracts.

Definitions. The policy defines what constitutes a valid grievance. The definition may be broad or narrow, depending on the style of the institution. The policy describes which employees have access to the grievance procedure. The description may specify which categories of employees are eligible and whether part-time or casual employees are eligible. Quite often different procedures are specified for different classes of employees. Unionized employees usually have a separate procedure.

Information discussion. Many policies require an informal first step in which the staff member takes up the problem with the administrator. This step provides for discussion and possible solution before a formal written grievance is submitted. Once a staff member puts the case in writing, he or she may be locked into a position that may make resolution more difficult.

Grievance form. If the staff member is not satisfied by the response to the informal discussion, he or she files a formal written grievance. Exhibits 58 and 59, pp. 278–281, present samples of grievance forms.

Time limits. The policy designates time limits for each step of the formal grievance procedure. For example, it states a time limit for initiating a grievance to disallow outdated grievances that can be difficult to resolve. The time limit may be expressed as the time from the incident causing the grievance or from the time that the employee could have had knowledge of the act that is the basis for the grievance. Second, to avoid supervisory dereliction, a time limit may be expressed for the number of workdays or calendar days in which the hearing must be held following receipt of the grievance. Third, once again to avoid supervisory dereliction, a policy may set a time limit, expressed as workdays or calendar days following the hearing, for answering the grievance. Fourth, the policy may state a time limit for the employee to request the next step in the appeal procedure. This limit is usually expressed as the number of workdays or calendar days from the date of the administrator's response following the last hearing. Simply not requesting the next step within the time allotted discontinues the case. It may avoid unnecessary confrontations. In addition, the policy should explain how employees' time off to attend hearings will be handled.

Hearings. The policy specifies a series of hearings through administrative channels following receipt of the written grievance. The policy usually indicates who may attend each hearing and who is responsible for providing a ruling. The number of hearings depends on scope of the organization and the layers of administration. Because solutions to grievances require that all parties fully understand all the factors that have caused the grievance, the various hearings serve to refine the issue. Before a grievance is sent to final arbitration, all parties should arrive at an agreement about the basis of the problem.

Final resolution. The policy specifies a final step of the procedure, which may be a hearing before an outside arbitrator or a panel of individuals selected by the parties. The policy may specify that the result of the final hearing is binding or that it be referred as a recommendation to the institution's top administration. If the result of the final appeal is made by an outside arbitrator and is considered binding, the arbitrator is forbidden to propose a solution that contradicts the institution's policy or practice.

Exhibit 60, pp. 282–288, presents policy guidelines on grievance and appeal procedures. Exhibits 61 and 62, pp. 289–295, present sample grievance procedures for staff employees.

How Are Arbitrators Selected?

Prior to arbitration, all parties must develop a clear understanding of the specific issue to be arbitrated. Parties may then select professional arbitrators from lists provided by the American Arbitration Association, the Federal Mediation and Conciliation Service, or state agencies with similar responsibilities. In selecting an arbitrator from such a list, the employee relations administrator has the responsibility to research the past decisions of each arbitrator, particularly in regard to the type of case under dispute.

When a union is involved, the process of selection usually follows this pattern: A specified number, usually an odd number, of names is selected from one of the arbitration agencies. The institution and the union alternately strike the names of arbitrators off the list until one remains, and he or she is invited to arbitrate. When a union is involved, the fees and expenses of an arbitrator are usually shared by the parties. In some agreements, the party that loses the case pays the fees.

Usually, the arbitrator decides the pattern for the hearings. Some are quite informal. Although the standard rules for presenting evidence do not apply at arbitrator hearings, the parties are given the opportunity to present testimony, present evidence, and cross-examine witnesses. Verbatim records may be required if the parties agree; the cost of preparation is then shared by the parties. The arbitrator may or may not request statements or briefs from both parties following the hearing, depending upon the nature of the case.

The arbitrator's decision is usually final and binding. In unusual cases, when one of the parties feels that the decision is inconsistent with the contract, that party may seek relief in court. However, courts are reluctant to overturn arbitration decisions—fearing that the courts may take the place of the arbitration process.

How Are Grievances Related to Discrimination Handled?

When grievances relate to discrimination, faculty and staff members have the right to file appeals with state and federal agencies. Therefore, any decision reached as a result of an internal appeal procedure is subject to being overturned by a state or federal agency. Nevertheless, an internal procedure is recommended, and institutions should attempt to solve such problems internally.

In some institutions, discrimination complaints are processed through the same procedure as other grievances. However,
we recommend a separate procedure be used because discrimination complaints differ from other grievances in two ways. First, all
faculty and staff members (including probationary, part-time, temporary, and casual) and applicants for employment may file
discrimination complaints. Second, since faculty and staff members can appeal any internal decision to federal and state agencies,
such decisions are not final and binding. In light of this, many institutions appoint advisory committees to study discrimination
complaints and to make advisory recommendations to the chief executive officer. These committees often include women and minority representatives who may bring special consideration to the
specialized nature of discrimination complaints. Exhibit 63, pp.
295–301, presents a sample policy for advisory committees charged
with reviewing discrimination complaints.

Exhibit 55. Guidelines for Policy on Disciplinary Procedures Including Termination of Employment

Federal and state mandates such as unemployment compensation laws and
civil rights legislation dictate the necessity for a procedure covering discipline and dismissal. Normally, the provisions of such a procedure apply to
employees after they have completed their probationary periods.

Disciplinary action should be corrective rather than punitive and a series of
actions (progressive discipline) usually results in dismissal, unless dismissal
is for a major act of misconduct. The action of discipline or dismissal
should never be a surprise to an employee.

Most institutions do not list specific offenses and penalties applicable
thereto on the basis that to list is to limit management's basic right to
manage. Causes for discipline are frequently listed in a general way such as
"failure to meet acceptable standards of conduct."

In most cases, a well-planned disciplinary program will improve the work
patterns of problem employees, or it will provide a record of progressive
action should the institution have to defend dismissal of an employee who
does not undertake corrective measures.

Policy items and sample policy language:

Disciplinary procedures usually don't apply to probationary or casual employees:
"This procedure applies to nonprobationary, regular employees." "This

Exhibit 55 (continued)

procedure does not apply to dismissal during the probationary period."
"At any time during the probationary period, an employee may be terminated. Employment may be terminated by either party at any time during
this initial period and no written notice will be required."

Discipline frequently is specified to be corrective in nature rather than punitive:
"The purpose of the discipline procedure is to provide a means of correction, not punishment." "Discipline should be designed to correct, not
punish. It should be fair, firm, and consistent." "It is the university's policy
that supervisory efforts should be concentrated on preventing serious personnel problems from occurring rather than on disciplining employees for
misconduct. If disciplinary measures are imposed, it is essential that: each
problem should be investigated, so that the facts of the situation are
known; any action taken be primarily corrective rather than punitive and
be appropriate to the offense; and that the dignity of the employee be
respected."

Often, causes for disciplinary action are stated in general rather than specific terms:
"The university shall have the right to discipline or summarily discharge
an employee for cause. The university may, in its discretion, issue warning
letters to an employee it intends to discipline." "Certain standards of performance and conduct must be maintained in any work group. Generally,
these standards are recognized and observed by individual members of the
work group without any need for action by the supervisor. When an employee does not observe these standards, counseling or an oral reminder
by a supervisor normally results in the employee doing so in the future.
When an employee does not respond to oral reminders, more formal
discipline may be necessary." "What is an appropriate discipline cannot be
decided in advance or with the precision of a slide rule. The immediate
supervisor must decide, based upon the circumstances in each case, what is
appropriate discipline. No two cases are identical."

In a few cases, examples of situations resulting in discipline or dismissal are listed:
"Some causes for discipline are: fraud in securing appointment, incompe-
tency, inefficiency, inexcusable neglect of duty, insubordination, dishonesty, drunkenness on duty, intemperance, addiction to the use of narcotics
or habit-forming drugs, inexcusable absence without leave, conviction of a
felony or conviction of a misdemeanor involving moral turpitude, immorality, discourteous treatment of the public or other employees, improper political activity, willful disobedience, misuse of state property,
refusal to take and subscribe to any oath or affirmation which is required
by law in connection with his or her employment, unprofessional conduct,
other failure of good behavior either during or outside of duty hours
which is of such a nature that it causes discredit to his or her agency or
employment." "These are the most common reasons for termination.
Insubordination—persons who give physical or mental resistance to au-

thority and work direction. Those who are unruly and disobedient are considered insubordinate. Alcoholism or narcotics—those staff members who are intoxicated on the job or bring liquor on the campus. The same applies to narcotics. Theft or dishonesty—the acquiring of university-owned items which do not belong to an employee or dishonest actions, for example, falsification of records. The same applies to long-distance personal calls charged to the university. Personal damage—willful damage of and to university property. Physical fights—employees engaged in fist fights, wrestling, and similar encounters. Absenteeism—absences without good cause and repeated absenteeism which lowers the working conditions. Accuracy—those employees in secretarial and related positions are required to maintain accuracy and confidentiality at all times. Lateness—tardiness detracts from one's value as a member of the staff. It is a very poor work habit which affects the smooth functioning of a staff member's work unit. A record of excessive lateness will, like absenteeism, be a factor in appraising dependability. Public relations—each employee represents the university both on and off the job. The image one portrays is a label for all persons to witness whether they be students, colleagues, faculty, administration, alumni, visitors, or townspeople. Good public relations includes a friendly smile, courteous manners and, above all, a cordial and well-mannered relationship to and with all with whom one comes in contact. Smoking and coffee—adequate provision is made for rest periods during which time smoking and coffee may be consumed. Employees may not smoke or drink coffee while on the job. Coffee and smoking are not allowed by staff members at their normal work locale. Others—it is impossible to detail all other potential reasons for termination. Among them include unheeded reprimands, gross neglect of work or duty, indecent conduct, horseplay, or other acts that jeopardize the safety of others."

Usually, discipline is progressive and starts with an oral warning: "If it appears that an employee has failed to perform the work or conduct him or herself in accordance with requirements, the supervisor should first talk to the employee about the matter and then, if necessary, informally inquire into the situation further. When the facts indicate the employee may have been at fault, the supervisor should discuss the matter with the employee privately and in a pleasant manner. The first objective should be to find out whether the employee understands the rules involved or the standard expected of him. If not, the supervisor should fully explain what is expected and should be open to consideration of whether special circumstances may have been involved." "Initial disciplinary action should be in the form of an oral discussion and warning. Disciplinary action should never involve the element of surprise to the employee." "For repeated, but relatively minor, incidents of substandard performance or misconduct, discipline should be progressive. For example, an employee who is developing a lateness problem should first be talked to about his problem. A written record of the date and content of such discussion should be kept."

Exhibit 55 (continued)

Commonly, a written reprimand procedure is part of a disciplinary procedure: "The university may, in its discretion, issue warning letters to an employee it intends to discipline, in accordance with the following procedure: A meeting between the employee and the supervisor shall be held at which time the supervisor shall review and develop the facts and if the facts warrant, shall inform the employee that the employee is failing to meet acceptable standards of performance and dismissal will result if such standards are not met. Within three workdays after the meeting, the supervisor shall give to the employee a warning letter." "For continued problems requiring further action beyond oral warnings, a formal warning in writing as to the extent of the problem, suggested courses of action, and the time period of resolution should be prepared and discussed with the employee." "If the problem continues, a more formal discussion should take place. This more formal discussion should be confirmed by a letter to the employee which is sufficiently detailed to let him or her know how he or she has failed to meet standards. The letter should also advise the employee in general terms of the possible consequences of continued substandard performance." "Reprimand—the reprimand involves both discussion with the employee and an official memorandum. The discussion should be similar to that described in the oral warning section, but should place greater emphasis on the possible effect of the employee's conduct or performance on his or her record and the opportunities for advancement. The memorandum should be written by the supervisor to the employee. In it, the employee's supervisor should review the facts of the case and notify the employee that a copy be placed in the personnel folder." "The issuance of a written reprimand is a serious step. It creates a negative record to be considered in connection with performance review, promotion, and similar actions. Placing the employee under a handicap to overcome, may, however, be the best way to motivate the employee to the desired improvement. Not calling shortcomings to the employee's attention, on the other hand, may mean not giving him or her the chance to better the record."

The policy may state what should be included in the warning letter: "The supervisor will give to the employee a warning letter informing the employee of the date of the disciplinary meeting, the manner in which the employee is failing to meet acceptable standards of performance, and that dismissal will follow if such standards are not met."

The warning letter may be signed by the employee: "A copy of the letter of reprimand should be sent to the director of personnel services for the official files. It should bear the employee's comments, if any, and signature. The employee should be advised that the signature indicates that a copy has been received, and not necessarily that the employee agrees with the contents of the reprimand letter." "The employee will be required to sign the provided statement, signifying receipt of such communication."

The policy may state when a warning letter becomes obsolete: "If an employee receives three warning letters, the employee shall be discharged; provided, however, that if an employee does not receive a warning letter for a twelve-month period, all warning letters received prior to said twelve-month period shall not be considered as one of three warning letters toward discharge, and such letters shall not be used in considering the employee for promotion or transfer."

A result of a disciplinary action may be suspension without pay: "Suspension—suspension involves removal from the payroll, normally from two to five workdays. Before suspension action is taken, the supervisor should discuss the situation with the supervisor, the employee, and the director of personnel services. The employee should be given advance notice in writing and an opportunity to request reconsideration." "An employee should not be disciplined or discharged in haste or anger. If a serious incident occurs which may warrant discharge, the employee should be suspended pending investigation. The supervisor should then proceed to check all the facts, hear the employee's side, and check the employee's complete employment history. The supervisor may also find it helpful to obtain staff advice from the university personnel office or higher management." "When appropriate, a supervisor may suspend an employee without pay pending review by the immediate administrative supervisor. An employee will be fully informed of the reasons for suspension or dismissal and afforded his or her rights of appeal pending final institution action." "In cases where dismissal may be too severe an action, suspension may be approved by processing a leave of absence without salary. Suspension means the interruption of active employment status (without compensation) pending investigation and a decision as to the extent of disciplinary action. Time off during a suspension may be considered part of a disciplinary layoff. The suspension should not be given for a predetermined period of time, but should last only long enough in the supervisor's judgment to permit time for the investigation or cooling off or for the formulation of a decision after the investigation." "Disciplinary layoff without compensation is a very serious form of corrective action. It should only be employed when supervision believes that by its use the staff member will correct the misconduct. In contrast to the suspension, the disciplinary layoff should be for a stated period of time but only of a duration sufficient to correct misconduct. It may range from the balance of a shift to several weeks. The staff member will be given a written statement of the reasons for disciplinary layoff."

Termination of employment is the final action to be taken in the disciplinary process: "Release—in the case of other than serious offenses, release from employment should be used as a last resort only. When it becomes necessary to release an employee, the employee, in effect, will have released him or herself by the record that has been established." "Dismissal of classified employees may be effected by the immediate administrative supervisor if an employee's performance of duty or personal conduct is unsatisfactory."

Exhibit 55 (continued)

"If an employee receives three warning letters the employee shall be discharged." "Any person terminated will receive a warning notice or notices in advance relative to the reasons and request to improve work habits."

Dismissal can be immediate for major acts of misconduct or serious dereliction of duty: "Discharge without prior warnings or suspension may be justified for very serious offenses, for example, serious dishonesty, including theft of university property." "Two weeks notice of dismissal normally is given, but this period may be reduced or waived in extreme cases with the concurrence of the director of personnel. The notice period may be paid in full with attendance at work not required." "In cases involving dereliction of duty or serious misconduct, an employee may be suspended without prior notice pending review within ten working days. In such cases, the salary of the employee may be terminated immediately."

Other forms of disciplinary action may include making up of lost time, withholding salary increases, demotion, and transfer to more suitable work: "Depending on the severity of the offense, disciplinary action may take the following forms: warning, making up of lost time, withholding salary increases, demotion, suspension, or termination of services." "If there is insufficient improvement within a reasonable period of time, the department should try to work out a transfer to more suitable work within the department or contact the personnel office about a transfer within the university."

A statement may be included regarding repayment of salary lost in the event of reinstatement: "Any employee who has been dismissed or suspended without pay and who is later reinstated after appeal shall be paid at his or her regular rate from the date of dismissal or suspension."

Discipline, particularly termination for cause, usually involves notice of, or approval by, the personnel office: "Disciplinary action involving withholding of salary increase, suspension, demotion, or termination of services is accomplished upon the recommendation of the department head and with approval of the staff personnel officer." "Intended dismissals for cause (dishonesty, subordination, habitual tardiness or absenteeism, unacceptable behavior, and so forth) are reviewed with the personnel director." "A copy of the disciplinary notice is to be sent to the office of personnel services for inclusion in the employee's records and the employee should be so advised." "Fairness and consistency require that certain general principles of administering discipline be followed by all supervisors and that a staff office coordinate the discipline of university employees. Representatives in the university personnel office are available to discuss what is the appropriate course of action in a particular case."

Source: College and University Personnel Association (1980b, pp. 19–28).

Exhibit 56. Sample Policy on Failure to Meet Acceptable
Standards of Performance

The following policy outlines the steps to be taken by a supervisor when a staff employee is failing to meet acceptable standards of performance as determined by the university and, in the judgment of the supervisor, formal action is warranted. Reason and good judgment will be used in the application of this policy. This procedure does not grant substantive contractual rights to an employee. This procedure does not apply to a new employee during the provisional period.

Performance improvement meetings:

A meeting between the employee and the supervisor shall be held in which the supervisor shall discuss wherein the employee is failing to meet acceptable standards of performance and, if the facts warrant, indicate that dismissal will result if such standards are not met. A future date shall be established by which the employee shall meet the acceptable standards. The supervisor shall give the employee a signed written summary indicating the date of the meeting and the points covered in the discussion.

In addition, if the supervisor deems the circumstances serious enough that dismissal will result if acceptable standards are not met, the documentation shall so indicate. In such instance, copies also shall be given to the dean or administrative officer, and the university's manager of employee relations. Additional meetings between the supervisor and employee may be held to review the employee's progress and, at the discretion of the supervisor, to extend the period within which the employee is to meet acceptable standards of performance.

Dismissal of employee:

If the employee fails to meet acceptable standards of performance within the period designated by the supervisor or any extensions thereof, and the supervisor desires to proceed toward dismissal, a final meeting shall be held with the employee. However, prior to this final meeting, appropriate approval must be obtained as outlined in the following section covering responsibility for dismissal. At the final meeting the supervisor shall review the manner in which the employee has failed to meet acceptable standards of performance, and inform the employee that approval for termination has been received and specify a future date of termination (normally not less than thirty days from the date of the final meeting, except as provided below).

A written summary of the final meeting shall be given to the employee by the supervisor, with copies to the dean or administrative officer, and the manager of employee relations. The written summary constitutes the employee's formal confirmation of termination.

Exhibit 56 (continued)

Immediate dismissal:

If an employee is guilty of theft or other major act of misconduct, the supervisor shall recommend immediate dismissal.

Responsibility for dismissal:

Dismissal shall be only on recommendation to and approval by the dean or administrative officer. However, the dean or administrative officer shall review the dismissal with the university's manager of employee relations before approving action.

Exhibit 57. Sample Appeal Procedure for Faculty Members

The following procedures may be followed when issues involving faculty rights and responsibilities have not been successfully resolved through the normal channels of administrative responsibility and procedure.

Scope:

The Committee on Faculty Rights and Responsibilities, established by the Faculty Senate, may review petitions from faculty members and administrators involving: (1) Any situation in which a faculty member asserts that he or she has suffered a substantial injustice resulting from a violation of academic freedom, professional ethics, or procedural fairness; and (2) any situation in which an administrator seeks a committee judgment as to appropriate action toward a faculty member who, in his judgment, may be failing to meet his or her responsibilities. The committee shall not consider the substantive academic judgment aspects of such matters as promotion, tenure, compensation, and evaluation of performance. In such matters as these, only procedural fairness may be reviewed. The committee may not review petitions which are being or have been processed in the courts or through affirmative action.

The committee on Faculty Rights and Responsibilities will normally consider only petitions which involve a faculty member as a direct party including the following types of cases: (1) Dismissal—any university academic employee may make use of these procedures upon receipt of notice of dismissal. A dismissal is a termination before the end of the period of appointment; (2) nonreappointment—any university academic employee who can demonstrate that considerations violative of academic freedom significantly contributed to a decision of nonreappointment may make use of these procedures; and (3) other matters—the Committee on Faculty

Rights and Responsibilities may, as it deems appropriate, review petitions of any university academic employee in matters beyond the above limitations, but formal hearings will not be held except in rare cases where there are compelling reasons for them. The committee shall not define other matters so as to include cases which are being or have been processed in court or through affirmative action.

Cases of substantive dispute involving the termination of a tenured appointment for cause or for reasons of financial exigency or program elimination or revision, or the release of a faculty member during the provisional appointment period with less advance notice than that specified in university policy, shall be considered at a hearing by the Standing Joint Committee on Tenure under the conditions set forth in the tenure policy.

Committee on faculty rights and responsibilities:

The Committee on Faculty Rights and Responsibilities will have nine members elected by the Faculty Senate: six faculty members and three members of the Council of Academic Deans. The term of office will be three years, with staggered terms for the initial committee. Six faculty members and three deans will be elected as alternates for three-year terms. The Senate Council will present a list of nominees to fill vacancies and expiring terms on the committee at the May meeting of the Faculty Senate each year. Additional nominations may be made from the floor at that time. Election of committee members and alternates will be by secret written mail ballot.

Operation of the committee:

The committee chairman will be elected by the committee from among its members at a meeting in June. The term of office will be for one year—from the July meeting of one year to the July meeting of the next year. At the May Faculty Senate meeting of each academic year, the chairman of the Committee on Faculty Rights and Responsibilities will present a brief general report of the committee's activities.

A quorum of the committee will be a majority of those remaining after disqualifications on a matter at issue, subject to a minimum of three members. A majority of those voting on a matter at issue will be faculty.

Upon receiving a petition, the committee will make a preliminary determination as to the extent of its review of the matter. This preliminary determination must include the committee's judgment that the appropriate department, college, or other unit administrative procedures have been exhausted prior to the point the committee decides whether to review the petition further. In making such a judgment, the committee shall consult

Exhibit 57 (continued)

with the ombudsman in the appropriate college or campus. The committee will reserve the right not to take up a complaint that it judges substantial or without merit or where it appears that other remedies should be sought before coming to the committee.

The committee may decide to have an informal review or to establish a hearing board. If a hearing board is not established, the committee may use its good offices in an attempt to bring about a satisfactory settlement. In the event the committee decides to review informally the case or hold a hearing, the petitioner, the university's provost's office, the appropriate college official, and the college ombudsman shall be notified immediately.

A hearing board will be established only when the issue is clearly serious, a prima facie case has been established by the complaining party, and the committee finds that reasonable efforts have already been made to solve the problem, and that no alternative way of attempting to settle the matter is appropriate in the circumstances. The burden of proof in establishing a prima facie case will be on the complaining party.

The committee should attempt to settle matters brought to it as quickly as possible without sacrificing fairness to all parties. Only in extraordinary circumstances should there be a time span longer than thirty days between the receipt of a complaint by the committee and a decision as to whether there will be a formal hearing.

The role of a hearing board:

For a particular case, a hearing board, consisting of two faculty members and one dean to be chosen from the committee by methods of its own selection, will be established to hear the case. The hearing board will elect its chairman from among its members. A member will remove himself or herself from a case by reason of bias or interest. Each party will have a maximum of two challenges without stated cause. If disqualifications and challenges make it impossible to set up a board with three members from the committee or elected alternates, the Senate Council will select substitutes for a particular case. Each party will have a maximum of two challenges of such substitutes without stated cause.

If a hearing is scheduled, notice will be served with a specific statement of the complaint at least twenty days prior to the hearing. The party complained against may waive a hearing or may respond to the complaint in writing at any time before the hearing. Hearings before a hearing board will not be public. Publicity and public statements about the case by either the faculty member or administrative officers will be avoided until the proceedings have been completed. The hearing board may have present at the hearing such assistance as it deems necessary.

During the proceedings the parties will be entitled to have an advisor and counsel of their own choice. The hearing board will not be bound by strict rules of legal evidence, and may admit any evidence or probative value in determining the issues involved. Every possible effort will be made to obtain the most reliable evidence available and to avoid excessively legalistic procedures. A verbatim record of the hearings will be taken and a typewritten copy will be made available to both parties.

The parties will be afforded an opportunity to obtain necessary witnesses and documentary or other evidence. The university administration will make all reasonable efforts to cooperate with the hearing board in securing witnesses and making available documentary and other evidence. Parties will have the right to confront and cross-examine all witnesses. The hearing board will grant adjournments to enable either party to investigate evidence as to which a valid claim of surprise is made.

The hearing board's findings of fact and conclusions will be based solely on the hearing record. The hearing board shall reach its conclusions by majority vote and shall submit these conclusions to the president of the university through the chairman of the Committee on Faculty Rights and Responsibilities. The president shall notify the chairman of the decision that has been reached. In the event that the president's decision is not in accord with the conclusions of the hearing board, the reasons for that decision shall be specified to the chairman of the Committee on Faculty Rights and Responsibilities who will inform the committee and the parties directly involved. After receiving the conclusions and recommendations on a case from a hearing board, the president of the university shall notify the parties directly involved, appropriate university administrative officers, and the chairman of the Committee on Faculty Rights and Responsibilities as to his decision. The chairman shall be responsible for informing the Committee on Faculty Rights and Responsibilities.

Definition of faculty:

The term *faculty member* shall include the Faculty Senate's definition of its electorate plus all research equivalent ranks. The definition is as follows: All persons who are not candidates for degrees at this university, who hold full-time academic appointments, and who fall into one of the following categories—those holding professorial, research, or librarian titles, those who are full-time instructors or assistant librarians, and those other full-time academic employees who are members of the Graduate Faculty, but who do not fall into either of the preceding categories. In addition, access to these procedures is afforded professional employees involved in teaching, research, or creative activities who are attached to a research unit or an

Exhibit 57 (continued)

academic college, including the following categories: part-time (with at least a six-months' appointment), visiting, clinical, and adjunct academic personnel.

Conciliation:

Each college and library should have a person or group to serve in the role of ombudsman. The ombudsman's objectives are to enhance communication and clarify possible misunderstandings in situations that involve potential disputes, to advise faculty members and administrators as to appropriate courses of action, and to help settle matters before they become hardened into serious disputes. The individual or group should be selected by procedures approved by a majority of the faculty in the unit.

The dean and the faculty shall jointly develop selection procedures for the ombudsman. Normally, the role of ombudsman will be performed by a single person, with a designated alternate. In unusual circumstances, a group of not more than three persons may be selected. No one who is a member of the Committee on Faculty Rights and Responsibilities shall serve as ombudsman.

The functions of the ombudsman are: (1) to clarify misunderstandings; (2) to advise faculty and administrators as to appropriate courses of action; (3) to assist in the informal resolution of differences; (4) to assure that appropriate department and college procedures are exhausted before referring the case to higher levels; and (5) to inform the university provost's office and appropriate college or campus officials if a matter cannot be resolved at the lower level and the case is to be referred to the Committee on Faculty Rights and Responsibilities.

The ombudsman shall *not:* (1) hold hearings; (2) exceed the role of conciliator and advisor; (3) substitute his or her judgment for that of appropriate administrative or faculty bodies; nor (4) serve as counsel for either party to a complaint before the hearing board.

Exhibit 58. Sample Employee Grievance Form

Employee: _____ _____ _____
              Name   Position   Agency

_____   _____
         Work Facility   Work Unit

Nature of grievance _____

_____

_____

_____

_____

Date grievance occurred _____ Relief requested _____
_____
_____
_____

Date of verbal presentation to supervisor _____
Date form submitted to supervisor _____

Step 1 Employee-supervisor
Supervisor's first-step reply _____
_____
_____
_____
_____

Date _____ Supervisor's signature _____
☐ Check this box if you wish to advance your grievance to the second step
   of the grievance procedure.
Employee's signature _____

Step 2 Employee–next higher level manager
_____ Date submitted to second step
Date of second-step meeting _____ Manager's second step reply _____
_____
_____
_____
_____

Date _____ Manager's signature _____
☐ Check this box if you wish to advance your grievance to the third step
   of the grievance procedure.
Employee's signature _____

Step 3 Employee–agency head or faculty director
_____ Date forwarded to third step
Date of third-step meeting _____ Manager's third step reply _____
_____
_____
_____
_____

Date _____ Manager's Signature _____
☐ Check this box if the grievance has not been satisfactorily resolved and
   you wish to advance the grievance to a panel hearing.
Employee's signature _____

Upon checking the above box, this form must be submitted to the agency
head within ten work days of receipt of the third-step reply.

Exhibit 59. Sample Grievance Form for Nurses in a Teaching Hospital

General Information
   Name of grievant(s) _____
   Work area _____
   Shift assignment _____
   Status (check one) _____ Full-time _____Part-time
   Date of hire _____
Statement of Grievance
   Date on which grievance arose _____
   Location at which grievance arose _____
   Brief statement of grievance _____
   _____
   _____
   _____
   _____

   Applicable article(s) of the agreement _____
   Signature of grievant(s) _____
   Local unit representative's signature (if requested)
   _____

Step 1. Present grievance to grievant's immediate supervisor, for discussion within seven calendar days after grievance arises.
   Supervisor's name _____
   Supervisor's title _____
   Date on which grievance presented _____
   The answer of the immediate supervisor shall be given to the employee within four calendar days following the discussion.
   Statement of grievance settlement or supervisor's answer _____
   _____
   _____
   _____

   Supervisor's signature _____
   Date of settlement or answer _____

Step 2. Appeal of unsettled grievance to the Director of Nursing within four calendar days following the step 1 answer. Presentation to the Director of Nursing *must* be in writing.
   Date on which grievance presented to the Director of Nursing _____
   Is a meeting requested by grievant(s) at this step?
                     _____ Yes   _____ No

   If meeting requested, what date? (Within ten calendar days of presentation of grievance to director)
   _____

   If meeting not requested by grievant(s) or Director of Nursing, an answer to the grievance is due within five calendar days after presentation.

Statement of settlement or answer of Director of Nursing _____

_____

_____

Signature of Director of Nursing_____
Date of settlement or answer _____

Step 3. Appeal of unsettled grievance to the office of the Hospital Director within four calendar days following the step 2 answer.
    Date on which grievance presented to Hospital Director _____
    Is a meeting requested by grievant(s) at this step?
                _____ Yes   _____ No
    If meeting requested, what date? (Within ten calendar days of presentation of grievance to Hospital Director)

_____

    If meeting not requested by grievant(s) or Hospital Director, an answer to the grievance is due within five calendar days after presentation.
    Statement of settlement or answer to Hospital Director _____

_____

_____

Signature of Hospital Director _____
Date of settlement or answer _____

Step 4. Appeal of unsettled grievance to the office of the Associate Provost for Administration within five calendar days following the step 3 answer.
    Date on which grievance presented to Associate Provost_____
    Is a meeting requested by grievant(s) at this step?
                _____ Yes   _____ No
    If meeting requested, what date? (Within ten calendar days of presentation of grievance to Associate Provost)

_____

    If meeting not requested by grievant(s) or Associate Provost, an answer to the grievance is due within seven calendar days after presentation.
    Statement of settlement or answer to Associate Provost _____

_____

_____

Signature of Associate Provost _____
Date of settlement or answer _____

   Note: An association grievance begins at step 3. Time limits may be waived only by mutual agreement. Any unresolved grievance may be referred to arbitration within ten calendar days of the step 4 answer.

Exhibit 60. Guidelines for Policy on Grievance or Appeal Procedures

A good affirmative action program has, as one of its ingredients, a procedure whereby an employee who feels aggrieved can seek redress. The grievance procedure should, of course, handle a variety of grievances, not only alleged discrimination grievances. Grievance procedures are usually not available to probationary employees (unless there is a claim of discrimination).

There are two distinct schools of thought regarding the definition of what is grievable. One is legalistic and limits a grievance to a breach of a contract or written policy. The second is broader and permits a grievance on any condition of employment. Personnel officers divide on their opinions on which is better.

The procedure itself should be designed to provide for hearings or reviews at various management steps. This has two virtues: (1) It refines the grievance. Sometimes an employee is obviously upset, and because of the emotion that permeates the atmosphere, it is difficult to determine exactly what solution is being sought. A review by steps affords the opportunity to explore solutions. (2) Having a case reviewed at a variety of management levels provides a broader look at the problem. A broader insight can provide a better solution.

Policy items and sample policy language:

The definition of a grievance may be very broad: "Any staff member has the right to present any personal concern or dissatisfaction regarding his employment to the university and have it considered on its merits." "Should a regular staff member have a grievance concerning any condition of employment (rates of pay, classification of position, hours of work, disciplinary action, and so forth) he or she may present an appeal." "The purpose of this procedure is to promote the orderly resolution of problems arising out of employment." "Fair and prompt consideration shall be given to all employee complaints, problems, suggestions and questions."

The definition of a grievance may be more restrictive: "The following procedures may be utilized by an employee who believes he or she has been discharged or disciplined without just cause, or discriminated against in connection with his or her employment because of sex, race, color, religion, national origin, or age." "All disputes concerning the operation or interruption of this agreement shall be settled in accordance with this grievance procedure." "A grievance within the meaning of this agreement shall be any difference, controversy, or dispute arising between the parties hereto or the members of the union employed by this university involving the application of interpretation of this agreement." "A grievance is a work-related problem or condition which an employee believes to be unfair, inequitable, discriminatory, or a hindrance to his or her effective operation. This grievance procedure is not designed to include changes in policy or demotions or terminations." ". . . that his or her rights under established university rules and procedures have been violated." "A grievance is defined as a claim of an individual employee, as well as a small group of employees, that the employee's rights under announced rules and regulations or past practices have not been respected." "Discharge and discipline cases do not include failure to extend employment beyond a previously established term or elimination of a position due to a reduction in force."

Time limits for initiating a grievance should be considered in order to avoid hearing outdated grievances which can be most difficult to resolve: "A grievance, other than one involving discharge, shall be presented not later than five working days after the occurrence of the event claimed to have given rise to the grievance. Any claim not presented within the time provided shall be deemed to have been waived." "Any grievance to be considered under this procedure must be brought up . . . within one calendar week of the time that the employee has knowledge of the act which is the basis for the grievance." "The employee may request a review of his or her case by submitting a letter to his or her supervisor within two weeks after the action was taken in the discipline or discharge case, or with reasonable promptness in a case of alleged discrimination." "The employee, within thirty calendar days of the time the specific incident leading to the alleged grievance occurred, shall file a written grievance."

The policy should designate which employees have access to the grievance procedure. Some institutions have different procedures for each classification group. Others combine classification groupings: "This procedure is applicable to salaried personnel. It is not applicable to members of a faculty or other instructional staff, or employees covered by a collective bargaining agreement unless the agreement so provides." "This complaint procedure applies to office, technical, professional, and administrative staff members." "This procedure will be applicable to grievances arising out of employment of a university employee, whether exempt or nonexempt provided: (1) such an employee is not a member of the university faculty or is not a senior research associate, a senior extension associate, instructor, lecturer, graduate assistant, teaching assistant, research assistant, extension or graduate research assistant; or (2) such employee is not a member of a bargaining unit certified for the purposes of collective bargaining." "This grievance procedure is applicable to all regular staff (nonteaching) personnel." "Members of the university staff including faculty, professional, classified, and student employees . . . are hereby provided grievance procedures." "Grievance procedure for regular employees and for employees designated as part-time continuing."

Normally, the grievance first must be discussed with the immediate supervisor. In some procedures this is the first formal step of the procedure. In others, it is a required

Exhibit 60 (continued)

step before the first formal step: "Step one: A problem should be taken first to the immediate supervisor(s). Most problems can be worked out here and the supervisor(s), after investigation of the situation, shall report his or her decision to the employee within forty-eight hours." "Since most grievances can be settled in conversation between the employee and the employee's supervisor, a written grievance will not be considered unless the grievance has first been discussed with the supervisor, and the supervisor has had two workdays to give an answer to the employee." "Whenever an employee feels improperly or unfairly treated by the university and has been unable to resolve the problem by informal means, he or she individually, or with another university employee as his or her representative, shall discuss the grievance with the immediate supervisor." "The employee may request a review of his or her case by submitting a letter to his or her supervisor. If the case remains unresolved a week after the request is received, the supervisor will attach his or her comments to the letter and forward the letter." "If you have a problem or grievance, you should attempt to work it out with your supervisor first. If you do not feel that your supervisor has handled your complaint satisfactorily, you should present it to his administrative officer in the presence of your supervisor, if you wish. If your complaint cannot be resolved as a result of this initial contact, the administrative officer is to direct a written acknowledgment of the problem to you with an indication of a timetable and steps for resolution." "When an employee has a question or complaint, or any difficulty with working relationships, he or she should first either (1) discuss it with his or her immediate supervisor; or, as an alternative, (2) discuss it with an employee advisor in the personnel office. Such advisors will attempt to mediate any difference that cannot be resolved between an employee and his supervisor."

Grievance procedures usually proceed through steps either formal or informal to a final step. Usually the grievance must be submitted in writing: "When the employee files a grievance, he shall submit a brief statement to the office of personnel services containing those relevant facts which form the basis of his complaint and the relief which he seeks. No particular form shall be required and the personnel office will, if necessary, prepare a copy for the employee to sign." "If the employee is not satisfied with the decision by the immediate supervisor(s), he or she shall present his or her grievance in writing to the director of personnel. The employee should provide the following: (1) A statement of the grievance and the facts upon which it is based. (2) The remedy or corrective action sought." "The first step in this procedure will be the filing of a memorandum in letter form by the aggrieved employee with his or her immediate supervisor. The document should include, but not necessarily be limited to, the following: (1) Statement and basis of the grievance; (2) date(s) of the occurrence(s); (3) attempts made to solve the grievance; (4) signature of the aggrieved employee and the date of the memorandum."

There are usually time limits for requesting the next step in the grievance procedure: "An appeal by either party to the next step must be made within three working days of the receipt of such answer." "If an employee gets an answer within the time limit at any step of the procedure and does not ask for further review of the grievance within the next four workdays, it will be assumed that particular grievance will not be considered any further." "Grievance shall be handled with 'reasonable promptness' both in submission and in processing at each level. 'Reasonable promptness' is defined as a maximum of five working days."

Frequently there are time limits by which a hearing is held: "A hearing must be held within five days after filing the written grievance." "The person to whom the grievance has been referred shall promptly, but in any event within five working days after the grievance has been submitted, meet with the employee."

Often there are time limits by which an answer must be given at the various steps of the procedure: "The director of personnel shall have twenty-four hours (three working days) in which to answer the employee in writing, providing reasons for his or her determination in the issue." " . . . provide the staff member with a written response to his or her complaint within seven calendar days of the review meeting." "If a mutually satisfactory adjustment is not reached within ten working days, the employee may submit the grievance to the proper person at the next supervisory level."

Sometimes time limits are defined where there are a variety of days on and days off for employees: "Saturdays, Sundays, and holidays shall not be applied in computing time limits under this procedure, nor shall the normal workdays off of the grievant or his or her immediate supervisor apply in computing such time limits."

Time limits may be extended: "All time limits may be extended solely by agreement of the parties in writing." "If there is a reasonable explanation why an employee has failed to seek a review within the required time limit, the time limit may be waived by the dean, administrative department head, or director of personnel. In some cases, additional time may be required for investigations and answers because of the complexity of the case and the availability of the people involved." "When warranted by unusual circumstances (illness, extended absence, and the like), the director of personnel may extend or modify the time limits indicated in the grievance procedure." "Time standards for review meetings and answers should only be adjusted if the university representative responsible for the discussion or the answer is absent from the office or if the staff member is unable to meet within the established time period."

Exhibit 60 (continued)

The aggrieved employee(s) may be represented by other persons at the hearing: "The employee may be accompanied by another university employee of the employee's own choosing from the employee's own department." "At the meeting, the employee may have representatives of the employee's own choosing not to exceed three in number." "The employee may be represented by the steward and a paid representative of the union." "In the case of a group grievance, up to three employees from the aggrieved group may attend the hearing." "An employee may select as a representative any university employee who is both willing to serve and able to arrange the work schedule so that he or she can discharge his or her obligations as a grievance representative without impairing significantly the work performance of the department. After filing a request for a hearing before an outside hearing officer, an employee may be represented, for purposes of selecting a hearing officer, preparing a submission agreement, and preparing and representing evidence and arguments before the hearing officer, by a person who is not a university employee." "The employee, if he or she so chooses, can obtain assistance from a member of the university or will be provided assistance by the university in presenting his or her case." "The employee may be represented at the hearing by a person of his or her own choosing. The director of personnel shall, if requested, help the employee find a suitable representative. Reasonable provisions will be made for other employees to appear as witnesses on behalf of either party without loss of pay."

The employee and his or her representatives (if they are employees) normally are paid for work time missed (but they are not paid if the hearing is at a non-work time): "Employees attending proceedings as grievants, representatives, or witnesses shall be reimbursed at their normal rates of pay for any normal work time missed for such proceedings." "A staff member may make an oral presentation, write a complaint, and attend the complaint review meeting during normal working hours without loss of time or pay."

The final step of the procedure is an important step which can be handled by arbitrators or panels. (The intermediate steps usually follow organizational channels with assistance from the personnel department. The intermediate steps should be tailored to meet each institution's structure): "If arbitration is requested, the parties shall attempt to mutually agree on an arbitrator. If such agreement cannot be reached, the Federal Mediation and Conciliation Service will be requested to send a list of seven suggested arbitrators. The parties shall select the arbitrator from such list by each party alternately removing one name from the list until one name remains. In a grievance concerning job evaluation, the seven arbitrators shall be experienced in matters relating to job classification and evaluation and familiar with job rating plans of the types then currently in effect at the university, and the arbitrator selected by the parties shall make a decision based on the principles of the job rating plan then currently in effect at the university." "The final appeal is to the University Complaint Review Committee which consists of the personnel director, or assistant to the vice president for academic affairs (or their designated representatives), as chairman, the head of the operating unit in which the complaining staff member works (or his or her representative) and other staff members who may be designated." "The hearing officer, who shall not be an employee of the university, shall be selected from a list of five names established by the president of the university. The list will be established from time to time and shall consist of persons experienced in labor arbitration recommended to the president by a panel of those persons similarly experienced chosen by the president from the faculties of other universities or colleges. The president shall submit the list of five names to the grievant and to the university's representative on the case. Within five working days after the list is provided, the parties shall select the hearing officer by the alternate striking of names (first by the grievant and then by the university representative) until one remains. If within two working days following the selection, the hearing officer selected is unable to confirm that he or she will hold a hearing, within two weeks, the selection process shall be repeated until a hearing officer is selected who can hold a hearing within two weeks following the selection." "The employee may appeal the grievance directly to an appeal committee. The three-member appeal committee shall be ad hoc and the members shall be appointed by the president from a list of six or more employees agreed upon by the appropriate dean and either the president or representative of the faculty association or of the classified employees association." "In cases involving suspension or discharge, the complaint may be referred to a three-member fact-finding committee appointed by the president. The committee members will be knowledgeable in employee relations matters and impartial to the case." "A grievance review board will be established to review all grievances which a classified employee feels have not been satisfactorily resolved within his or her own organization or the personnel services division. This board will, for each grievance hearing, consist of three members selected from a group of fifteen university employees and administrators appointed by the president. The membership of the board and method of selecting representatives for a specific grievance will be as follows: *Membership*—five members appointed from nonadministrative classified employees; five members appointed from administrative classified employees and from administrative offices; five members appointed from the faculty. *Selection*—the grieving employee will select one member from the fifteen; the director of personnel services will select one member from the fifteen; the two selected will select the third from the fifteen." "The grievance board is composed of a chairperson and four members appointed by the president from a panel of persons recommended by bodies which represent the three major employee groups of

Exhibit 60 (continued)

the university: faculty, professional, and classified. Twelve persons are elected by each representative council in a manner determined by each council. Terms are for two years except that initially six persons are to be elected to one-year terms by each council so that half the membership may be renewed annually." "The employee can appeal to the committee in charge of nonfaculty personnel which consists of the vice president for business and finance, the director of personnel, and another annually appointed member of the administration."

The results of the final appeal step are then defined: "The decision of the arbitrator shall be final and binding on the parties." "The appeal committee shall hear the grievance and make a recommendation directly to the president." "The staff council will present its findings and recommendations to the president for final action." "The recommendation of the board of review shall be forwarded to the president for final decision. If the problem cannot be resolved to the satisfaction of the employee at the institutional level, the employee may file a written appeal with the board of regents within twenty days following the written notification of the president's decision." "The decision of the hearing committee shall be final and binding."

A statement regarding arbitration expenses is frequently used. Usually the expenses are borne by the university in a nonunion situation and split with the union when there is one: "Tape recordings will be used, but a written transcript will not be made unless the grievant secures the services of a competent court reporter and pays the cost thereof." "Stenographic service may be employed in connection with the arbitration at the discretion of either party at its expense. If the parties mutually agree upon stenographic service, the expenses therefore shall be borne equally by the university and the union."

Usually grievance procedures are not available to probationary employees (except for alleged discrimination): "This procedure does not apply to an employee during his or her probationary period."

Source: College and University Personnel Association (1980b, pp. 29–40).

Exhibit 61. Sample Appeal Procedure for Staff Employees

The following procedure may be used by an employee classified as staff exempt or staff nonexempt who is not a probationary employee to appeal that his or her rights under established university rules and procedures have been violated. An employee can use this procedure without fear of prejudice. This procedure shall not be used for a claim of discrimination, which will be covered by the Equal Opportunity Staff Discrimination Review Committee procedure. Nothing contained herein shall negate the right of the university to augment or change its policies applicable to staff exempt and staff nonexempt employees.

Time limits:

Any matter to be considered under this procedure must be discussed initially between the employee and the employee's immediate supervisor within one calendar week from the date the employee first has knowledge of the circumstances giving rise to the issue. If an employee does not request further review within the time limits specified at any point in this procedure, it shall be assumed that the employee is satisfied. The time limits specified in this procedure may be extended only by mutual agreement in writing between the employee and the university.

Dismissal appeal:

An appeal concerning dismissal shall be heard directly at the second level in the procedure.

First level:

The employee shall submit the appeal in writing and give two copies to the employee's immediate supervisor (one copy to be given immediately to the designated personnel representative by the supervisor). The written appeal shall state facts, dates, and policy or procedure involved if applicable. A hearing shall be held within eight workdays following receipt of the written appeal and shall be attended by the employee, the employee's immediate supervisor, a supervisor at a higher level in the department if applicable, and the designated personnel representative. The employee may be accompanied by another regular university employee of his or her own choosing. A written answer shall be provided to the employee within eight workdays following the hearing.

Second level:

If the issue is not settled at the first level, the appeal may proceed to the second level, upon written request of the employee to the dean or adminis-

Exhibit 61 (continued)

trative officer, with a copy to the university's director of personnel relations, within eight workdays following the written answer to the first-level hearing. A hearing shall be held within eight workdays following receipt of the request. The hearing shall be attended by those persons present at the first-level hearing and the dean or administrative officer and the director of personnel relations or their designees. The university or the employee may invite such other persons as appropriate to present testimony in the hearing in order to ascertain the facts or resolve the issue. Before the answer is given to the employee, the facts of the case shall be reviewed by the cognizant vice president. Subsequently, written answer shall be given to the employee by the dean or administrative officer, or the designee of the dean or administrative officer, within eight workdays following the hearing.

Appeal review board:

If the issue is not settled at the second level, the employee may appeal to a tripartite board for review, upon written request to the director of personnel relations within eight workdays following the answer to the second-level hearing. The review board shall consist of a member selected by the employee (excluding a representative of any organization or association acting as bargaining agent for any other classification of university employees), a member selected by the university, and a third, impartial member selected by the other two members. The impartial member shall serve as chairperson. In the event the first two members cannot agree on a third member, a list of seven names shall be requested from the Federal Mediation and Conciliation Service, and the third member shall be selected by the other members' alternately removing one name from the list until one name remains.

The review board shall schedule a hearing as soon as possible at a time mutually agreeable to all parties concerned. The employee may have a representative of his or her own choosing (excluding a representative of any organization or association acting as bargaining agent for any other classification of university employees) at the hearing, and other university representatives as appropriate shall attend. The board may at its discretion summon such other persons as necessary for testimony to determine the fact or merit of the appeal. The review board shall make its findings and recommendations for action as expeditiously as possible to the president of the university, applying and interpreting existing university rules and regulations applicable to the case at hand. The president shall make a ruling after considering the panel's recommendation. The university shall bear the cost, if any, for the review board members.

Special meetings:

By mutual agreement, special meetings between the employee and university representatives involved may be scheduled on an informal basis at any time during this procedure in order to seek resolution of the matter.

Group appeal:

In the event an issue involves a group of employees, up to three employees from the group may participate in presenting the appeal at hearings or meetings specified in this procedure.

Time off for appeal hearings:

Employees shall not lose pay for any time not on the job if their presence is required at appeal hearings or special meetings with the university as provided by this procedure. An employee shall not be paid for any time present during the processing of an appeal if such time falls outside the employee's normal work hours.

Exhibit 62. Sample Grievance Procedure for Staff Employees

Policy:

A staff member shall be afforded the opportunity to file a grievance on matters directly associated with the staff member's employment relationship with the university. Filing a grievance will not cause any reflection on the individual's status as a staff member nor will it affect future employment, compensation, or work assignments. An allegation that a staff member's rights under this policy have been violated also will be subject to review under the grievance procedure. This policy applies to regular and temporary office, technical, professional, administrative, and primary staff members except those covered by approved unit grievance procedures.

Pregrievance counseling:

A representative of the personnel office, or in cases dealing with discrimination, a representative of the affirmative action program office, will be available to counsel staff members who believe they have a grievance. Pregrievance counseling is not judgmental. The role of the counselor is to help the grievant identify the source of the problem. A personnel office representative provides the grievant with information concerning university policies and standard practice guides, as well as protective laws and regulations related to the potential grievance. In cases dealing with a potential discrimination grievance, an affirmative action program office representative may also inform the grievant concerning university policies as well as protective laws and regulations as they may apply.

Exhibit 62 (continued)

Pregrievance resolution:

The university will make a good faith effort to seek resolution of a problem informally brought to the attention of the personnel office representative, or, in the case of alleged discrimination to an affirmative action program office representative, through discussion and communication with the department or unit involved and with appropriate university officials.

Definition:

The grievance procedure is a three-step review process whereby a staff member may exercise the right to address matters directly associated with employment in accordance with the procedures set forth in this standard practice guide.

Time standards:

Time limits set forth for filing and appealing grievances, holding review meetings, and issuing answers must be strictly followed. Mutually agreeable adjustments in holding a review meeting and in issuing an answer may be made due to the unavailability of a necessary party. In any event, such time limit adjustments shall not be in excess of five days beyond the stated limits. The grievance is considered withdrawn if the grievant fails to appear at a scheduled review meeting or does not appeal on a timely basis.

Modification:

The orderly progression from steps 1 through 3 may be modified by the university by reducing the number of steps for grievance resolution where the origin of the grievance, the operational unit involved, or the content and scope of the grievance makes that progression impractical.

Assistance in review meetings:

A staff member may select any individual (except a staff member who is included in a university collective bargaining unit or the grievant's immediate supervisor) to assist in the review meetings at steps 2 and 3. If the assistant is a university staff member, the assistant will not lose time or pay for attending meetings held during the assistant's normal working hours.

No loss of time or pay:

A staff member's attendance at a grievance review meeting held during normal working hours shall be with pay. Any other time spent in formulating or preparing a grievance shall be done outside the regular work schedule and shall be without compensation.

Discipline grievances:

Grievances concerning discharge or disciplinary layoff will be heard directly at step 3.

University grievance review committee:

The University Grievance Review Committee will consist of the university personnel director, or assistant to the vice president for academic affairs, or their designated representative, as chairperson; the head of the operating unit in which the grieving staff member works, or a designated representative; and other staff members who may be deemed appropriate in the review process by the chairperson because of their special sensitivity or expertise. A representative of the general counsel's office will be available to advise the review committee. When unlawful discrimination is alleged, the University Grievance Review Committee also will include a representative from the university affirmative action programs office.

Failure to appeal:

If a staff member does not appeal a grievance within the time requirement set forth in the following procedures, the grievance shall be considered settled on the basis of the university's last answer.

Liability:

Except as otherwise specifically provided, the university shall not be liable on a grievance claiming back wages or other financial reimbursement for any period prior to thirty calendar days prior to knowledge of the facts giving rise to the grievance.

Procedures:

Responsibility	*Action*
Staff member	Consider involvement in pregrievance counseling and pregrievance resolution.
Representative of the personnel office or affirmative action program office	Counsel the employee concerning university policies, practices, standard practice guides, and protective laws and regulations.
Representative of the personnel office or affirmative action program office	Work to informally resolve a grievance. In no event shall this effort void the time limits established in the procedure outlined in this standard practice guide.
Staff member (step 1)	Within fifteen calendar days (thirty calendar days if the grievant works with a

Exhibit 62 (continued)

Responsibility	Action
Staff member (step 1) (cont.)	representative of the personnel office or affirmative action program to informally resolve a grievance) of knowledge of the facts giving rise to the grievance, discuss grievance with immediate supervisor.
Supervisor	Reply orally to staff member within three mutual working days from date of discussion.
Staff member (step 2)	If not satisfied with oral answer, or none received within three mutual working days, may appeal in writing to department head. Complete grievance form. Obtain advice as needed from staff and union relations office. Present grievance form to department head (or equivalent level of supervisor) or designated representative within seven calendar days following a timely, but unsatisfactory answer or no answer at step 1.
Department head	Upon receipt of written appeal: (1) Notify personnel office representative and send copy of grievance; (2) schedule review meeting and hear oral presentation of grievance within seven calendar days of receipt of written grievance; and (3) provide staff member with a written response to grievance within seven calendar days of review meeting.
Staff member (step 3)	If not satisfied with the answer may appeal to the University Grievance Review Committee within fourteen calendar days after receipt of step 2 answer. If no step 2 answer is received within seven calendar days of review meeting, may appeal to the University Review Committee by presenting grievance form to the Committee. (Grievance involving lost time, discipline or discharge begins at step 3.)
Chairperson of the University Grievance Review Committee	Upon receipt of written appeal: (1) Schedule review meeting within fourteen calen-

dar days of receipt of written grievance; (2) review the record and any additional pertinent new information; and (3) answer grievance in writing within sixty days from date of hearing (thirty days when the grievant is appealing a discharge or a lost time disciplinary action), provided that if the grievance involves alleged unlawful discrimination, the answer will be reviewed by the president with no extension of time, before being issued.

Staff member

No further appeal is available unless unlawful discrimination is alleged (in which case appeal, if timely, may be to an external agency).

**Exhibit 63. Sample Policy on Equal Employment
Opportunity Discrimination Review Committees**

Purpose:

To systematically and appropriately examine complaints by academic or staff employees who contend that discrimination has occurred on the basis of race, creed, color, national origin, handicap, age (as provided by law), or sex, and to recommend to the president corrective measures if the evidence so indicates.

Major principles:

The review and adjudication of complaints related to discrimination shall occur at the lowest administrative level and in the least formal manner possible contingent on the satisfaction of both parties. Procedures for resolving such grievances in a progressively more formal way and at higher administrative levels shall, however, be made available to either party if necessary.

The review of complaints shall be conducted by the appropriate committee of professional peers whose constituency shall include minority and female members. Such members are to serve as jurors and not assume an advocacy position for either party. The committee shall include appropriate representatives from both faculty or staff and administration. All complaints shall be reviewed and recommendations made with promptness and dispatch. The president shall be informed with promptness and dispatch of the actions and recommendations of review committees.

Exhibit 63 (continued)

Legal counsel for the complainant or the university shall not be present at any hearing; however, a legal advisor selected by the review committee may be present to assist with procedural matters. Also, prehearing briefings by legal counsel to the contending parties are permissible; however, transcripts of the preceding testimony will not be available.

The committees shall serve in an advisory capacity to the president. Their report to the president will note the judgment of the committee surrounding the grievant's claim. Other relevant comments may be made if the committee wishes.

Confidentiality shall be maintained at all levels of the review.

Charges of discrimination shall be directed to the university. Persons serving as administrative officers shall always be viewed as agents of the university and any charges shall not be directed to them personally. When, however, a particular person is alleged to be the responsible party, for the discriminatory practice, that person may be named in the charge together with supporting evidence of instances of such action. The officer responsible for the person so charged shall be notified of the charge and given an opportunity to participate in the hearing as a witness. The charged person shall have the right to be present at all times during any formal hearing and defend himself or herself.

Academic staff discrimination review committee:

The Academic Staff Discrimination Review Committee shall review complaints filed by academic staff members. The membership and selection procedures for the committee are as follows: (1) Two members selected by the provost from four nominees submitted by the Council of Academic Deans, provided, however, that should a particular administrator be named in a charge or alleged discrimination, he or she shall (for purposes of this investigation) be considered a witness rather than representative of the administration; (2) two members selected by the provost from four nominees submitted by the University Senate Council; and (3) one member appointed by the provost from the academic community at large. Minority representation is considered an important criterion for appointments.

Staff discrimination review committee:

The Staff Discrimination Review Committee shall review complaints filed by employees in the administrator, staff, clerical, and service categories. The membership and selection procedures for the committee are as follows: (1) Four employees who are representatives from the above staff categories, two appointed by the provost and two appointed by the senior vice president for finance and operations; and (2) one clerical employee selected by the vice president for business from three nominees submitted by the committee of personnel representatives. Minority representation is considered an important criterion for appointments.

Committee members shall serve on their respective committees for two fiscal years. A committee member whose term expires shall continue to serve on the committee for any case brought before the committee during that member's term. Committee members may be reappointed. Each year the committee shall elect one of the members to serve as chairperson during that fiscal year. If the chairperson has a second year remaining in his or her term of appointment, or if reappointed, he or she shall qualify for reelection.

Staff assistance:

The Affirmative Action Office shall serve as staff for the committees or appeal board. Staff assistance from various university offices, such as the Office of Personnel Administration, shall be made available following a request by the committee or appeal board.

Committee responsibilities:

The committees shall deal with cases involving alleged violations of the university's policy of nondiscrimination (as defined in the university's Affirmative Action Program and Fair Employment Practices Policy) filed by individuals who allege that they were the victims of such discrimination. The committees also shall review situations involving alleged or apparent patterns of discrimination. Apparent patterns of such discrimination may emerge as the committees hear witnesses on a particular case. Committees shall not engage in search for such patterns beyond the issue of concern on a specific case. The committees shall *not* consider any petition for which another procedure has been initiated by the grievant.

Committee procedures:

Within ten days of a request for committee action, the appropriate review committee shall be convened. Upon receipt of a written claim of discrimination by an individual, or a written charge of a pattern of discrimination, the committee shall investigate the claim. Every reasonable effort shall be made to achieve a settlement of the dispute or charge during the investigation. Informal styles of investigation may be utilized by committees; teams may request conferences with various people involved in the case. No investigation of a case may be done by a single member, nor any action taken without the concurrence of the committee. The Office of Personnel

Exhibit 63 (continued)

Administration shall be available to assist with coordinating a response to the grievant's allegations. Such decision shall be made within thirty days of the initial filing of the complaint.

The appropriate review committee shall decide, based on the investigation, whether or not to conduct a formal hearing. The committee shall notify all parties of the committee's decision relative to holding a hearing and the reasons for that decision. If a formal hearing is held, the parties shall have full due process rights. The intention is to permit the committee or board to secure evidence from reliable sources without necessarily meeting the requirements of an unbiased and fully informed source usually required in legal proceedings. The major principles listed at the beginning of the policy and the general rules of procedure described in the following section shall be used in the conduct of all hearings. They are designed and should be interpreted to provide substantial justice without being restricted to rules concerning evidence and burden of proof as defined in actions taken in the courts. If a formal hearing is not held, the committee will advise the president of the university of its conclusions within sixty days from receipt of the claim.

The review committee or appeal board shall render its findings and (if appropriate) conclusions following a formal hearing. If a claim lacks merit, the committee may dismiss the case. If, however, the committee finds evidence to support the claim, the findings shall so state. Findings which support or reject the claim of discrimination by the committees shall be submitted to the president and to the complainant in writing. In certain instances recommendations could be given to the president. Except in extraordinary circumstances, agreed to by both parties, the review committee shall submit its report within thirty days after the conclusion of the hearings.

Procedure for formal hearings:

The following rules shall be used to guide formal hearings and are to be applied in such a way to assure fair, orderly, and expeditious proceedings. While they provide general guidelines to direct hearings by discrimination review committees and appeal boards, additional specific rules of procedure may be applied by agreement of both parties. (Additional rules pertaining exclusively to appeal boards are presented in the section of this policy entitled "Appeal Procedure.")

Written notice of specific charges (including the specific acts forming the basis thereof) shall be filed with the chairperson along with the charging party's recommendation for a solution to the problem should the claim be upheld. Where a pattern of discrimination is alleged to exist, the complainant shall provide incidents to support the charge. The charges shall be signed by the charging party and presented in sufficient detail to set forth clearly the charges which must be defended. Such written notice must be filed with the chairperson within thirty days of the date a formal hearing is approved. If the committee finds the charges insufficiently explicit, it will direct the complainant to clarify them. Copies of the charges shall be provided to the provost of the university, to all members of the hearing committee or board through the chairperson, and to the individual administrators charged with discrimination.

Legal counsel shall not be permitted access to hearings, nor shall the hearings be interrupted solely for purposes of either party consulting with legal counsel or other advisors. Observers shall not be permitted in the hearing room unless requested by appropriate university officials or the complainant. In all instances, the members of the review committee shall have the right and authority to dismiss observers from the hearing room by consensus. Tape recordings of the hearing proceedings shall not be permitted by observers. The university shall have the right to have an official representative present at all times throughout the hearing. The news media shall not have access to hearings. The Affirmative Action Office, in its role as staff to the committees, will have the same privileges as those of the university's official representative.

The written statement of specific charges shall constitute an official part of the record. The entire hearing shall be tape-recorded, under the control of the chairperson of the committee, and the tapes shall become an official part of the record. Additional documents pertaining to the hearing and submitted by the university, charging party, or witnesses shall be entered into and become part of the official record. When copies of these documents are made for the committee members, those copies shall be retrieved at the end of the hearing. Neither the tapes nor those documents that are part of the official record shall be made available to any persons other than the complainant, the university, other parties charged with discrimination, and the committee in the hearing, except in response to legal subpoena or by court order.

Witnesses for the university (as designated by the provost of the university or vice president for finance and operations) and for the charging party may be called by request of either party and following the approval of the committee. In all cases, the number of witnesses to appear on behalf of either party shall be left to the discretion of the committee. All witnesses shall swear or affirm the truthfulness of their testimony. Witnesses testifying on behalf of either the charging party or university shall be permitted in the hearing room only while presenting their testimony. Following the testimony of each witness, the members of the committee may question the witness. Under the discretion of the chairperson, members of the commit-

Exhibit 63 (continued)

tee may secure additional testimony from either contending party or other sources and relate such testimony to the responses of the witness. Administrators charged with discrimination have the right to be present during the entire formal hearing.

A hearing date and time shall be established following consultation with and at the convenience of all relevant parties. In all instances, however, the committee must convene within ten days following the receipt of written notice of a specific charge(s) and schedule a hearing (if appropriate) for shortly thereafter.

All testimony before a discrimination review committee must be heard by at least four of the members. The chairperson shall be responsible for entertaining the adoption of specific rules of procedures for the hearing from members of the committee. Any rules or procedures shall be compatible with general principles and rules in this document, and their adoption shall be by the mutual consent of the charging party, the university, and members of the committee or boards. Those rules must be finalized and adopted prior to the time of the actual hearing.

The chairperson shall open the hearing by stating the procedures to be followed and reading to the committee the written notice of specific charges. The chairperson shall have responsibility to: (1) rule on questions of procedure, with the advice of legal counsel for the committee, if desired; (2) deny admissibility of testimony from unknown or unidentified witnesses; (3) rule on the admissibility of evidence, and the appropriateness of questions directed to either party; (4) advise witnesses of the consequences of presenting false and misleading testimony; and (5) assure that all witnesses have been heard.

The university shall be provided an opportunity to respond to all charges. Following the statement of charges and the response of the university, the committee shall secure all relevant testimony reasonably possible by direct presentation and questioning witnesses. Neither party may directly question the other; all oral comments must be directed to the chairperson and committee members. Briefs and memorandums from either side may be submitted at any time with copies provided to both parties.

The committee shall present its findings and conclusions to the president in writing within fifteen days of the date of the final hearing. Except in extraordinary circumstances, the entire hearing should be completed within thirty days. Such report shall describe findings and conclusions, including any suggested redress to the complaining party, if appropriate. Copies of the report of the committee shall be made available to the charging party and to any individual administrator(s) charged with discrimination.

Appeal procedure:

An appeal board is established by request of a complaining party when a discrimination review committee has refused to conduct a formal hearing or when a discrimination review committee has dismissed a case. In addition, an individual administrator has the right to appeal a finding by a discrimination review committee that he or she has discriminated. In both instances, the request for the appointment of an appeal board is filed with Affirmative Action Office, under whose office the administration of review and appeal procedures are organized. The appeal board shall serve in an advisory capacity to the president and shall take whatever steps are necessary to review the discrimination review committee's action including, but not limited to, holding hearings, interviewing employees, and examining records.

Selection of appeal board members:

One member is chosen by the charging party; one member is selected by the provost of the university; a third member is chosen by the other two members. After the third member has been identified, the provost of the university shall have responsibility for contacting that individual to determine his or her willingness to serve. The appeal board shall elect one of the members to serve as chairperson. Each appeal board shall serve until a report has been submitted to the president. Upon receipt of the report and after proper review, the board shall be dismissed from further responsibility in the case.

Appeal board rules of procedure:

The principles and general rules of procedure for discrimination review committees pertain to and are to be applied in all aspects of the appeal procedure. These are to include the time periods which have been established for each stage of the process. The appeal board shall have available for review the official records of the hearing before the discrimination review committee, if such a hearing was held. If the case was dismissed, the appeal board will hear the case anew. All members of an appeal board must be present to receive testimony. After all relevant evidence has been presented, the charging party and the university shall have an opportunity to argue orally before the appeal board.

Reimbursement of costs:

The cost of the proceedings, including that of legal counsel to the committee, shall be the responsibility of the university. The rates shall be established by the university and agreed upon prior to the hearings.

❧ 14 ❧

Developing and Implementing Personnel Policies

An overabundance of policy stifles action, precludes flexibility, and discourages both supervisors and their subordinates. Some guides are necessary, however, for without them chaos would result as decisions would be based on emotion rather than institutional standards. To avoid inconsistencies and inequalities, institutions must have policies on sick leave, vacation, holidays, leaves of absence, time off for death in the family, and so forth. All such policies should be reviewed regularly. Obsolete policies that are no longer enforced should be deleted from the institution's policy manual lest managers suspect the validity of other policies in the manual. As new policies are introduced, old policies should be reviewed to see if they should be eliminated or modified to conform to new policies.

Four general guidelines should govern the establishment of new policies. First, one should avoid establishing policies that cover one-time situations. Second, one should test existing and new policies for practicality and usage with those who are to implement them. Third, one should not introduce policies that cannot be adequately monitored; such policies can create an atmosphere of distrust of other policies. Fourth, one should review relevant existing policies when establishing new policies; a specific program for regular review of policies is essential. Policy makers should also realize that policies cannot substitute for good management; policies are only as effective as the people who implement them.

What Are the Differences Between Policy and Procedure?

A policy is a clear statement of a philosophy. A procedure is the implementation of that philosophy. An example of a policy is "We shall promote employees from within the institution whenever feasible." An accompanying procedure for that policy would be the plan for an internal announcement program for vacancies. Groups such as boards of trustees or presidential executive committees, after consultation with appropriate institutional personnel, are responsible for determining personnel policies. Usually such governing groups are not (and should not be) sufficiently aware of the day-to-day procedures of the institution to develop implementation procedures for newly formed or revised policies. Implementation of the personnel policies, the determination of procedures, should be the responsibility of the personnel officer, after consultation with those affected by the procedures. Thus, the personnel officer is accountable for proper implementation procedures for all personnel policies, but he or she should not independently establish personnel policies. Rather, the personnel officer should make effective recommendations to proper authorities for needed changes. Indeed, the chief academic officer and the personnel officer should be particularly mindful of the need for new or revised policies or procedures and should consider it their responsibility to originate such recommendations.

Who Should Review and Approve Policies and Procedures?

Prior to implementation, a proposed policy or procedure should be reviewed by a number of people. The nature of the review process depends on the size, complexity, and protocol of the institution. Essential to the success of the review is that all who participate feel their viewpoints have been heard, whether or not their ideas are adopted.

Almost all policy reviews require the participation of legal counsel because policies are binding documents and the consequences of unclear wording can be devastating. For example, one statewide policy on rest periods stated that employees were to be granted two fifteen-minute rest periods a day. However, prison guards and some other employees in that state worked eight-hour shifts without breaks. These employees filed a grievance, and an arbitrator awarded them back pay for rest periods missed and an increase in pay to cover future rest periods that they would not be able to take. That error in exceptions to policy and procedural statements cost the state nearly $1 million. Had the policy treated rest periods as a privilege rather than a right, the appeal might have been denied.

In addition to legal review, each institution must have its own hierarchy for policy approval. Some institutions require the board of trustees to approve all personnel policies. Other institutions delegate such approval to the chief executive officer. However, executive approval of a personnel policy is only one step in the process of establishing a new policy. One should treat such approval as a license to sell the policy within the institution, rather than as a mandate that all personnel follow the policy. Because an institution of higher education is composed of a variety of relatively autonomous units, individuals in all units must have an opportunity to understand the policy's purpose. Misuse of the chief executive officer's approval may backfire and make future institutionwide approval more difficult to attain. The review of new policies by such groups as the faculty senate, the council of academic deans, the president's advisory council, as well as personnel representatives from the various academic and administrative units can facilitate institutionwide understanding and acceptance.

How Should the Elements of a Policy Be Developed?

In *College and University Personnel Policy Models,* the College and University Personnel Association (1980b) outlines sample policy statements on a variety of policies. The approach illustrated in these policy models requires one to first make a list of the policy elements that need to be addressed in the policy. Consider, for example, the development of a policy on rest periods. Policy questions that might be considered include the following:

Are rest periods a right or a privilege?
How long will rest periods be?
How many periods will be allowed per day?
Are there to be any restrictions on the scheduling of rest periods? For example, can they be used to lengthen a meal period or to shorten the workday?
Are they to be cumulative if not used?
Are they to be granted to part-time or temporary employees?
How are conflicts in scheduling to be resolved?
Will employees be permitted to leave their work areas?

Once one has compiled such a list and outlined the behavioral objectives to be realized from implementation of the policy, one must answer each question in clear language. Policy writers who begin writing without taking this orderly approach may find themselves composing loose and ineffective policy. Exhibit 64, pp. 308–309, presents a sample policy on rest periods based on the approach outlined here. For a detailed discussion of the development of a policy manual, see Dartnell (Lawson, 1967).

How Are Policies Effectively Disseminated?

Faculty and staff members need to be kept informed about the policies that affect them. Indeed, institutions are advised to review carefully the content and format in which the policies are disseminated as such can be a matter of concern in litigation. The authors recommend that information on policies be disseminated in two kinds of publications: a detailed and controlled personnel policy manual (in loose-leaf form) should be supplied to each administrative unit and a summary handbook should be distributed to each faculty and staff member. Two handbooks are usually necessary, one for faculty and one for nonfaculty.

The controlled personnel policy manual should contain the full statement of all policies and procedures affecting all categories of faculty and staff members. It may also contain forms used to initiate personnel actions. The handbook need only contain summaries of the policies with references to appropriate sections of the institution's policy manual. The handbook should not resemble a contract in appearance, and it is prudent to indicate that it is not intended to be a contract, but rather a ready reference guide to the policy statements in the policy manual. The handbook should include a disclaimer statement; for example, "This handbook is prepared as a convenient first reference for university policies. However, the exact and official text of each policy is found in the university's personnel policy manual found in each departmental office. If there appears to be conflict between the handbook and the personnel policy manual in interpretation of a policy, the personnel policy manual shall prevail. The university reserves the right to change its policies and procedures as appropriate."

Specific details such as names, office addresses, and telephone numbers should not appear in policy manuals and handbooks. To list them is to necessitate frequent updating. For other suggestions on policy manuals and staff handbooks, see Chapter Thirteen.

The details of faculty and staff benefits, such as hospital, surgical, and major medical insurance or life insurance, may change frequently. Therefore, it may be desirable to publish, or request the carrier to publish, an inexpensive pamphlet on each such benefit rather than include the details in the employee handbook. The handbook should include a brief statement about each benefit and reference to the appropriate pamphlet. Pamphlets should be reissued as the details of the plans change, and the institution's house organ can provide notice of changes in the various programs as well as periodic reminders of benefits.

Any changes in the personnel portion of the institution's policy manual should be monitored by a central personnel staff member. When a change is approved, that staff member should examine the manual to determine if the approved change requires changes in other policies. All policy changes should be issued in standard format. (For a sample standard format, see Exhibit 65,

p. 310.) Changes should be coded by number, and each page should be numbered and dated. Notice of changes should be sent to the holder of each policy manual with instructions to "delete policy number _____ and replace it with the revised _____." A brief explanation of the change may accompany the revision. The use of an arrow or other visual marker to identify specific changes will help the holders of policy manuals more readily note those changes.

One caution is offered. The revised policies or procedures sent to offices for insertion in manuals may be read by the clerical employees who insert them but not read by the administrators who need to know of the changes. Therefore, it may be necessary to address a notice and a copy of the policy or procedure to the administrative officers at the same time one is submitted for insertion into the manual. Or the personnel office could suggest to administrators that the clerical employee be instructed to summarize the policy and present a summary to the administrator.

What Policies Are Peculiar to Educational Institutions?

One policy peculiar to educational institutions concerns sabbatical leaves of absences, which are usually granted faculty following seven years of service in a professorial rank. However, some institutions grant them for lesser service. Sabbatical leave is usually a privilege rather than a right and is granted only if a faculty member submits a program of activity that will result in professional growth. Most institutions grant salary support during a sabbatical leave at full salary for half a year or one half salary for the entire year. Exhibit 66, pp. 311–314, presents guidelines for a policy on sabbatical leave.

Similarly, educational institutions need policies on emeritus rank (see Exhibit 51, p. 241), academic ranks (Exhibit 67, pp. 315–316), private consulting practice (Exhibit 68, pp. 316–317), affiliate academic appointments (Exhibit 69, p. 318), and named professorships (Exhibit 70, p. 319).

Exhibit 64. Guidelines for Policy on Rest Periods

Practically all employers provide employees with breaks in their work shifts. However, not all employers make written statements about such breaks. For those who do make written statements, the breaks may be specified as an employee right, or they may be specified as a privilege which may or may not be granted depending on conditions.

When rest periods become official and are committed to writing, and thus become formalized, several facets of the policy should be considered as outlined under the policy items for consideration.

Policy items and sample policy language:

In some cases, rest periods are stated as an employee right: "A full-time employee is entitled to two rest periods of fifteen minutes each in each day's work schedule." "The university allows a fifteen-minute rest period in the middle of each half of an eight-hour day."

In other cases, rest periods are considered a privilege which may or may not be granted: "If your work situation permits, your supervisor may authorize you two fifteen-minute breaks. . . . Remember the needs of the job must be met first, and in some areas 'breaks' are not possible. In some areas the work situation has its own built-in 'breaks' such as frequent changes of pace." "Most departments allow rest periods or coffee breaks if the work involved can be interrupted even though the college does not provide formal rest periods for employees." "There is no law covering compulsory rest periods in an educational institution. Therefore, it is within the authority of each department to establish its own policy on this subject. Certain guides should be followed." "There is no specific policy governing rest periods. Provision for rest periods is left to the discretion of the individual supervisor." "Employees shall be allowed rest periods (or coffee breaks) of fifteen minutes each per half day worked, provided such interruption in the work does not interfere with the performance of the employee's responsibilities or the efficiency of the department." "Supervisors may request that you not take a break during heavy or emergency work periods."

The length of the rest period is usually defined: "A rest period should not exceed fifteen minutes." "Rest periods should be limited to two fifteen-minute breaks per day away from your work station." "The rest period will be with pay and will not exceed fifteen minutes for each four hours of work."

The scheduling of rest periods is usually indicated: "The university allows a fifteen-minute rest period in the middle of each half of an eight-hour day." "One in the morning and one in the afternoon if you are on an 8 A.M. to 5 P.M. schedule. Employees on other shifts should have the supervisor specify times for rest periods." "Insofar as practicable, the rest period should be taken in the middle of each work period." "The first rest period shall occur during the work session prior to the meal break, and the second rest period shall occur in the work session after the meal break." "When rest periods are taken, they should be at times within the workday to be arranged by the supervisor, normally midmorning and midafternoon."

Restrictions are indicated regarding using rest periods at the beginning or ending of work periods or adjacent to meal breaks: "The rest period is a recess; it is not to be used to extend the starting time or advance the departure time of a work session." "A rest period will not be granted during the first or last hours of a work period." "A rest period may not be added to the lunch hour or other off-duty time." "Employees who do not take rest periods are not permitted to use the time to shorten the day." "The rest period is intended to be a recess to be preceded and followed by an extended work period. Consequently, it may not be used to cover a staff member's late arrival or early departure or to extend a lunch period."

Work breaks not used are not cumulative: "Rest period time cannot be accumulated to provide for a prolonged time-off period." "Rest periods are for your benefit during working hours and may not be accumulated or used for lost time away from the job or for any other purpose." "It is not possible to forgo breaks to accumulate extra time off in the future."

Rest periods for part-time employees may be covered: "Part-time employees are entitled to a rest period during any work session of three hours or more."

Conflicts in scheduling employee breaks may be covered: "In offices where more than one individual is employed, the taking of breaks at the same time by both employees is not permitted." "Supervisors will stagger the breaks for employees within the same office in order to maintain uninterrupted service."

A statement about leaving the work area may be included: "If there is a convenient place to buy refreshments, you may leave your work area during the break."

Source: College and University Personnel Association (1980b, pp. 89–91).

Exhibit 65. Sample Policy on University Appointments Without Remuneration

Eligibility:

Persons appropriately qualified who perform a service to the university without remuneration for such services may be recommended for an appointment.

Titles:

Three series of titles may be used to designate such personnel, as follows:

1. Adjunct status: The term *adjunct* is to be used only with normal academic titles.
2. Clinical faculty appointments: This series of titles is to be used only for medical doctors. The discipline indication shall not be in conflict with department designations at the medical center. Advance concurrence by the dean and provost of the medical center shall be obtained.
3. Faculty associate: The title *faculty associate* is available for use in conjunction with university cooperative programs with representatives of agencies or communities or with similar programs. The term *faculty associate* is used with the discipline designation; for example, Faculty Associate in Welfare Services. Professorial ranks are not used in conjunction with the faculty associate title.

Procedure for recommendation and termination:

In making appointment to any of the above categories, deans are to follow established procedures. Termination of such an appointment, likewise, is to follow established procedures.

Benefits available:

A person appointed to any of the above categories is not eligible for tenure nor does he or she participate in the benefits programs of the university.

Annual review:

The appropriate administrative officer in each area is responsible to review annually the appointments without remuneration in his or her area of responsibility to determine whether or not the appointment should be continued.

Exhibit 66. Guidelines for Policy on Sabbatical Leave
of Absence with Salary

While policies covering sabbatical leaves of absence with salary are generally written for faculty members, some institutions provide such leaves for staff personnel. Normally such leaves are a privilege rather than a right and are dependent upon: (1) meeting a length of service requirement, and (2) submitting a plan for a significant program of accomplishment during the leave. The leaves are generally granted for one year with half salary or six months with full salary. Normally, reports of accomplishments on the leave are required, and the faculty or staff member must give service to the institution for a specified period following return from the leave.

Policy items and sample policy language:

The purpose for providing sabbatical leaves is usually stated: "The university expects faculty members to maintain continuous professional growth. In order to assist in this growth, faculty members are encouraged to take periodic leaves of absence for further study or scholarly work which will increase their effectiveness as members of the faculty." "Recognizing the necessity for faculty members to acquire new experiences to enrich their teaching and also to provide time for research projects and writing, the university supports the principle of sabbatical leave." "The purpose of the sabbatical leave program is to make it possible for members of the teaching faculty to take time off from normal academic duties to engage in activities of professional value that could not otherwise be undertaken."

Sabbatical leaves may be provided to all faculty members, to only certain faculty members, or to others besides faculty members: "Leaves of absence with pay may be granted to full-time members of the faculty." "Members of the regular instructional staff who have completed six years of service in professorial ranks are eligible for a sabbatical leave." "When unusual circumstances warrant, staff members who have served the university effectively for a minimum of six calendar years may apply." "Professional leaves are granted to any instructional staff member, instructional staff member assigned to administrative responsibilities, or professional staff member."

A length of service requirement before becoming eligible for a sabbatical usually is stated: "A faculty member who has served six or more consecutive years as a full-time member of the faculty is eligible for consideration for a sabbatical leave." "The Board of Regents ordinarily will not approve a request for a leave with pay if the applicant has been employed for a period of less than three years." "Eligibility for sabbatical leave may be established by having served seven years in addition to holding a continuing contract."

Service time not to be counted toward length of service may be mentioned: "Time spent on leave without salary, absence by reason of illness, and full-time

Exhibit 66 (continued)

nonteaching service normally are excluded in counting sabbatical leave credit." "Leaves of absence without salary are not considered in determining years of service."

One year is usually the maximum length for a sabbatical leave, but optional modes of salary payment are available: "A professor may choose to take one half year of leave at full salary instead of one full year at half salary." "The staff member granted a sabbatical leave for the entire appointment period shall receive one half of the staff member's regular salary. A sabbatical leave granted for one half of the annual appointment period provides full salary." "Stipend conditions: (1) one semester at full salary; (2) one academic year at one half of full salary."

Limitations on the sabbatical stipend may be imposed when other remuneration is received by the recipient of the sabbatical: "In the case of a sabbatical leave granted to a faculty member who will receive a salary, grant, or stipend from another source for his work while on leave, the university may reduce the normal sabbatical salary accordingly." "If the activity being undertaken during the leave is accompanied by a salary or grant that is adequate to pay travel expenses and a normal level of living, then a leave of absence without salary may be granted rather than a sabbatical leave." "Compensation received from acceptance of a fellowship or other assistance in research including the sabbatical leave salary may not exceed the regular salary of the staff member." "Should the president have evidence that the employee on paid leave status is employed regularly by another school system or agency, the salary payments may be discontinued."

The institution may impose limitations on the granting of sabbatical leaves: "In any given year, a sabbatical leave will be granted to not more than five percent of the total faculty. In general, the order of selection will be determined by seniority." "Such leave shall be limited to one percent of the total certified instructional, supervisory, and administrative staff." "A leave with pay is not granted to an individual after the fiscal year in which the sixty-seventh birthday is reached." "It is a general principle that sabbatical leaves shall not be granted for study toward a master's or doctoral degree if the opportunity exists within the general geographical area for faculty to earn such a degree on a part-time basis." "A faculty member may apply only after having attained tenure."

The policy usually requires a return to full-time service for a specified period of time at the completion of a sabbatical. A penalty clause may be included for violations: "Any faculty member shall be required to sign an agreement that he will return the full amount of compensation he received while on leave if he should not return to the university for at least one year of service." "Employees granted sabbatical leave must serve a minimum of one additional contract year following the expiration of their leave." "It is expected that those granted sabbatical leave will return to duty at the university for at least one year. Those who do not return in order to accept employment elsewhere are expected to remit to the university any salary paid to them while on leave or to arrange for the new employer to reimburse the university for such salary." "Individuals granted leaves with pay are required to return to full-time active service with the university for two consecutive contractual years or, if they do not remain for the full two years, to refund all of the salary received from the university during the leave. There will be no proration of the amount to be returned if an individual remains for any time less than the two years."

The process of applying for a sabbatical leave is often formal: "Application for sabbatical leave is made by letter to the appropriate dean prior to the term preceding the term during which the leave is desired. Copies of the application are sent by the applicant to the president and to the department head concerned." "Sabbatical leave is granted by the president or the provost following receipt and approval of a letter of request addressed to the provost and bearing indication of approval by the dean of the school involved." "Requests for leave must be submitted in writing to the appropriate department head, with a copy to the academic dean, as far in advance as possible of the requested effective date of the leave, but in no event later than six months in advance." "Invitations formally to apply for a sabbatical leave are issued by the academic vice president on a faculty seniority basis." "Application for leave with pay shall be made on a form provided by the university and shall be submitted with the recommendation of the department head and dean to the president via the Staff Committee on Academic Leaves."

The applicant is usually required to specify what he or she intends to accomplish while on sabbatical leave: "The application must be accompanied by a statement of a well-considered plan for the sabbatical which includes its significance as a contribution to the professional effectiveness of the applicant and the best interest of the university." "Each application shall include a detailed statement describing the program to be followed while on leave and indicating the contributions it is expected to make to the staff member's professional improvement and to his ability to serve the university." "It is essential that the applicant submit a carefully developed plan for the use of the leave indicating how the completion of the plan will enable the applicant to improve research or teaching ability and other services to the university."

The policy may state who is responsible for approving requests for sabbatical leave: "The decision on applications for leaves with pay will be made by the president after consideration and recommendation by the Staff Committee on Academic Leaves." "Sabbatical leave is not automatic. Sabbatical leave is granted by the president or the provost following receipt and

Exhibit 66 (continued)

approval of a letter of request addressed to the provost, and bearing indication of approval by the dean of the school involved." "Requests for leave must be recommended by the department or division head, approved by the dean, and submitted by the president to the Board of Trustees." "Final approval is to be given in writing by the president. Likewise, final disapproval for stated cause is to be given in writing by the president."

A statement may be made regarding fringe benefits while on leave: "An individual who is granted a leave is required to maintain membership in the university's insurance program during the leave. If the individual is a member of the retirement plan in effect at the university, the individual is required to continue to contribute to that plan." "Subject to, and consistent with the group health insurance plans and the group life insurance plan, coverage may be continued during a sabbatical leave of absence." "Retirement plan contributions will continue during a sabbatical leave." "Disability plan protection will continue during sabbatical leave." "Sick leave plan benefits will continue during sabbatical leave." "A person who is on leave of absence with pay and who is eligible for educational privileges will retain these privileges during the period of the leave. Dependents of faculty or staff members who are eligible for grants-in-aid will retain the eligibility during the time that the staff member is on leave with pay."

Following completion of the sabbatical, the individual granted the leave may be expected to submit a report of activity and accomplishment: "At conclusion of the leave, individuals are required to submit a report of the work accomplished during the leave and indicating how they believe that the experience has improved their capacity to serve the university." "A detailed report or the actual results of the project must be filed within ninety days after the beginning of the term immediately following the end of the sabbatical leave." "Upon completion of the sabbatical leave, the recipient shall submit a report of the results of the leave within ninety days following return from leave. The report shall include: (1) an account of activities during the leave, including travel itineraries, institutions visited, and persons consulted; (2) a statement of progress made on the sabbatical leave program as proposed in the application and an explanation of any significant changes made in the program; and (3) an appraisal of the relationship between the results obtained and those anticipated in the sabbatical leave program statement."

Source: College and University Personnel Association (1980b, pp. 105–111).

Exhibit 67. Sample Definitions of Academic Ranks

The following definitions provide guidance on the qualifications necessary for appointment or promotion to the various academic ranks.

Lecturer. The title of lecturer is to be employed for temporary appointments of teaching faculty members to whom it is not feasible to assign a specific rank.

Assistant librarian. The assistant librarian should possess the bachelor's degree and a graduate library school degree or equivalent graduate degrees in other professional or scholarly field where appropriate.

Instructor (or research assistant). The instructor should possess the bachelor's and master's degrees and at least two years of graduate work (or equivalent) in the field of his or her specialization. Experience in teaching, while desirable, is not necessary. The research assistant rank is limited to a faculty member in an academic unit who devotes a major fraction of time to the personal conduct of research, in which individual initiative, creativity, and responsibility are required. The research assistant should possess a master's degree or equivalent or be an active candidate for an advanced degree in an academic field related to his or her research.

Senior assistant librarian. The senior assistant librarian should possess the same degrees as the assistant librarian. He or she should have previous professional library experience or experience in another profession or discipline. The senior assistant librarian must demonstrate: the ability to apply modern library techniques, competence in reference or bibliographical work, and the ability to give creative and imaginative direction to areas of library service.

Assistant professor (or research associate). The assistant professor (or research associate) should possess a doctor's degree or its equivalent in organized research or professional practice, must have demonstrated ability as a teacher or research worker, and must have shown definite evidence of growth in scholarship. The research associate rank is limited to a faculty member in an academic unit who devotes a major fraction of time to the personal conduct of research, in which individual initiative, creativity, and responsibility are required.

Associate librarian. The associate librarian should possess the same qualifications as the senior assistant librarian but should in addition demonstrate exceptional competence in reference or bibliographical work and exhibit proven leadership abilities. The associate librarian should also give evidence of an established reputation in scholarly or professional achievement.

Associate professor (or senior research associate). The associate professor (or senior research associate) should possess the same qualifications as the

Exhibit 67 (continued)

assistant professor (or research associate), but must also give evidence of an established reputation in scholarly, artistic, or professional achievement.

Librarian. In addition to possessing the characteristics of the members of the lower ranks, the librarian must give evidence of marked capacity for creative work and of leadership in his or her field of specialization. The rank of librarian is reserved for persons of proven stature in the library profession or in a field of scholarly specialization.

Professor. In addition to possessing the characteristics of the members of the lower ranks, the professor should give evidence of a marked capacity for creative work and of leadership in his or her field of specialization. The rank of professor is reserved for persons of proven stature in teaching or research.

Exhibit 68. Sample Policy on Private Consulting Practice

Definition:

For an outside activity to be considered legitimate private consulting, this activity must be in the faculty member's field and be of a professional nature.

Consulting time:

A member of the faculty may engage in a limited amount of private consulting with the understanding that this privilege pertains only if the outside activity does not interfere with the performance of regular university duties. A faculty member is expected to perform his or her university duties in the most effective manner of which he or she is capable. The faculty member's first duty and first responsibility is to the university. Outside service should not be undertaken, whether with or without pay, that might interfere with the discharge of this paramount obligation.

Required approval:

Faculty members are to inform their department heads of the type and extent of their outside activities whether undertaken for compensation or otherwise so that the department head may judge the appropriateness of the activity in relation to the performance of the faculty member's regular duties. A faculty member may not provide special service to the state for additional compensation without prior written approval of the president of the university. A faculty member requesting approval for such service to the state shall submit his or her request to the president describing the service, the approximate time required, personal compensation expected, and the effect of such service on the faculty member's regular work.

Required reporting:

Annual reports shall be submitted by department heads to their vice president, dean, or director, who shall in turn submit a summary report to the provost, concerning the levels and amount of private consulting by those faculty and staff within their administrative authority. The reports shall not identify individuals by name. Reports from department heads to their vice president, dean, or director are due by June 1. Summary reports from those officials to the provost are due by July 1.

Responsibility for private professional services:

The university assumes no responsibility for private professional services performed by members of its faculty. The name of the university is not in any way to be connected with the service rendered or the results obtained. The faculty member must make it clear that his or her consulting work is a personal matter. He or she must not use the official stationery of the university nor stationery having a university address or a university telephone number. A faculty member shall not accept or retain employment that would bring him or her, as an expert or in any other capacity, into conflict or in competition with the interests and purposes of the university or the state and federal agencies.

Internal consulting:

Faculty members are ineligible to serve as paid consultants on university programs whether funded from general university or external grant or contract monies. When such collaboration is required, the faculty member should participate directly in the project and his or her salary should be distributed accordingly.

Exhibit 69. Sample Policy on Affiliate Academic Appointments

Purposes of the policy:

This policy serves to recognize the academic qualifications of certain administrative or staff members (other than academic deans and academic department heads) who may on occasion perform educational services, yet whose primary responsibilities do not involve teaching and research and who, therefore, are not eligible for tenure.

Eligibility:

Individuals are eligible for affiliate academic appointments if appropriately qualified for a regular academic appointment if the individual's primary responsibilities are other than academic, and if such status for them is recommended by the appropriate dean.

Titles:

Academic appointments authorized under this policy are to be designated as follows: affiliate professor, affiliate associate professor, affiliate assistant professor, and affiliate instructor.

Approval and appointment:

Appointment to an affiliate faculty rank is made in an academic department, and must have the approval of the department head and the college dean.

Tenure eligibility:

Affiliate faculty appointments are not subject to the university's tenure regulations.

Review:

The appropriate academic officers are responsible for providing a regular review of affiliate faculty appointments to determine whether a continuation of the appointment is academically warranted.

Exhibit 70. Sample Policy on Named Professorships

Purpose of appointment:

To supplement departmental support for outstanding university faculty in order to provide a holder of the professorship with the resources necessary to make even more outstanding contributions in teaching, research, and public service. Following presidential approval, the support monies will be used for such purposes as graduate student salaries, secretarial assistance, travel expenses, and so forth. By supporting the establishment of a named professorship, the benefactor directs attention to a continuing commitment to support scholarship within the university.

Designated titles:

The designated title is *(name of benefactor)*, Professorship, or Librarianship, in *(field)*.

Source of funds:

Funds for a named professorship are provided by benefactors from outside the university. To establish this position, either a one-time grant of not less than $250,000 or an annual grant of not less than $15,000 is required.

Qualifications and length of appointment:

The holder of a named professorship must be a full-time member of the university faculty holding the academic rank of professor or librarian. The duration of the appointment will be until retirement of the faculty member or termination from the employ of the university, and in all cases is contingent on the continuing support of the benefactor.

Responsibility for appointment:

Appointments will be made by the president of the university upon recommendation of the dean of the appropriate college.

❧ 15 ❧

Organizing
Personnel Records

The management of personnel records is an important function that is more than clerical in nature. Maintenance of such records is costly in terms of storage space, equipment, and personnel. Because these records are used in decision making relative to the granting of tenure and promotions, the resolution of disciplinary matters, the defense of employment decisions, and the compliance with legal requirements, personnel records must be managed effectively.

The establishment of a management system for personnel records must begin with decisions about the purpose of each record maintained. Decisions about what documents will be retained in official personnel files should not be delegated to clerical staff members, since they may be inclined to save materials rather than risk discarding them. Personnel administrators should establish policies for retention, realizing that the excessive retention of files is expensive. Recent advances in management information systems are intended to streamline management's need for data. For a detailed discussion of management information systems, see Sisson and Canning (1976).

Why Are Personnel Records Kept?

There are seven principle uses of personnel records:

1. For decision making relative to a faculty or staff member's promotion, tenure, recognition, discipline, dismissal, and the like.
2. For personnel research. Personnel records can and should be used for institutional planning. Personnel records are valuable sources of information for a variety of institutional research studies. (A list of such studies is presented in Chapter One.)
3. For legal requirements; for example, under the Fair Labor Standards Act it is necessary to maintain a file on an individual's work schedule. In addition, it is necessary to maintain records to show the basis of evaluation of one position as exempt and another as nonexempt. Tax laws require the maintenance of payroll and tax-deduction records. Affirmative action legislation requires the maintenance of records of the applicants considered when filling a particular position. Most personnel-related laws and regulations specify the obligations for recordkeeping both in regard to content and time limits.
4. For participating in surveys on personnel data with other institutions or associations. (See Chapter Five for a discussion of interinstitutional salary surveys.)
5. For communicating with faculty and staff members or with their next of kin in case of death or emergencies.
6. For providing necessary faculty and staff information for such publications as a telephone directory or an institutional catalogue or bulletin.
7. For preparation for collective bargaining with employees; for example, employees' request for payment of a shift differential requires data on the numbers of employees working those shifts selected for differential payments.

Which Personnel Data Should Be Collected and Retained?

The following list suggests elements that are usually included in a personnel data base:

Name
Social security number (and employee identification number, if different)
Home address and telephone number
Campus address and telephone number
Sex
Ethnic or racial identity
Person to contact in case of emergency
Date of birth
Education and degrees
Classification category and position title
EEO-6 category (see Chapter Six)
Pay grade
Salary
Date of employment
Type of appointment (standing, fixed-term; ending date if fixed-term appointment)
Number of months of contract
Full-time or part-time (if part-time, percentage of time)
Fair Labor Standards Act code (exempt or nonexempt); see Chapter Three)
History of positions held within institution
Tenure status
Benefits plans enrollments
Dependents covered in benefits plans
Veteran status
Handicapped status, if applicable
List of publications
Vacation and sick leave record
Performance evaluation
Faculty teaching load reports
Union membership status

Most of these elements can be collected immediately following appointment of a faculty or staff member by having the employee complete a biographical data form. While some of the elements could be collected in advance of employment, to do so may invite some legal problems because of equal employment legislation. The information stored in the personnel data base should be periodically sent to faculty and staff members for verification of accuracy.

Security of the data elements is important. Security systems are needed to avoid unauthorized changes in records, unauthorized entry into the file, unauthorized or unlawful uses of the data, and unauthorized purging of data elements.

What Are the Requirements of an Effective Records Management Program?

The following principles should govern the management of personnel records:

- Each record to be maintained must have a stated specific need, objective, or purpose. If one cannot specify the purpose of a data element, one should seriously question maintaining it.
- The system should be designed to minimize handling costs. In some cases, a machine record meets that criterion; in other cases, keeping the hard-copy record may be effective and less expensive.
- The system must have updating mechanisms for all records. A data base that lacks integrity is not worth maintaining. Similarly, the system must have mechanisms for the removal of outdated or otherwise obsolete data.
- The records should be maintained by individuals who use those records. If personnel data elements are to be added to a payroll data base maintained by payroll people, the personnel data may not be properly maintained. For example, a payroll clerk may not place a high priority on entering tenure data into the file when under pressure to meet payroll deadlines.
- The personnel data base elements must be available to the personnel administrators in a timely manner. If an administrator cannot gain access to needed data, the system is ineffective.
- The maintenance cost of each data element should be compared to its administrative value to assure that the system is cost effective.

- Personnel data elements should not duplicate other departments' data. For example, historical payroll records need not be duplicated in the personnel office provided that the personnel office has reasonable access to the payroll office's records. However, it may be desirable to maintain in the personnel office a master personnel file on each faculty member even though a similar file is maintained by the academic department. Such decisions should be based on the size of institution, the sophistication of the mechanized records, and the physical availability of the records to others who need them.
- Systems should be devised so that the document presented for a personnel action can be filed directly into the central file. It should not be necessary either to make a machine copy, which is costly, or to reenter data elements by hand, which may cause errors.

Even small institutions should consider converting hard-copy records into computer records if at all feasible. While larger institutions find it to be cost effective to operate their own computers, small institutions may be able to purchase computer services. Personnel data computer software systems are on the open market, so institutions need not write their own programs. Such ready-made data systems can reduce the cost of installation considerably, and software packages are available through many vendors and users. The College and University Systems Exchange (737 29th Street, Boulder, CO 80303) has information regarding systems available for higher education.

By placing records in computers, an institution should be able to reduce duplication of records stored in different offices. Because there is a natural overlap in the records needs of the payroll, budget, accounting, and personnel offices, all these should be consulted in the design of the system and all should have access to needed records within the system. Thus, the data base system will be effective in response to the management needs of the institution.

Institutions that are too small to use computerized records can used color coding to expedite the retrieval of data for studies. Researchers need not open each file if adhesive color-coded symbols are placed on the outside edge of each employee's file. For example, the outside (visible) edge of the file folder could contain the employee's name, job title, and date of hire, and colored stickers for the following elements (each element is assigned a specific location on the folder):

Basic classification category
Rank
Tenure status
Academic or administrative unit
Leave of absence status
Racial or ethnic identity
EEO-6 classification category (see Chapter Six)
Pay grade
Type of appointment (standing or fixed-term)
Full-time or part-time status
Fair Labor Standards Act code (exempt or nonexempt)

A color-coding system would thus enable a researcher to look at the edges of the files to determine how many professors with tenure there are in the College of Education or how many individuals are currently on sabbatical leave of absence. A color-coding system is easy to install, inexpensive to maintain, and simple to change to meet new needs.

How Can One Avoid Starting Unnecessary Files?

The best method to avoid having cluttered files is not to start them in the first place. For example, an administrator receives a letter asking for an appointment from someone with whom he or she regularly does business and responds by writing the date and time of the appointment. The administrator's secretary then files the original letter and a carbon of the response. Such files are unnecessary. Indeed, had the transaction taken place on the telephone, the only written record of it would have been a notation on the administrator's appointment calendar.

Principles of effective time management dictate that one attempt to handle each piece of paper one receives only once. To achieve that goal, one needs a program for handling each paper that crosses one's desk. The following list suggests such a program:

Documents that cross the desk of personnel administrators	*How to handle them*
Carbon copy of an outgoing letter	1. First, try to throw it away. Decisions to discard paperwork are management, not clerical, responsibilities.
	2. If one cannot throw it away, perhaps one should send it to someone else.
	3. If 1 and 2 do not apply, mark it for some future date (a week or ten days hence) and place it in a come-up (or suspense) file.
	4. Only as a last resort should one place it in a "permanent" file. However, all such files should have an automatic procedure for review and subsequent purging. A reminder note in the come-up file may be useful.
Incoming letter	1. First, consider throwing it away. It is not necessary to retain every letter one receives.
	2. Then consider sending it to someone else who should handle it.
	3. If 1 and 2 do not apply, respond to the letter or place it in a come-up file.
An item from the come-up file.	1. First, take action on it.
	2. Second, try to throw it away.
	3. Mark another future date on it and reassign it to the come-up file.
Periodicals, magazines, circulars, and the like	1. First, take action on it.
	2. Second, consider sending it to

		someone else who may find it useful.
	3.	Retain it for reference and assign it a future throw-away date.
Directives, policy statements, contracts, and legal documents	1.	Retain in a file.
Regular periodic reports	1.	Retain for a fixed period of time and assign a future throw-away date.

This rather simple approach to file storage is effective in avoiding the initiation of unnecessary files. Of course, once in a while, an administrator will discard paperwork only to later find that it should have been retained. But an administrator who has never been inconvenienced by having discarded a needed record is likely to be retaining too many documents and not managing files prudently.

Should Employees Have Access to Their Personnel Files?

There is no federal legislation regarding the access of faculty and staff members to their personnel files. However, because there is public concern that improper information stored in records might have a negative effect on individuals, some states have passed legislation permitting faculty and staff members to have limited access to their personnel files and to raise objections if they disagree with the contents. Such legislation, of course, varies from state to state. Typically, employees are granted access to:

- Personnel action forms such as appointments, transfers, promotions, leave of absences, changes in salary, changes of title, layoff, and the like
- Internal correspondence addressed to the faculty or staff member
- Attendance records
- Letters of commendation and letters of reprimand
- Insurance forms and retirement forms
- Employment application forms and biographical data forms

- Grievance forms and responses
- Official management performance evaluations

The laws in many states, however, forbid employees access to:

- Letters or memorandums of reference solicited for appointment, promotion, or tenure review
- Information relating to the investigation of a possible criminal offense
- Information developed or prepared for use in civil, criminal, or grievance procedures
- Medical records

Most states' laws permit the institution to develop a procedure for employees to use in requesting to review their personnel file. (Exhibit 71, p. 329, shows a sample form for such requests.) Institutional procedures may outline time limits for producing the record or may limit the rights of employees to routinely request copies of all the materials in the file.

Some institutions have adopted access policies although not legally required to do so. However, it may be only a matter of time before federal legislation requires access to personnel files. Therefore, personnel administrators responsible for files should work toward assuring that materials maintained in the files will stand the scrutiny of access. The principles outlined in this section should be considered in planning a policy on access.

How Should Personnel Inquiries Be Answered?

Institutions receive both written and telephone inquiries regarding present and past faculty and staff members from potential employers and from organizations seeking credit information. An institution should designate a specific office to respond to such inquiries in order to assure that legal requirements are met. For example, while it is helpful to provide employment information on behalf of a faculty member who is seeking credit or another position, an individual's salary should not be disclosed unless the faculty or staff member provides written authorization for its release.

Responding to questions regarding the ability of an employee or former employee is a delicate matter. The respondent should provide only first-hand information regarding quality of work, attendance record, dates of employment, and the like. The respondent should be prepared to defend any statements made should any legal action ensue. Information about an employee's record with a former employer should not be provided.

Some credit agencies make numerous interruptive calls to the personnel records office for information. Some institutions request that such agencies limit their calls to one a day to avoid such interruptions.

Exhibit 71. Request to Review Personnel File

I hereby request permission to review my personnel file.

a. The purpose of my request is: _____

_____

_____

b. The particular parts of my personnel file I wish to inspect are: _____

_____

_____

_____

_____

Signature   Date

_____

Title

_____

Department

I understand that my personnel representative (or campus business manager) will inform me of the time scheduled for me to review my personnel file in accordance with the university's policy on access to personnel files.

❧ 16 ❧

Preparing for Collective Bargaining

Although unionization of non-academic personnel dates back to the 1930s and 1940s, two comparatively recent new conditions have led to a proliferation of union activity, and such activity has extended into some sections of the country where previously it had not been common. First, in 1970, the National Labor Relations Board asserted its jurisdiction over private colleges and universities that participate in interstate commerce and have annual budgets of $1 million or more. This action did not require a change in law as the board simply asserted a jurisdiction that might have been asserted at any earlier date. Second, approximately thirty-five states have passed public employee relations acts that affect public institutions of higher education in regard to collective bargaining. Some of the laws specifically concern labor relations in postsecondary institutions; other laws cover public employees without specific reference to colleges or universities. In many of the states that passed public employee relations acts, unionization followed rather quickly.

By the early 1980s, dealing with labor unions, along with affirmative action and equal employment opportunity, had become one of the most active functions of higher education personnel

330

administrators. The following figures illustrate the proliferation of union activity. By June 1980, faculty bargaining units had been certified on 681 campuses and bargaining had been rejected by 82 faculties. Of the 681 campuses, 415 are two-year institutions and 253 are four-year institutions, and 585 are public institutions and 96 are private. Of the 82 faculties who rejected unionization, 65 are from four-year institutions and 17 from two-year institutions. (See "Faculty Bargaining Agents on 681 Campuses," 1980). The unions most active in organizing faculties have been the National Education Association (NEA), the American Federation of Teachers (AFT) and the American Association of University Professors (AAUP). In some cases organization has been achieved by a combination of unions, for example, the AAUP-AFT organized 14 campuses and the AAUP-NEA, 9. Nonacademic employee classification categories that have become organized include the trades, and custodial, maintenance, food service, professional, clerical, and supervisory personnel.

Why Are Employees Unionizing?

Higher education, government, and the health care field have been seen by major unions that have experienced drops in membership in industry as appropriate new areas for organization. Among the unions that have organized employees in these areas are the Teamsters Union, the Steelworkers Union, the American Federation of State, County, and Municipal Employees (AFSCME), the United Mine Workers, and the Service Employees International Union.

A variety of reasons have led some higher education faculty and staff members to unionize. Recent turns in the economy have led some employees to feel that only a coordinated union effort will enable them to keep pace with inflation and avoid retrenchment and arbitrary displacement of personnel. In public institutions some faculty and staff members join unions to pressure state government and legislatures for higher appropriations. Too, although within any group there is a variety of attitudes regarding unionization, some faculty and staff members join because of peer pressure; others are impressed by unions' image, by the respectability unions attained when they began organizing high school teachers and other professionals.

What Is Unique About Collective
Bargaining in Higher Education?

Situations unique to higher education have become obvious as faculty and staff members have petitioned for recognition as exclusive bargaining representatives. Unit determination hearings have brought to light a variety of special unit determination questions.

What is the status of a faculty member? Since faculty members through various governance procedures may take an active role in making institutional policy, are they employees under labor relations law or are they uniquely different and part of the management? In the case of Yeshiva University, the U.S. Supreme Court ruled that Yeshiva's faculty are not covered by the National Labor Relations Act because of their role in such management functions as formulating, determining, and effectuating the institution's policies. The decision raises significant questions about faculty collective bargaining at private colleges in the future. However, since the Court did not propose any general rules for determination, the question of other faculties with a smaller role in governance is unanswered. (For details about the Yeshiva vase, see Douglas, 1979; Daponte, 1980; Roots and Shepard, 1980.)

What is the status of a department chairperson? In some institutions, the department chairperson operates as a committee chairperson of the departmental faculty. In these institutions, the chairperson is merely the faculty member who chairs the faculty, and most issues are settled by a vote of the entire faculty. In such cases, department chairpersons have been included in a faculty bargaining unit. However, in other institutions, the department chairperson makes effective recommendations regarding selection of faculty members, salaries, promotion, tenure, and the like. The chairperson may consult with the departmental faculty, but he or she makes the effective recommendation. In such cases, the chairperson is not included in the faculty bargaining unit. Each case requires specific testimony to determine the functional relationship between the chairperson and the faculty.

What is the status of student employees? In most cases, student employees are excluded from participation in unions of regular institutional faculty and staff members. Some states' labor relations acts specifically exclude them.

What is the status of part-time and temporary employees? Higher education uses more continuing part-time, temporary, and casual employees than most other employers. Some states' labor relations acts include continuing part-time faculty or staff members, while others leave the issue open for debate. Temporary or casual employees are usually excluded. In the absence of clear-cut institutional definitions of what constitutes continuing part-time employment, a definition is likely to be reached by a labor board following a unit determination hearing.

What is the status of students' spouses? Some institutions consider students' spouses employed by the institution as individuals receiving student financial aid. If a unit determination hearing were held at such an institution the labor board would have to make a determination of status.

What is the status of domestic workers? Domestic workers in areas such as the institution's chief executive officer's residence have unique working conditions and an effort should be made to exclude them from a bargaining unit.

What is the status of employees on grants and contracts? Employees on grants and contracts compose a unique group because of funding differences. Some contracts are renewed often and, therefore, provide more than short-term employment. If in all ways such individuals are appointed and paid like other continuing faculty or staff members, to exclude them from a union would be difficult unless they are truly very temporary.

What is the status of volunteers? Nonpaid volunteers in areas like university medical schools are not usually considered as employees, and therefore, are not eligible for unionization. However, their presence may cause a problem with unions within the organization if such unions are experiencing cutbacks of personnel and volunteers are doing the work normally performed by the bargaining unit employees.

These aspects of unit determination in higher education are presented as a caution to personnel administrators in higher education. The authors believe that it is realistic for administrators to believe that unionization might soon happen. To prepare for this eventuality, personnel administrators must make decisions regarding what types of bargaining units would be most effective and in the best interest of the institution. Is it advisable to have faculty and professional staff in the same unit; to have the skilled trades and the unskilled in the same unit? Should there be separate bargaining units for the same types of employees at satellite campuses? What about department chairpersons? What is the institution's definition of continuing part-time employment? After administrators decide which units would be in the best interest of the institution, they can recommend personnel policies and procedural rules to strengthen the integrity of such units. Such preparation cannot guarantee suitable unit determinations at a hearing, but failure to prepare can only lead to less desirable outcomes.

Should Institutions Voice a Point of View Regarding Unionization?

Institutions should express their attitude toward the unionization of their employees. Ideally, the chief executive officer and the board of trustees should either publicly or privately express the institution's view. Such a statement might indicate that employees are free to organize under the proper statute; that the institution hopes that employees do not feel a need to organize; and that, if an organization attempt is made, the institution feels obligated to provide information and arguments against unionization. By this suggestion, we do not mean to deprecate unionization. Indeed, many institutions enjoy reasonable relationships with unions, and employees have the right to unionize. However, the excessive costs of legal feels, arbitration, and management time that are devoted to employee organizations divert the institution's limited resources from other essential expenditures.

How Does the Organizing Process Work?

Normally, unions are invited on campus by employees, perhaps disgruntled employees or employees who have always worked in a union environment. Usually, the union sends specially trained organizers to assess the situation and to organize interested employees to convince other employees to sign statements indicating their desire to have that particular union represent them. Alert administrators may be able to detect incipient organizing by watching for the following kinds of incidents:

- Small gatherings of employees, perhaps in unusual places such as the restrooms
- A dead grapevine—suddenly
- Presence of a former employee (one who has quit or been fired) talking with employees
- "Busyness" during breaks, before and after work, and during lunch
- New groups forming and new informal leaders suddenly emerging
- The clam up—a group of people who are deep in conversation but suddenly clam up when a supervisor or administrator approaches
- Sudden increase in questions about policies and benefits
- More assertive complaints
- A previously popular employee is suddenly unpopular
- A new employee (probationary) is overly expressive of his or her loyalty and enthusiasm
- A poor worker becomes a model employee

If a union receives signed statements from at least 30 percent of the potential unit it is claiming for organization, it may file a petition with the appropriate labor board and request an election. Normally, if an election is held, a majority of those voting is required to certify a union for collective bargaining purposes. Therefore, most responsible unions do not file for an election until many more than 30 percent of the employees appear interested.

When the labor board receives the petition, it first considers the following questions:

Is the institution an "employer" under the act?
Is there a sufficient show of interest?

Does the petitioning organization meet the act's definition of
a "labor organization"?

Has there been intervention by another union claiming to
represent the same faculty or staff members?

What is the scope of the bargaining unit sought?

Next, the board schedules an informal conference between
representatives of the union and the institution to determine what
differences of opinion exist between the parties. The purpose of
this meeting is to identify, narrow, or limit issues. This informal
conference is followed by a formal hearing, before a representative
of the appropriate labor board, during which both parties testify on
the scope of the unit in question. Traditionally, labor board
examiners consider the following factors in determining units:
(1) The unit has centralized organization and management;
(2) the members of the group have a community of interest
and centralized personnel policies, procedures, and practices; and
(3) the unit has an integration of location, services, operations,
and facilities. In addition, the examiner considers the history of
collective bargaining within the institution and the possibilities of
extension of the bargaining unit schoolwide, campuswide, statewide, or systemwide.

In many cases certain individuals are excluded by law or
labor board ruling from inclusion in units with other employees.
Excluded employees may include guards, supervisors, members of
other bargaining units, student employees, casual or temporary
employees, confidential employees, and managerial employees.

When an institution presents an argument at a unit determination hearing, the unit it suggests should be a logically created
unit and not one put together according to management's predictions of how employees will vote in the election. Management
should not make assumptions about voting patterns and it should
be prepared to live with the unit, should the union win the election.

If an election is to be held, it is directed by the appropriate
labor board in a way that assures employees freedom of choice.
The board sets the date, time, and polling places for the election.
Each side may have observers at the polling places to challenge

votes. Ballots are usually manual and are secret. At the conclusion of the election, the board counts the ballots. Challenged ballots are resolved only if they would affect the outcome of the election. The winner is determined by a majority of the votes cast. If the union wins, it is declared as the certified bargaining agent for the employees and collective bargaining begins. (For a detailed discussion of the organizing process, see Beal, Wickersham, and Kienast, 1972.)

Should the Institution Campaign Against Unionization?

Prior to an election, a union usually holds employee meetings, hands out leaflets, and conducts mailings and visits. The union's message, of course, is to vote for the union. Should the management of the institution also conduct a campaign? Management should consider the ways in which the mission of the institution and the goals of the union are likely to conflict. For example, an institution has many constituencies including students, faculty, trustees, alumni, and nonunionized employees; however, a union has a single constituency and will try to divert a major share of the institution's resources to its membership. An institution has a variety of educational uses for its resources, while a union thinks of its members' compensation. An institution must be able to accommodate to changes in economic, social, and political realities, while a union wants to protect its members' jobs. An institution needs to have continuity of its operations, while a union wants the right to strike. An institution wants to have external competitiveness and internal equity for *all* jobs, while a union wants more for its members and is not concerned about others. An educational institution has a style that tends toward decentralized authority; a spirit of collegiality, persuasion, and reason; diversity and academic freedom; flexibility and accommodation to individuals. The style of a union tends toward the practical, with centralized authority, and a concern with results, power, majority rule, rigidity of contract, and equity for all.

With these evident conflicts of thought and purpose, it seems appropriate that faculty and staff members be told both sides of the issue. The union will tell its side, and management should, too. Exhibit 72, pp. 345–347, provides guidelines about what supervisors can and cannot say or do during the campaign. Simply stated, the don'ts are don't threaten, don't promise, don't interrogate, and don't spy.

Professional legal assistance is recommended during an organizational campaign. Because the regular legal counsel probably is not experienced in this specialized field of law, the institution should retain specialists in labor law. During a campaign an institution also needs a top-level advisory committee to plan strategy and tactics. Clearly defined policy enables administrators to more easily make the day-to-day campaign decisions. The total institutional management team should be kept abreast of all activities.

In planning its campaign, the institution should be prepared to counter the union's argument. The union's campaign will focus on the following issues:

- Employees have a legal right to organize. The institution cannot prevent employees from asserting that right, and the union seeks to help employees exercise that right.
- Unionization will lead to higher pay, better benefits, and greater autonomy for employees. Unions represent employees' interests and have been successful in achieving real gains for their members.
- Management will not act to protect employees against layoffs, dismissals, or other actions. The institution is concerned only with its overall cost effectiveness, not with the situation of individual employees.
- In unity employees gain strength. The union's international office has the resources to help individual members.

The institution's campaign should be positive rather than defensive. The campaign should encourage employees to vote on election day, reminding them that the majority of those voting will decide the issue. To point out the potential disadvantages of unionization, the institution's campaign literature might pose a series of questions about the union, such as: What is the cost of union dues and fees? What are the consequences of an employee's failure to pay union dues or fines? Will employees have to go on strike? What experience has this union had in higher education? What do the union leaders earn? How much does the union provide in strike benefits? Can employees collect unemployment compensation while on strike? Can the union really protect employees against layoffs? Will individual rights be protected against the majority? Are personal problems handled confidentially by the union?

The institution can also establish a telephone information center to answer employees' questions. Such a service allows employees to ask questions without having to identify themselves. Letters to employees at work or at home, employee meetings, articles in the institution's house organ, and posters are other ways for the institution to campaign.

While the techniques just mentioned are effective in communicating with nonacademic employees, some may not be appropriate in a campaign against an attempt to organize faculty members. Since faculty members by nature are individualists who participate in the management of their institutions through various forms of governance, they may resent a strong campaign from the top management of the institution. Such resentment is particularly likely in a research-oriented institution.

In many institutions whose faculty members have voted against unionization, a strong group of faculty members against unionization emerged and led the campaign against the union. In such cases, the institution can assist by providing opportunities for debate, organizing a library of literature on unionization, and publishing low-key statements. The administration should make its view known, but perhaps not as forcefully as in nonfaculty campaigns. Obviously, local conditions dictate the kind of campaign that will be most effective.

In sum, to prepare a campaign against unionization, the institution must, in consultation with a labor lawyer, carefully assess the particulars of the situation: the institution's weaknesses and the union's weaknesses. The effectiveness of the institution's campaign depends on how well the administration analyzes the situation and communicates its point of view to employees. The institution must also prepare its public information office, since the union may attempt to wage its campaign through the local media. The institution should issue prepared statements through its public information office; individual interviews and other unprepared public announcements should be discouraged.

Are Strikes and Other Work Interruptions Legal?

Under the National Labor Relations Act and some states' public employee acts, strikes are permitted after other remedies have been exhausted. Institutions should have a standard emergency plan for operation in the event of a strike. The institution must evaluate whether it will be able to operate in the face of a strike and the legal actions it will pursue in the event of an illegal strike or improper picketing. Such emergency planning should be undertaken even if state legislation prohibits strikes, since historically the presence of no-strike legislation has not prevented strikes.

How Does Collective Bargaining Work?

If a union wins the election, collective bargaining follows. The first negotiated agreement is extremely important because any omissions from that first contract are generally difficult to correct later.

Usually, the institution's negotiating committee is relatively small, although the union may use a relatively large committee. The institution's committee may include a top administrator from the personnel, financial, and operational areas, and a lawyer. Some institutions appoint the lawyer as the chief negotiator, but we recommend that the personnel officer be the chief negotiator and the lawyer serve in an advisory capacity. The chief executive officer of the institution should not be on the committee because he or she is the final authority on all issues.

The institution's committee should study the backgrounds of the members of the union's negotiating committee: their ranks or grade levels, their lengths of service, their tenure status, their promotion and disciplinary history, their education and work experience, and the like. Such knowledge helps the committee to understand the reasoning behind the demands, statements, and questions that arise at the bargaining table. Such knowledge also helps the committee to construct arguments that will convince the union's negotiating committee.

In conducting bargaining, the institution's committee should carefully consider the following strategies:

- The institution's committee should submit demands just as the union does.
- The institution's committee need not respond to all the union demands. Lack of response is a form of a negative response that may avoid argument.
- The committee should decide the order in which to consider the issues. Difficult issues may be held until rapport has been established at the bargaining table.
- The committee should make a cost estimate for each demand. Committee members should never give off-the-cuff figures or statistics.
- The committee should review all the union demands and prepare a list of questions on each. Committee members should not assume that they know what is meant by a demand nor what response the union expects.
- The committee should try to create a wholesome attitude. At best, negotiation is an adversary relationship; however, it can be reasonably harmonious.
- The committee should always phrase any concessions in a tentative way, pending complete agreement; for example, "We'll consider doing that."
- The committee should not reach conclusions on money issues if the other issues are not settled.
- The committee should recognize that the political nature of unions often necessitates the appearance of conflict.
- The committee should keep supervisors informed.

Exhibit 72, pp. 345–347, presents suggestions for preparing for collective bargaining.

What Is Covered in an Agreement?

An effective agreement services the employee, the union, and the institution. The agreement serves employees by covering such subjects as: hours of work, wages (labor grades or negotiated rates), promotional opportunities, benefits, and security (seniority and grievance procedure).

The union seeks union security rights such as: a definitive statement that defines the bargaining unit, a statement on the type of union representation, a provision for dues checkoff, and an agreement on the duration and renewal of the contract. The major types of union representation are as follows:

1. Maintenance of membership: Any employee who voluntarily joins the union must remain a dues-paying member throughout the life of the contract.
2. Union shop: All employees must join the union within a specified time.
3. Modified union shop: Some current employees who are not members of the union are excluded from the union-shop requirement.
4. Agency shop: Employees who choose not to join the union are required to pay the equivalent of union dues and fees for the union's services.
5. Modified agency shop: Some current employees who are not covered by agency-shop provisions remain free of obligation.
6. Closed shop: The employer may hire only members of a particular union.

The institution is served by the provisions of the agreement that stipulate management's right to exercise flexibility in management: freedom to schedule, to use student employees, to discipline and discharge employees, to change job content, to change the make-up of the work force, to transfer employees, to hire and promote qualified persons, and to make and enforce work rules. The institution's needs are also served by a no-strike clause.

Once the agreement is approved by the institution and ratified by the union membership, all supervisory personnel should be thoroughly trained in the details of the contract. Working under a contract is a new experience for supervisors accustomed to making independent decisions. They need to understand the importance of complying with the contract, and they should not allow practices that result in giving away gains made at the bargaining table. They must learn to consult the agreement and members of the personnel department for interpretation of the agreement so that the institution does not break the provisions of the agreement.

There are two main approaches to interpreting an agreement. The legalistic approach focuses on the letter of the contract; the other approach considers the intent of the agreement. Because agreements are sometimes hastily conceived in the frantic last moments of bargaining, errors of commission and omission are evident in many contracts. In those areas, we recommend that interpretation be based on the intent rather than any vagueness in the wording of the agreement. Those who use the agreement as a legal weapon in settling grievances find future bargaining very difficult.

Impasse During Collective Bargaining

The various laws covering collective bargaining differ in the steps taken if the parties reach an impasse during the collective bargaining process. Most provide for a form of mediation in which a mediator is appointed either from the Federal Mediation and Conciliation Service (FMCS) or from a similar state agency if the institution is covered by state legislation. Mediation is the process of seeking a voluntary solution or compromise through persuasion; thus, the mediator has no power to force a decision.

Another step in the process applicable to the public sector in an attempt to avoid strikes is fact finding. Such a step may be written into a state public employee relations act. The fact finder, like the mediator, has no decision-making authority. Usually, the process involves hearings and investigations that result in the fact finder's specific written recommendations for settlement. The process is designed to put public pressure on the parties for settlement, but the parties have the right to accept or reject the fact finder's recommendations.

Finally, some state statutes stipulate binding arbitration as the final step to resolve an impasse in collective bargaining. Such arbitration, referred to as interest arbitration, is found most often in laws governing collective bargaining for police and fire fighters and serves to preclude a strike. Interest arbitration differs from the arbitration used to settle differences of opinions about the interpretation of a portion of a contract. In those cases, the arbitrator interprets already agreed upon contractual language. In binding arbitration, the arbitrator studies the final positions of parties at an impasse and makes a binding decision for settlement.

Variations of interest arbitration include total-package arbitration, item-by-item arbitration, and independent-position or compromise arbitration. In total-package arbitration, the arbitrator studies the final positions of both parties and then selects one of them in its entirety as the binding position. In item-by-item arbitration, the arbitrator studies the final positions of the two parties on each item and gives a binding decision by selecting the union's position on some items and the institution's position on others. Under compromise arbitration, the arbitrator's decisions on issues may be new positions that fall between the final positions of the two parties. (For details on impasse resolution, see Birnbaum, 1980; Lee, 1979; Levine, 1978.)

Obviously, the nature of the binding arbitration to be used must be decided prior to the parties' reaching an impasse. The process and strategy of bargaining is affected by the type of arbitration to be used. Of course, the institution must remember that binding arbitration puts the final decision concerning the institution's expenditures in the hands of an outsider.

Exhibit 72. Guidelines for Supervisors During a Union Organizational Campaign

College and university employees who are covered by the National Labor Relations Act or similar state legislation are permitted to organize, form, join, or assist in employee organizations; to engage in lawful concerted activities for the purpose of collective bargaining or other mutual aid; and to bargain collectively through representatives of their own free choice. Since employees are provided free choice in the matter of union organization, representatives of management must be careful to refrain from any conduct that interferes with the employees' rights in this respect. All management representatives also must remember that anything that is said or done by them in connection with union organization activities may be considered to have been said or done by the university itself. The following is a summary of permissible and prohibited activities by an institution's supervisors and other management personnel.

Supervisors can:

1. Tell employees that members of management are always willing to discuss with them any subject of interest to them.
2. Tell employees about the benefits they presently enjoy, but avoid veiled promises or threats.
3. Tell employees some of the disadvantages of belonging to a union: the expense of initiation fees and monthly dues, membership rules restricting freedom, and their loss of the right to make their own decisions on matters involving wages, hours, and other working conditions.
4. Tell employees that in negotiating with the union the institution does not have to agree to all the union's terms and certainly not to any terms that are not in the interest of the institution.
5. Tell employees about any personal experience with unions, especially the union seeking to represent the employees.
6. Tell employees about any untrue or misleading statements made by a union organizer or in any union literature.
7. Tell employees that an international union may try to dominate the local union, or at least try to influence local members.
8. Tell employees that they are free to join or not to join any organization without prejudice to their status at the institution.
9. Tell employees that signing a union authorization card or application for membership does not mean that they must vote for the union in an election.
10. Make or enforce any rules requiring that oral solicitation of membership or discussion of union affairs not be conducted during work-

Exhibit 72 (continued)

ing time. (Employees can solicit and discuss unionism on their own time, even on the institution's premises, as long as they do not interrupt work.)

11. Lay off, discipline, and discharge employees for cause following customary practice and without regard to an employee's participation or nonparticipation in union activities.

12. Make assignments of preferred work, overtime, and shift preference following customary practice and without reference to the employee's participation or nonparticipation in union activities.

13. Impartially enforce rules in accordance with customary action, irrespective of the employee's membership or activity in a union.

14. Tell employees they do not have to talk with union organizers at their home or anywhere else unless they want to.

Supervisors cannot:

1. Promise employees a pay increase, promotion, betterment, benefit, or special favor if they do not join the union or vote against it.

2. Threaten loss of job, reduction of income, discontinuance of privileges or benefits presently enjoyed, or use intimidating language that may influence an employee in the exercise of his or her right to belong, or refrain from belonging, to a union.

3. Threaten or actually discharge, discipline, or layoff an employee because of his or her activities in behalf of the union.

4. Threaten, through a third party, any of the foregoing acts of interference.

5. Threaten to drastically reduce operations if a union is selected as a representative.

6. Spy on union meetings. (Parking across the street from a union hall to watch employees enter the hall is suspect.)

7. Conduct themselves in a way that would indicate to employees that they are being watched to determine whether they are participating in union activities.

8. Discriminate against employees who actively support the union by intentionally assigning undesirable work to them.

9. Prejudicially transfer employees because of union affiliation.

10. Engage in any partiality favoring those employees not active in behalf of the union.

11. Discipline or penalize employees who actively support a union for an infraction for which other employees are not likewise disciplined.

12. Make any work assignment for the purpose of causing an employee who is active in behalf of the union to quit his or her job.

13. Take any action that is intended to impair the status of, or adversely affect, an employee's job or pay because of his or her activity in behalf of the union.

14. Intentionally assign work or transfer employees so that those active in behalf of the union are separated from those who are not interested in supporting a union.

15. Select employees to be laid off with the intention of curbing the union's strength or discouraging affiliation with it.

16. Ask employees to express their thoughts about the union or its officers.

17. Ask employees how they intend to vote in a union election.

18. Ask employees at time of hiring or thereafter whether they belong to the union or have signed a union application or authorization card.

19. Ask employees about the internal affairs of unions such as meetings and so forth. (It is not an unfair labor practice to listen to employees who volunteer information, but supervisors must not ask questions to obtain additional information.)

20. Ask employees what they expect to gain by joining the union.

21. Make a statement that supervisors or management will not deal with the union.

22. Indicate to employees that they will be discharged or disciplined if they are active in behalf of the union.

23. Urge employees to try to persuade others to oppose the union or stay out of it.

24. Prevent employees from soliciting union members during their free time on the institution's premises so long as such does not interfere with work being performed by others.

25. Visit the homes of employees for the purpose of urging them to reject the union.

26. Speak privately to employees in any institution's office about the union campaign in order to urge them to vote against the union. (The best place to talk to employees about such matters is at their work stations or in work areas or in public areas where other employees are present.)

27. Ask employees about the identity of employees favoring the union.

28. Prevent employees from wearing union buttons.

Exhibit 73. How to Prepare for Collective Bargaining

By Robert E. Keane
University of Maine

Purpose:

The primary objective of collective bargaining is to reach mutually acceptable agreements on wages, hours, and other terms and conditions of
employment while maintaining the most harmonious relations possible
between employer and employee. During negotiations, this objective often
is obscured by a communications breakdown between the parties. In many
cases, such breakdowns can be avoided if the management team anticipates
the problems and makes adequate preparations beforehand to cope with
them. It is difficult to anticipate, and subsequently prepare for, all contingencies, but adequate preparation can substantially contribute to successful collective bargaining.

Preparation for negotiations:

Although preparations immediately preceding negotiations for a new
contract typically generate the highest concern, long-range preparations
should start immediately after a new contract is signed. Management's
techniques in administering the new contract, in handling grievances and
employee problems, and its attitude toward labor after a contract is signed
are important considerations which directly affect the conduct of future
bargaining sessions as well as the general climate of employee relations.

In short-range preparations, attention should be given to an agenda of
bargaining items which management would like to discuss. Many organizations are adversely affected by hamstringing contract clauses which cause
operational inefficiencies and by other contract language which, perhaps
by improper interpretation, has resulted in costly precedent-setting practices. Managerial problems, such as these, are prime items for negotiations,
and it is worth the effort to prepare a case for their elimination. Line
supervision and operational staff personnel should be queried before negotiations to pinpoint costly areas of operating inefficiencies which could
be eliminated by a change in contract language. Then, with the help of
legal counsel, new contract language can be drafted to replace undesirable
phraseology.

Agenda items should be analyzed then to determine the savings which
could be achieved if they were bargained for successfully. The costs involved give management an extremely useful bargaining tool which could
be used as a buffer if negotiations reach an impasse on economic issues.
Also, as soon as the list of union demands is received and before formal

bargaining commences, the demands should be evaluated and decisions and estimates made regarding the importance each item represents to the respective parties.

Cost-factor analysis:

It is important to develop standardized conversion data for use in translating and computing the cost impact of anticipated union proposals before negotiations begin. The preparation of this information well in advance of the first bargaining session will not only facilitate a thoroughly briefed, knowledgeable management team which understands its organization but will allow valuable planning time for management to analyze the conversion data, verify their accuracy, and cover all possible cost contingencies.

For example, standardized conversion data which can be calculated easily and accurately are the costs of each cent-per-hour increase in wages, each cent-per-hour shift differential, an additional holiday, vacation day, and the like. Other conversion data are more difficult to calculate because trend and experience analyses are needed to determine accurate costs, but they are data worth preparing. Increasing sick leave accrual time, overtime pay premiums, call-in pay, hospitalization coverage, and tuition refund payments are only a few examples of valuable knowledge which can be effectively used at the bargaining table. The fact that union proposals may not include many of these items does not mean that calculating their cost impact was wasted effort. On the contrary, knowledge of the cost implications in these areas enables management to offer compromise proposals to costlier demands.

In addition, the development of other data valuable to effective bargaining includes comparative wage surveys of organizations engaged in the same endeavor, historical data on the organization's trends in personnel standards, and the number of employees by department and job classifications, to mention a few.

The bargaining team:

Structure of the bargaining team varies, depending upon the type of organization involved. The bargaining team should be as small in number as possible but should as a minimum include the top administrators from the financial, personnel, and operations segments of the organization. Subordinate managerial personnel could be included to make informational searches, to coordinate the routine arrangements incidental to negotiations, and, in general, to do the leg work needed by the trio of top administrators. The subordinate group also should be small in number and, if possible, be representatives of the personnel function. The latter recommendation is based on the assumption that personnel-oriented managerial types have an understanding of labor relations and its implica-

Exhibit 73 (continued)

tions in negotiations. They will also be heavily involved in the administration of the contract.

There also should be an organizational lawyer on call to forestall legal entanglements and to review recommended language in the contract. When the employee bargaining group has a lawyer present at the bargaining sessions, the institution should be similarly represented. However, the lawyer should act as an advisor and have no decision-making responsibility over and above calling for a caucus. In addition, someone other than the chief negotiator should be designated to take complete notes on the discussions and to record tentative agreements and concessions.

Conduct at the bargaining table:

Of the three top administrators on the bargaining team, the representative from the personnel function should be the chief negotiator. This individual should be experienced in negotiations, should conduct the bargaining sessions, and articulate positions for the institution. Other team members should be heard at the table only when information or clarification is needed. During negotiations, a direct line of communication should be maintained between the chief negotiator and the institution's highest policy-making body, which can make the decision to hold or yield when a breakdown in bargaining or a strike threat occurs.

On all other issues, the authority to make binding commitments must be delegated to the decision makers, and this authority should encompass administrative and economic matters. The three top administrators should have this responsibility and authority. When differing viewpoints prevail on critical issues, a majority vote of the three should settle the matter.

Decisions made in good faith at the bargaining table should never be rescinded, except for an undisputed break in faith initiated by the other party. However, it is not advisable to reach final agreement on any one item until discussion has taken place and tentative agreement has been reached on all items. Money should be the last item discussed.

Conclusion:

Careful preparation for collective bargaining enhances the process, facilitates efficient, effective, and expeditious negotiations, and provides that knowledge which can act as a catalyst to creative and imaginative alternatives which result in contract resolutions if job actions appear inevitable.

Source: College and University Personnel Association (in press).

❦ 17 ❧

Staffing for Personnel Administration

The personnel function has always existed in any organization with more than two employees. For example, decisions that one person receives more pay than another, that someone is paid while absent for illness, or that vacation is granted—all are personnel decisions. In the 1930s a very few institutions of higher education established formal personnel offices. During the 1940s and 1950s, an era of growth for higher education, more personnel administration offices were established and offered the necessary systematized methods for dealing with the growing numbers of faculty and staff members. However, many institutions did not formally create personnel functions until the 1960s and 1970s. More recently the term *human resource management* has replaced the term *personnel administration* in some institutions. This change reflects the expansion of the personnel function.

Today a typical personnel office fulfills the following functions:

Recruitment and appointment (including equal employment opportunity and affirmative action)
Salary administration, position evaluation, and analysis
Employee benefits
Employee relations
Personnel records and procedures
Performance evaluation
Orientation, training and management development
Communications
Personnel research

Some few institutions include safety and security as a personnel function; however, that practice is followed more in industry than in higher education. Too, some institutions assign responsibility for the payroll to their personnel departments. However, more frequently that function is placed under the jurisdiction of the controller or chief business officer. We recommend that payroll not be assigned to the personnel office. While the personnel office should provide the audited and approved personnel documents to the payroll office for payment, the actual payroll procedures are more appropriate to offices assigned the responsibilities for accounting, budgeting, and cash control.

Figures 5 and 6 illustrate recommended functional personnel organization charts for a large and a midsized institution, respectively. In a large institution, management of each function listed should be assigned to one individual. In midsized and smaller institutions, functions can be combined for management assignments. Logical combinations include: compensation, benefits, and personnel records; or employment, employee relations, and affirmative action; or performance evaluation, training, and development. The backgrounds and talents of the personnel staff and the work loads of the functions may dictate other acceptable combinations. The important principle is that each function is adequately recognized.

Figure 5. Sample Personnel Office Organization Chart for a Large Institution

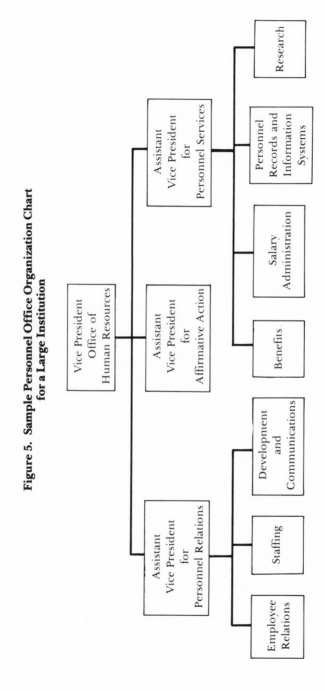

**Figure 6. Sample Personnel Office Organization Chart
for a Midsized Institution**

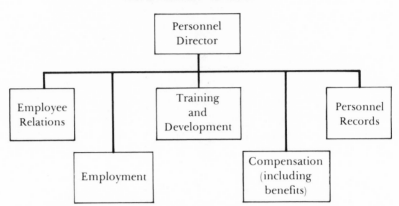

The placement of the affirmative action function is a controversial issue. (Note that in Figure 5, the affirmative action function reports to the vice president responsible for human resources. The affirmative action function is not shown as part of the personnel function in Figure 6.) Federal agencies, in an effort to emphasize affirmative action, often urge institutions to create a separate affirmative action office whose administrator reports directly to the chief executive officer of the institution. The federal agencies argue that because the affirmative action function audits the work of the personnel office, it should not be part of that office. Some institutions have created separate offices reporting to the president (or to another senior officer), while other institutions have assigned affirmative action to the personnel office. An argument for assigning it to the personnel office is that the personnel office is responsible for recommending personnel policy and for monitoring all personnel activities and, therefore, affirmative action and equal employment opportunity should be integrated into all aspects of the personnel program. To have the affirmative action officer report to a higher official in the institution than the one to whom the personnel officer reports may dilute the effectiveness of the personnel office.

We have discussed this organizational problem with personnel officers in a variety of institutions and find that both organizational philosophies seem to work successfully. The effectiveness of an affirmative action program depends on how cooperatively the personnel officer and the affirmative action officer coordinate their programs, not on the hierarchy of supervision.

Should the Central Personnel Office Be Responsible for Academic Personnel?

The scope of the responsibilities of the personnel office varies from institution to institution. Very often, the personnel office is responsible for all nonacademic personnel matters but only for the handling of benefits for academic personnel. However, in a number of institutions, the personnel office has considerable responsibility for academic personnel matters.

Academic personnel enjoy a unique relationship with an institution, particularly in a fully integrated research institution. The faculty senate usually gives faculty members a voice in the shared governance of the institution, and faculty members serve on committees that choose new faculty members and make effective recommendations on tenure. Some faculty members, through grants and contracts, bring their own fiscal support to the institution.

If the personnel office is responsible for matters concerning academic employees, that office should maintain a low profile in such matters. The office should work with the chief academic officer and the deans of the colleges in technical personnel areas. For example, assisting a dean with the termination of a faculty member, making recommendations to the chief academic officer regarding needed changes in the sabbatical leave policy, monitoring all academic appointments for the chief academic officer, and handling affirmative action matters—all are areas in which the personnel office can give effective assistance. Indeed, not to use the professional expertise of the personnel office in the handling of such personnel matters is inefficient since the personnel staff is already knowledgeable about relevant policies and procedures.

The handling of the personnel function for support staff can be reasonably standardized. In fact, large groups of similar staff positions in various parts of an institution dictate the need for some form of standardized fair treatment for such employees. Additionally, personnel policies can be quite specific for most support staff, whereas policies for faculty need to be more general and flexible because of the nature of the individual contributions of faculty members to higher education.

What Is Unique About Academic Personnel Administration?

Although similarities among employees in all work environments abound, distinct differences exist between personnel administration in business and industry and in higher education. The major difference involves the nature of the members of the academic community. Because most academic administrators rose through the faculty ranks, they identify themselves with the faculty. Essential to successful human resource management in colleges and universities is an understanding of the academic personality. The following broad generalizations are offered in a positive spirit to facilitate communication and understanding. (For a more detailed discussion, see Fortunato, 1979, the source of many of these suggestions.)

Many faculty members are independent mavericks. Their academic training encourages them to question authority in all areas and requires independent thinking, scholarship, and innovation. Too, many faculty members are adroit entrepreneurs; they independently engage in consulting, research, writing, and grantsmanship. This independence and maverick nature are positive factors that build an excellent faculty. Thus, some conflict may be created when these independent free thinkers are required to adhere to rules others, including personnel administrators, have developed.

Faculty members tend to react to situations in relation to their disciplines, and most faculty members' first loyalty is to their discipline. For example, consider performance evaluation. A faculty member in engineering will probably accept a detailed performance evaluation instrument that provides for multiple choices and numerical ratings, while a liberal arts faculty member may prefer to write paragraphs about the individual being evaluated. The personnel administrator should be sensitive to such differences. Faculty members' loyalty to their discipline is not to be interpreted as disloyalty to the institution. As independent professionals, faculty appreciate the institution to the extent that it allows them to pursue knowledge.

Most faculty members prefer to obtain information by written rather than oral communication. They are likely to give more attention and credence to written material. And, as trained researchers who document and annotate their material, they expect others to do the same. Thus, when preparing a presentation for faculty, personnel professionals should document the research that preceded the policy decision. For example, if a survey was conducted, the presentation should document the results so that faculty members can evaluate whether the final recommendations are justified.

Faculty members do not consider themselves to be only employees, and collective faculty judgment is used to make recommendations normally regarded as management responsibilities (selection of new faculty, tenure, and promotion). Indeed, faculty are unique in their employee-employer relationships. Personnel professionals should learn all they can about the shared governance model and how to improve it.

Generally, rules regarding faculty should be more flexible than those for staff because there are so many variables among faculty members and their proposals. Personnel administrators need not worry too much about setting precedents when responding to faculty requests for exceptions to rules. Personnel administrators must demonstrate that they understand the need for flexibility, although they must attempt not to create a backlash in which academic administrators question why personnel professionals do not grant staff employees the same flexibility granted faculty.

Faculty members and senior administrators who rose through the academic ranks tend to think of their profession at its highest level of integrity. Personnel administrators should be careful not to make any recommendations that might appear to question academic integrity. Of course a personnel administrator who hears that a faculty member is taking advantage of the profession will want to devise policies to correct the situation. However, all suggestions will be reviewed by faculty members and administrators who will consider the adverse effects of those recommendations on the faculty members of high integrity, and they may well scorn any proposal that does not respect their integrity.

Faculty members recognize that nonacademic staff perform essential duties; however, they tend to think of their own mission as the most important mission of the institution. Personnel administrators will accomplish little by debating this subject. Rather, they should reinforce that idea and remind faculty that everyone's mission is to serve the academic community. Because faculty members view academic activities as most important, they may not want to deal with a central personnel office that does not have a sufficiently academic look. Personnel administrators should consider ways in which to conduct personnel affairs that will gain the faculty's respect for the personnel function.

Faculty members constantly challenge each other, often in negative and forceful ways. Personnel administrators should not misunderstand faculty members' motives or style when challenged. Similarly, faculty members are jealous of their prerogatives. Personnel administrators should not appear to make a value judgment of an article published by a faculty member or of the significance of particular research.

In summary, faculty members have an unusually strong voice in their own destiny. Decisions about what they teach and what research they do are influenced greatly by their personal wishes. Faculty members, proud of and loyal to their discipline, usually take seriously their role in governance, particularly their contribution to and responsibility for the recruitment, appointment, tenuring, and promotion of colleagues. To recognize these conditions is the first step toward working successfully with the academic community.

To Whom Should the Personnel Office Report?

Most frequently, the personnel officer reports to the chief business (or fiscal) officer. The workability of that arrangement depends on the nature and priorities of the chief business officer. In many cases it works very well; however, if the chief business officer is fiscally oriented to the exclusion of having a positive interest in the personnel function, the personnel function may receive less-than-adequate support. A few educational institutions, recognizing the importance of the personnel function, have created vice presidencies for personnel. In many cases, those institutions have expanded the responsibility of the personnel office to include academic personnel administration.

In any case, the personnel officer should report high enough in the organization so that he or she has the opportunity to personally present new programs or reports to the chief executive officer of the institution. Three suggestions for a reporting line are to the chief executive officer, to the senior officer for administration, or to the chief academic officer and the chief business officer. Although split reporting lines can cause communications problems, the complexity of a major university is such that the split reporting line may be an ideal arrangement.

How Large Should the Central Personnel Office Be?

A 1975 survey of fourteen major institutions by the Office of Personnel Administration at The Pennsylvania State University compares the size of their personnel staffs to the numbers of their total faculty and staff (see Fortunato and Lozier, 1975). The institutions surveyed were Cornell, Harvard, Indiana, Michigan State, Purdue, Pennsylvania State, Georgia, Maryland, Michigan, Missouri, Pennsylvania, Pittsburgh, Temple, and Yale.

The coded results of the survey appear in Tables 2 through 7. (Note: These data include individuals performing the central personnel function whether or not they are organizationally part of the personnel department.) Data are provided for the total personnel staff and for each of the following functions: employment, salary administration and classification, personnel benefits, personnel records, and employee relations.

While institutions vary in mission, location, and complexity which make standard staffing formulas difficult to project, these data offer some basis for comparisons of personnel staff size. For example, Table 3 shows the ratio of the number of full-time equivalent personnel staff members in the central employment function to the number of full-time vacancies that staff assists in filling annually. The extremes indicate that in institution N each central

Table 2. Relationship Between Size of Central Personnel Staff and Total Full-Time Faculty and Staff Members

Rank/Institution		Ratio of Central Personnel Employees to Full-Time Faculty and Staff Members
1.	H	1:120.0
2.	F	1:128.0
3.	G	1:143.6
4.	J	1:150.5
5.	C	1:160.0
6.	N	1:166.9
7.	M	1:178.4
8.	A	1:186.5
9.	L	1:194.4
10.	K	1:210.1
11.	D	1:256.2
12.	I	1:258.3
13.	B	1:260.7
14.	E	1:273.6
	Median = 182.5	

Source: Fortunato and Lozier (1975, p. 41).

Table 3. Relationship Between Size of Central Personnel Employment Staff and the Total Number of Full-Time Vacancies Filled Annually

Rank/Institution		Ratio of Central Employment Staff to Full-Time Vacancies It Assists in Filling Annually
1.	N	1:42
2.	E	1:74
3.	G	1:112
4.	H	1:126
5.	C	1:133
6.	J	1:146
7.	K	1:159
8.	M	1:173
9.	B	1:197
10.	L	1:215
11.	F	1:221
12.	I	1:253
13.	D	1:367
14.	A	1:411
	Median = 166	

Source: Fortunato and Lozier (1975, p. 43).

**Table 4. Relationship Between Size of Central Personnel Salary
Administration and Classification Staff and Total Full-Time Staff
Members Evaluated**

Rank/Institution		Ratio of Central Classification Staff to Staff Members Whose Jobs Are Evaluated
1.	G	1:313
2.	F	1:490
3.	C	1:505
4.	M	1:531
5.	L	1:532
6.	H	1:566
7.	N	1:680
8.	I	1:698
9.	J	1:765
10.	K	1:796
11.	D	1:837
12.	E	1:1027
13.	B	1:1325
14.	A	1:1516
	Median = 689	

Source: Fortunato and Lozier (1975, p. 45).

**Table 5. Relationship Between Size of Central Personnel Benefits Staff
and Number of Faculty and Staff Members Served**

Rank/Institution		Ratio of Central Benefits Staff to Full-Time Faculty and Staff Members Served
1.	G	1:564
2.	A	1:568
3.	H	1:629
4.	B	1:757
5.	F	1:896
6.	L	1:923
7.	D	1:950
8.	C	1:960
9.	I	1:971
10.	J	1:979
11.	M	1:1300
12.	K	1:1308
13.	N	1:1475
	Median = 950	

Note: One institution's benefits administration is handled by state
government.
Source: Fortunato and Lozier (1975, p. 44).

**Table 6. Relationship Between Size of Central Personnel Records
Administration Staff and Total Full-Time Faculty and Staff on Whom
Hard-Copy Records Are Kept**

Rank/Institution	Ratio of Central Personnel Records Staff to Full-Time Faculty and Staff on Whom Hard-Copy Records Are Kept
1. J	1:534
2. A	1:559
3. G	1:658
4. F	1:701
5. C	1:840
6. E	1:848
7. H	1:916
8. B	1:1042
9. D	1:1267
10. L	1:1343
11. M	1:1394
12. K	1:1569
13. N	1:1769
14. I	1:2674
	Median = 980.5

Source: Fortunato and Lozier (1975, p. 42).

**Table 7. Relationship Between Size of Central Employee Relations Staff
and Total Numbers of Union Members**

Rank/Institution	Ratio of Central Employee Relations Staff to Number of Union Members
1. A	1:67
2. K	1:150
3. C	1:283
4. N	1:487
5. F	1:494
6. H	1:511
7. E	1:536
8. J	1:566
9. I	1:744
10. M	1:777
11. G	1:1150
12. D	1:1670
	Median = 523.5

Note: Two institutions that have no unions are not included in this
comparison.
Source: Fortunato and Lozier (1975, p. 45).

employment staff member assisted in filling only 42 full-time positions a year, whereas in institution A each central employment staff member assisted in filling 411 full-time positions. The median ratio is 1:166. If we assume that a reasonable band encompasses the ratios for the three institutions immediately above and below the median, an institution with a ratio above or below the band should examine its staffing needs.

As Tables 2 through 7 illustrate, the size of the central personnel staff that performs the various personnel functions of a college or university varies considerably both within and between institutions. This variance is likely to be a function of the types and number of functions served, and the procedures used in performing these functions. The data presented in the tables should aid institutions in their critical self-analysis. (For more information on this study, see Fortunato and Lozier, 1975.)

What Is the Role of the Personnel Staff?

The personnel office staff members are part of the institution's management. They are charged with the responsibility to attain, train, and retain the best institutional staff possible. They are responsible for helping to meet the institution's goals for cost reduction and productivity. They are employee advocates only to the degree of promoting sound employee relations; caution should be exercised in such advocacy so as not to undermine the authority of the deans and administrative officers. While personnel staff members have a service role in some of their activities, they have a monitoring role in other activities. The personnel staff implements, monitors, and controls the institution's commitments to affirmative action, equal pay, equal opportunities for employees, and related policies. Thus, the personnel staff's role is a delicate mixture of service and control that creates and maintains positive employee relations.

Can the Personnel Function Be Decentralized to Some Extent?

Middle-sized and large institutions are made up of a number of highly diversified and quite independent units. In such institutions, it is difficult for a personnel officer in central administration to be aware of personnel actions and problems in all units of the institution. Normally, these units are under the control of academic administrators who devote their time and effort to academic programs and problems. These administrators need to understand the personnel policies and procedures, yet they are too busy to become completely familiar with the details of the personnel program. In this situation, it is helpful for each dean or other major administrative officer to designate an administrative or professional staff member to be the personnel representative for that area. In most units, such an assignment would constitute one-quarter to one-half of the workload of the staff member selected. That staff member should have regular access to the administrative officer and should have authority to speak for that officer.

After a personnel representative has been named in each area, almost all contacts between the central personnel office and the units can be conducted through the personnel representatives. Those contacts and special training and regular monthly meetings will enable those representatives to become very knowledgeable about personnel processes. Such a system provides special assistance to academic employees who can address to their personnel representative any requests for new positions, replacements for current staff, and any other personnel matters. The personnel representatives can take the requests to the personnel staff and begin the appropriate procedures to respond to the requests.

As such a system matures, the personnel representatives provide a knowledgeable group for recommendations and responses to new or changed policies. In that way, each dean or administrative officer and the personnel officer are assured that a policy under consideration will be critiqued by representatives of all segments of the institution. The personnel representatives can assume other responsibilities such as: (1) describing the institution's benefits to new faculty and staff members and enrolling them in the benefits programs; (2) ensuring that employees within the unit are provided promotional opportunities; (3) ensuring that development opportunities are made available; (4) counseling faculty, staff, and administrators about employee relations problems; (5) assisting in monitoring unemployment compensation costs;

(6) interpreting policies within the unit; and (7) assisting in the collective bargaining process by providing necessary data.

Such a decentralized program creates an awareness throughout the institution about the goals of the institution's personnel program. It provides trained, responsible personnel people in each unit, which fosters excellent communication between the central administration and the units and allows a consistent administration of policies. Decentralization also assists in the identification of employee problems before they become major crises, provides for equity in resolving job evaluation programs, and ensures that all units participate in the review of policy. Finally, decentralization frees up the time of the central personnel staff so that they can devote their attention to important human resources management functions.

In summary, a successful human resources management program in higher education starts with positive attitudes on the part of the chief executive officer, the deans, and other administrators. By their actions, they must establish a climate in which all constituents of the institution's family know that consultation before decision making is standard, that faculty and staff members will have developmental and promotional opportunities, that effective performance by faculty and staff is an expectation, that remuneration and benefits will be administered fairly and equitably, and that a positive approach to affirmative action and equal employment opportunity will be enacted. In such an environment, the professional personnel officer can be an effective leader toward the goals of the institution.

⚜ References ⚜

AAUP/AAC Commission on Academic Tenure. *Faculty Tenure: A Report and Recommendations.* San Francisco: Jossey-Bass, 1973.

American Association of University Professors. "Academic Freedom and Tenure, Statement of Principles." *Bulletin of the American Association of University Professors,* 1941, *27,* 421.

American Association of University Professors. "Procedural Standards in the Renewal or Nonrenewal of Faculty Appointments." *Bulletin of the American Association of University Professors,* 1970, *46,* 21–25.

American Association of University Professors. "Evaluating Teachers." *Bulletin of the American Association of University Professors,* 1977, *65,* (entire issue).

American Management Association. *Programmed Instruction for Management Education (How to Master Job Descriptions).* New York: AMACOM, 1979.

Anderson, S. B., and Ball, S. *The Profession and Practice of Program Evaluation.* San Francisco: Jossey-Bass, 1978.

Angell, G. W., Kelley, E. P., Jr., and Associates. *Handbook of Faculty Bargaining.* San Francisco: Jossey-Bass, 1977.

Babbie, E. R. *Survey Research Methods.* Belmont, Calif.: Wadsworth, 1973.

Baird, L. S. "Self and Superior Rating of Performance." *Academy of Management Journal,* 1979, *20,* 291–300.

Beal, E. F., Wickersham, E. D., and Kienast, P. *The Practice of Collective Bargaining.* Homewood, Ill.: Irwin, 1972.

Beatty, R. W., and Schneier, C. E. *Personnel Administration: An Experiential Skill-Building Approach.* Reading, Mass.: Addison-Wesley, 1977.

Birnbaum, R. *Creative Academic Bargaining.* New York: Teachers College Press, 1980.

Blackwell, T. E. *College and University Administration.* New York: Center for Applied Research in Education, 1966.

Bosley, H. E. *Administration of Faculty Personnel in State Teachers Colleges.* Oneonta, N.Y.: American Association of Teachers Colleges, 1946.

Bouchard, R. A. "Experiences with Proposition 13 and Other Retrenchment Conditions." *Journal of the College and University Personnel Association,* 1980a, *31* (1), 61–65.

Bouchard, R. A. *Personnel Practices for Small Colleges.* Washington, D.C.: National Association of College and University Business Officers in conjunction with the College and University Personnel Association, 1980b.

Boxx, W. R., and others. "Duties and Responsibilities of the Academic Personnel Director." *Journal of the College and University Personnel Association,* 1978, *29* (1), 10–20.

Boyd, J. E., and Schietinger, E. F. *Faculty Evaluation Procedures in Southern Colleges and Universities.* Atlanta, Ga.: Southern Regional Education Board, 1976.

Brubacher, J. S. *The Courts and Higher Education.* San Francisco: Jossey-Bass, 1971.

Bureau of National Affairs (BNA) County of Washington v. *Alberta Gunther. Law Week 49* (No. 48) No. 80–429, 1981, 4623–4635.

Carlsen, R. D., and McHugh, J. F. *Handbook of Personnel Administration Forms and Formats.* Englewood Cliffs, N.J.: Prentice-Hall, 1979.

Carnegie Council on Policy Studies in Higher Education. *Making Affirmative Action Work in Higher Education.* San Francisco: Jossey-Bass, 1975.

Carnegie Council on Policy Studies in Higher Education, and others. *Faculty Bargaining in Public Higher Education.* San Francisco: Jossey-Bass, 1977.

Castetter, W. B. *The Personnel Function in Educational Administration.* (2nd ed.). New York: Macmillan, 1976.

CBI Publishing. *Training Perspectives: Conversations and Opinions.* Boston: CBI Publishing, Vistasonics, Inc., 1978.

Chesler, D. J. "Reliability and Comparability of Different Job Evaluation Systems." *Journal of Applied Psychology,* 1948, *32,* 465–475.

Claxton, S. C. *Community College Staff Development: Basic Issues in Planning.* Atlanta, Ga.: Southern Regional Education Board, 1976.

College and University Personnel Association. *Women and Minorities: A Supplement to the Administrative Compensation Survey.* Washington, D.C.: College and University Personnel Association, 1975–1976.

College and University Personnel Association. *Personnelite,* 1979, *6* (46), 2–3.

College and University Personnel Association. *Administrative Compensation Survey.* Washington, D.C.: College and University Personnel Association, 1980a.

College and University Personnel Association. *Personnel Policy Models.* (2nd ed.) Washington, D.C.: College and University Personnel Association, 1980b.

College and University Personnel Association. "Tenure and Retrenchment Practices in Higher Education." *Journal of the College and University Personnel Association, 31* (3 and 4), Fall-Winter, 1980c.

College and University Personnel Association. *Personnelite,* 1980d, *7* (9), 1–2.

College and University Personnel Association. *Guidelines to Better College and University Personnel Administration.* Washington, D.C.: College and University Personnel Association, in press.

Commerce Clearing House. *Guidebook to Federal Wage-Hour Law (Labor Law Reports).* Chicago: Commerce Clearing House, 1970.

Commerce Clearing House. *Topical Law Reports.* Chicago: Commerce Clearing House, 1979.

Cook, T. A., and Zucchi, D. M. *College and University Employee Benefits Cost Survey.* New York: Teachers Insurance and Annuity Association, 1979.

"Court Faces Issue of Equal Pay for Comparable Work." *Washington Post,* June 4, 1981, 1–2.

Craig, D. P. *Trainer's Handbook.* Austin, Tex.: Learning Concepts, 1978.

Craig, R. L., and Bittel, L. R. *Training and Development Handbook.* New York: McGraw-Hill, 1967.

Daponte, K. J. "Practical Implications of the Yeshiva Decision." *Journal of the College and University Personnel Association,* 1980, *31* (2), 45–49.

Davidson, W. *How to Develop and Administer an Effective Wage and Salary Program.* Chicago: Dartnell Corporation, 1979.

Dorfman, L. T. "Emeritus Professors Review University Retirement Policies." *Journal of the College and University Personnel Association,* 1979, *30* (2), 13–25.

Douglas, J. M. "NLRB Versus Yeshiva University." *Journal of the College and University Personnel Association,* 1979, *30* (3), 27–35.

Dressel, P. L. *Handbook of Academic Evaluation.* San Francisco: Jossey-Bass, 1976.

Duryea, E. D., Fisk, R. S., and Associates. *Faculty Unions and Collective Bargaining.* San Francisco: Jossey-Bass, 1973.

Eiben, R., and Milliren, A. *Educational Change: A Humanistic Approach.* San Diego: University Associates, 1976.

Elkin, R., and Hewitt, T. L. *Successful Arbitration: An Experiential Approach.* Reston, Va.: Reston, 1978.

"Faculty Bargaining Agents on 681 Campuses." *Chronicle of Higher Education,* July 7, 1980, 7–8.

Fiedler, J. *Field Research: A Manual for Logistics and Management of Scientific Studies in Natural Settings.* San Francisco: Jossey-Bass, 1978.

Fine, S. A. "Functional Job Analysis: An Approach to a Technology for Manpower Planning." *Personnel Journal,* 1974, *53* (11), 813–818.

Fitz-Gibbon, C. T., and Morris, L. L. *Program Evaluation Kit.* Beverly Hills, Calif.: Sage, 1978.

Fortunato, R. T. "Working Successfully in an Academic Environment." *Journal of College and University Personnel Association,* 1979, *30* (3), iii–v.

Fortunato, R. T., and Lozier, G. G. "How Large Should the Central Personnel Function Be in a College or University?" *Journal of the College and University Personnel Association,* 1975, *26* (4), 39–47.

Galloway, S. W., and Fisher, C. F. *A Guide to Professional Development Opportunities for College and University Administrators.* Washington, D.C.: American Council on Education, 1980.

Garrison, R. B., and England, C. M. *Retirement: A Time for Fulfillment*. Washington, D.C.: College and University Personnel Association, 1979.

Goldhaber, G. M. *Organizational Communication*. Dubuque, Iowa: William C. Brown Co., 1974.

Grote, C. N. "The Personnel Structure and Function in Community Colleges: In Retrospect and Prospect." *Journal of the College and University Personnel Association*, 1976, *27* (4), 1–4.

Grunig, J. E. "A Multi-Systems Theory of Organizational Communication." *Communication Research*, 1975, *2* (2), 103–107.

Guyon, R. *Meeting Leading*. Cleveland, Ohio: Professional Development, Inc., 1979.

Hammons, J. O. (Ed.). *Proceedings: The Conference of Staff Development Programs*. ERIC ED 111 462. University Park, Pa.: Center for the Study of Higher Education, 1975.

Harris, A. F., and Matson, G. A. "Job Evaluation with the Position Analysis Questionnaire." *Journal of the College and University Personnel Association*, 1976, *27* (3), 90–95.

Harrison, J. F. *Improving Performance and Productivity*. Reading, Mass.: Addison-Wesley, 1978.

Herman, J. J. *Developing an Effective School Staff Evaluation Program*. West Nyack, N.Y.: Parker Publishing, 1973.

Holley, W. F., Jr. "The Personnel Function in the Eighties." *Journal of the College and University Personnel Association*, 1980, *31* (2), 25–29.

Hoover, K. H. *College Teaching Today: A Handbook for Postsecondary Instruction*. Boston: Allyn & Bacon, 1980.

Hue, N. H., and others. *Statistical Package for the Social Sciences*. (2nd ed.) New York: McGraw-Hill, 1975.

Huegli, J. M., and Eich, R. K. "The Administrator Search Process." *Journal of the College and University Personnel Association*, 1979, *30* (2), 1–12.

Johnstone, W. A. "Faculty Retrenchment in the 1980s." *Journal of the College and University Personnel Association*, 1980, *31* (1), 22–30.

Kaplowitz, R. *The Selection of Academic Administrators*. Washington, D.C.: American Council on Education, 1973.

Kilberg, W. J., and Fort, L. S. "National League of Cities *v.* Usery: Its Meaning and Impact." *George Washington Law Review*, 1977, *45*, 613–632.

Lawson, J. W., II. *How to Develop a Company Personnel Policy Manual.* Chicago: Dartnell Corporation, 1967.

Lee, R. D., Jr. *Public Personnel Systems.* Baltimore: University Park Press, 1979.

Levine, M. J., and others. "A Comparison of Impasse Procedures in the Public and Private Sectors." *Public Personnel Management,* 1978, *7,* 108–118.

McCarthy, R. J., and Buck, J. A. *Job Evaluation and Pay Administration in the Public Sector.* (Harold Suskin, Ed.). Chicago: International Personnel Management Association, 1977.

McConnel, J. H. *How to Audit the Personnel Department.* New York: AMACOM, 1977.

McCormick, E. J. *Job Analysis: Methods and Applications.* New York: AMACOM, 1979.

McKeachie, W. J. "The Evaluation of Teachers in Higher Education." In F. N. Kerlinger (Ed.), *Review of Research in Education,* no. 3. Itasca, Ill.: Peacock, 1975.

MacKenzie, R. A. *New Time Management Methods.* Chicago: Dartnell Corporation, 1975.

Mager, R. F., and Pipe, P. *Analyzing Performance Problems.* Belmont, Calif.: Fearon, 1978.

Marks, J. R., and others. *Handbook of Educational Supervision: A Guide for the Practitioner.* (2nd ed.) Boston: Allyn & Bacon, 1978.

Marsh, H. W., and others. "Validity and Usefulness of Student Evaluations of Instructional Quality." *Journal of Educational Psychology,* 1975, *67,* 833–839.

Miller, R. I. *The Assessment of College Performance.* San Francisco: Jossey-Bass, 1979.

Millman, J. (Ed.). *Handbook of Teacher Evaluation.* Beverly Hills, Calif.: Sage, 1981.

Mortimer, K. P., and McConnell, T. R. *Sharing Authority Effectively.* San Francisco: Jossey-Bass, 1978.

Nadler, L. *Developing Human Resources.* (2nd ed.) Austin, Tex.: Learning Concepts, 1979.

National Association of College and University Business Officers. "Employee Performance Appraisal." The Administrative Service (a subscription service): *2:7:2,* Washington, D.C., 1978.

National Education Association. *Tenure Policies and Procedures in Teachers Colleges.* Washington, D.C.: National Education Association, 1943.

Newell, C. A. *Human Behavior in Educational Administration.* Englewood Cliffs, N.J.: Prentice-Hall, 1978.

O'Banion, T. (Ed.). *New Directions for Community Colleges. Developing Staff Potential* no. 19. San Francisco: Jossey-Bass, 1977.

Odiorne, G. S. *Personnel Administration by Objectives.* Homewood, Ill.: Irwin, 1971.

Pajer, R. G. "A Systems Approach to Results Oriented Performance Evaluation." *Personnel Administration and Public Personnel Review,* 1972, *1,* 42–217.

Personnel Management Training Center. *Performance Appraisal: Setting Performance Standards.* (Instructors' Guide). Washington, D.C.: Personnel Management Training Center, 1979.

Pfeiffer, J. W., and Jones, J. E. *Structured Experiences for Human Relations Training.* La Jolla, Calif.: University Associates, Vol. 1, 1966; Vol. 2, 1970; Vol. 3, 1971; Vol. 4, 1973.

Pondrum, C. "Faculty Retrenchment Problems and Possible Solutions." *Journal of the College and University Personnel Association,* 1980, *31* (1), 47–55.

Prentice-Hall. *Personnel Management: Policies and Practices.* Englewood Cliffs, N.J.: Prentice-Hall, 1966. (Update, 1979).

Richardson, R. C., Jr. "Staff Development: A Conceptual Framework." *Journal of Higher Education,* 1975, *46* (1), 303–311.

Rigby, S. "The Work May Be Equal But Is the Pay?" *Journal of the College and University Personnel Association,* 1974, *25,* 14–21.

Robinson, D. C., and others. "Comparison of Job Evaluation Methods: A 'Policy Capturing' Approach Using the Position Analysis Questionnaire (PAQ)." *Journal of Applied Psychology,* 1975, *59,* 633–637.

Rock, M. L. (Ed.). *Handbook of Wage and Salary Administration.* New York: McGraw-Hill, 1980.

Rodin, N., and Rodin, B. "Study Evaluation of Teachers" *Science,* 1972, *177,* 1164–1166.

Roots, D. H., and Shepard, I. M. "Yeshiva: Legal Analysis." *Journal of the College and University Personnel Association,* 1980, *31* (2), 51–55.

Schmuck, R. A., and Runkel, P. J. *Handbook of Organization Development in Schools.* Palo Alto, Calif.: Mayfield, 1972.

Scigliano, V. S. "The Search Committee." *Journal of the College and University Personnel Association,* 1979, *30* (3), 36–45.

Seldin, P. *Successful Faculty Evaluation Programs.* Crugers, N.Y.: Coventry Press, 1980.

Shaw, B. N. *Academic Tenure in Higher American Education.* Chicago: Adams Press, 1971.

Sikula, A. F. *Personnel Management.* New York: Wiley, 1977.

Sisson, R. L., and Canning, R. G. *Computer Applications.* New York: Wiley, 1976.

Smith, G. W. *Quantitative Methods of Research in Education.* Washington, D.C.: College and University Press, 1975.

Smith, J. B. *Job Analysis: An Outline of Five Common Methods.* Washington, D.C.: Office of Personnel Management, 1979.

Smith, L. "The EEO's Bold Foray into Job Evaluation." *Fortune,* September 11, 1978, 58–61.

Solomon, L., and Berzon, B. *Employee and Team Development.* San Diego: University Associates, 1976.

Thayer, L. *Fifty Strategies for Experiential Learning.* Vol. 1. San Diego: University Associates, 1976.

U.S. Department of Labor. *Handbook for Analyzing Jobs.* Washington, D.C.: U.S. Government Printing Office, 1972.

U.S. Department of Labor. *Dictionary of Occupational Titles* (4th ed.) Washington, D.C.: U.S. Government Printing Office, 1977.

Verduim, J. R., and others. *Adults Teaching Adults.* Austin, Tex.: Learning Concepts, 1977.

Wesolowski, Z. P. *A Humanistic Approach to Evaluation of Community College Noninstructional Personnel.* ERIC ED 099 074. Arlington, Virginia: NOVA University, 1974.

Williams, R. C. "Tenure Practices—Redefined." *Junior College Journal,* May 1969, pp. 26–29.

Woodburne, L. S. *Faculty Personnel Policies in Higher Education.* New York: Harper & Row, 1950.

Zawacki, R. A., and Warrick, D. D. *Organization Development: Managing Change in the Public Sector.* Chicago: International Personnel Management Association, 1976.

❧ Index ❦

A

Academic administrator, definition of, 42

Academic freedom: statements of, 167–168; and tenure, 176; in tenure-eligible contract, 174; and unionization, 337; violation of, 274

Academic rank, 42; definitions of, 315; tenure eligibility and, 169, 172, 176–177

Adjunct status, of faculty, 310

Administrative compensation survey, 72, 80–82

Adverse impact, in the selection process, 92–95

Advertisements: age and sex restrictions for, 97; minority recruitment in, 114; techniques for, 114–118

Affiliate Academic Appointments, 307, 318

Affirmative Action, 86–105; appeal procedures, 274–275, 282, 301; applicant identification form, 104–105; definition of, 87; goals and timetables, 89–100; grievances, 294; legal base, 87–88; plan, 88–89; plan index, 99–100; program, 291–293; record-keeping requirements, 90–91; recruitment report, 101–103; reporting categories, 40–41; sample policy, 98–99

Age Discrimination in Employment Act, 37, 87–88; maximum age, 148–149; and retirement policies, 235

American Arbitration Association, 266

American Association of University Professors (AAUP), 166, 197, 199, 331

AAUP/AAC Commission on Academic Tenure, 172

American Federation of State and Municipal Employees (AFSME), 331

American Federation of Teachers (AFT), 331

American Management Association (AMA), 21

American Speech and Hearing Association Journal, 113

Appeal procedures: for faculty, 274–278; for formal hearings, 298; for staff, 289–290

Applicant documentation form, 103

Applicants for employment: recruitment of, 114–118; selection of, 128–129; as a source of salary information, 71; from within, 111

Application for employment form, 92; questions on, 117–118. *See also* Employment

Appointment. *See* Employment

Appointments without remuneration, 310

Apprenticeship, 41, 97, 143